IMAGES
*of America*

# Jackson Parish

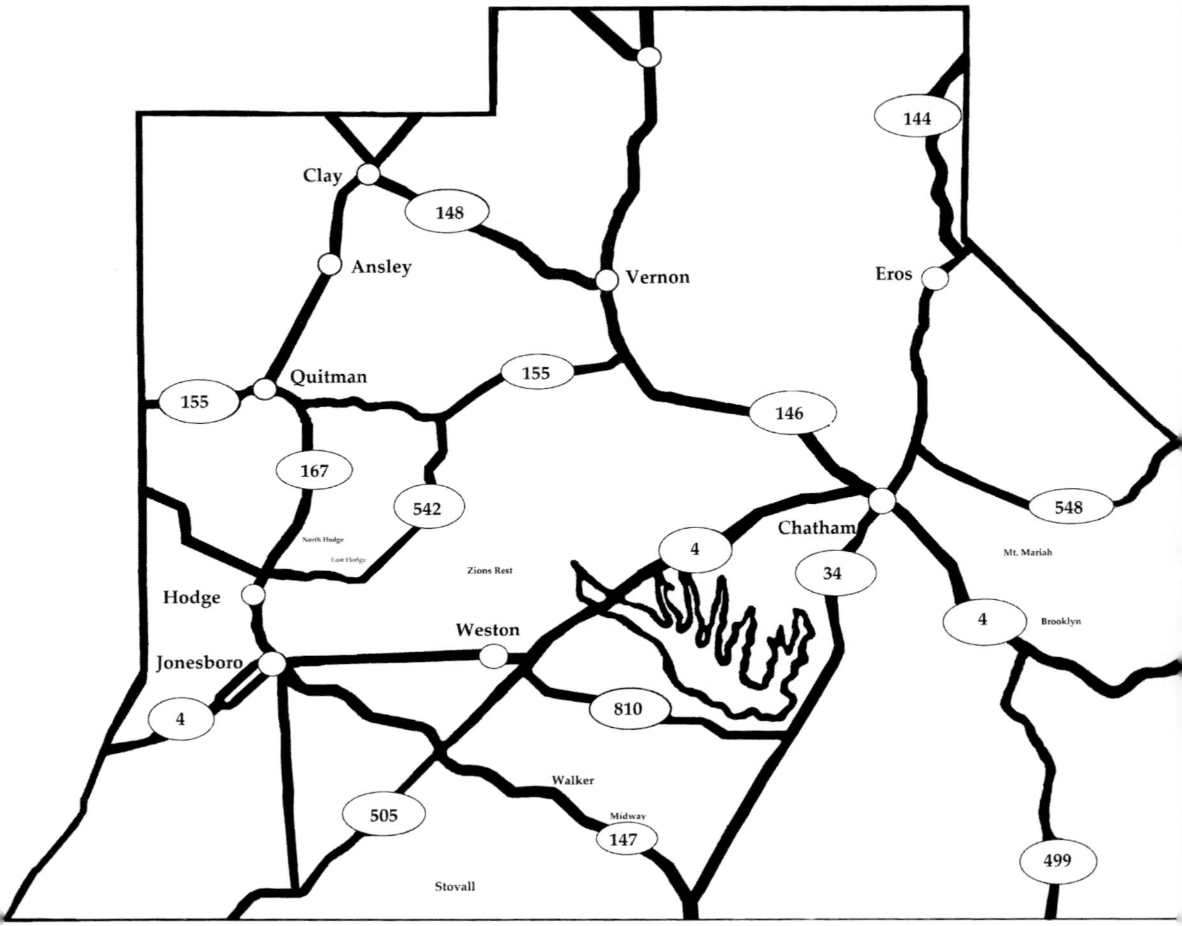


Jackson Parish is in north central Louisiana and covers 583 square miles. This map shows the towns represented in the following pages. (Courtesy of Katherine Rowell.)

**On the Cover:** Pictured is one of the early sawmills in Jackson Parish. This one is thought to have been in the Jonesboro community. Oxen were the choice for bringing the large trees that once grew in the parish to the sawmills and railroads. These trees, once thought a hindrance, became the parish's livelihood and continue to be to the present day. (Courtesy of the *Jackson Independent.*)

IMAGES
*of America*

# JACKSON PARISH

Katherine Smith Rowell

ARCADIA
PUBLISHING

ISBN 978-1-4671-1446-2

Published by Arcadia Publishing
Charleston, South Carolina

Printed in the United States of America

Library of Congress Control Number: 2015932696

For all general information, please contact Arcadia Publishing:
Telephone 843-853-2070
Fax 843-853-0044
E-mail sales@arcadiapublishing.com
For customer service and orders:
Toll-Free 1-888-313-2665

Visit us on the Internet at www.arcadiapublishing.com

*I dedicate this book to those who work so hard to preserve the past for future generations.*

# Contents

# ACKNOWLEDGMENTS

I would like to sincerely thank everyone who allowed me to reproduce their photographs for this book: Glen Nash, T.J. Hurst (T.L. Colvin estate), Patricia Maxwell, Johnny Culpepper, Sylvia Pagan, Patsy Nix (Ebenezer Baptist Church), Clyde Pointer, Kane Pullig (Jackson Parish Sheriff's Department), Kat Hamm (Jackson Parish *Independent*), Ellen Stephenson, Sandy Waits, Leah Beth Johnston (Jackson Parish Museum), Trot Hunt (the Hunt family), Helon Earle (the Allen family), Debbie Pender (Weston High School), Holbrook McLean, Herman Lenard, Mary Alice Williams (Hodge Methodist Church), Kay Barr, Ronnie Spillers, Sonda Womack, Yvonne Peel, Lucille Anderson, Eddie Ruth Wyatt, Judy Brown, Nella Robison, Phyllis Moore (Jackson Parish Library), Jim Tolar, D.E. Hatten, Friends of Chatham, Sue Henderson, Mrs. Judd Brown, Jud Rogers, Pat Heard, Patricia Maddox, Harrell Bond (Jackson Parish Sports Hall of Fame), Joan Teat (Jackson Parish Bank), Sherry Harvenston (Jonesboro Baptist Church), Karon Garlington, and James Pierce.

I want to express gratitude to my grandmother Pearl Hampton for contacting contributors and spending time with me telling me what she knew, and my parents, Cade and Mary Smith, for contacting contributors, answering question after question, and letting me use their home as a base of operations.

Thank you to those who helped by allowing me to endlessly talk about the book, my sisters Kathy Jordan and Annie Persilver, and especially my husband, Shane Rowell, for dealing with all the late nights and missed dinners. I apologize if I have missed naming someone; there were so many contributors, and I did my best to make note of everyone to say thank you.

# INTRODUCTION

Before the Louisiana Purchase, Jackson Parish was part of the Natchitoches Country, possessed by Spain and France. This great expanse of territory was ceded to the United States by France in 1803. In 1804, the territory was divided by Congress into two parts; the portion to the south was known as the New Orleans territory, and to the north was the District of Louisiana. The Jackson Parish area, along with most of what would become the state of Louisiana, was a part of the territory of Orleans until Louisiana was admitted to the Union in 1812.

Most of the early transportation in north Louisiana was by water, though there were some well-used trails. The Old Natchitoches Road ran from Lake Providence to Natchitoches and was used extensively by the Indians to transport salt from Louisiana salt works to the many Indian villages along the route. It was also a part of Sieur de Bienville's route in 1700 on his trip from Lake Providence to Natchitoches.

Many of the early arrivals to this area were hunters, trappers, or traders bartering with Indian tribes. There was no settlement in the area until John Stowe arrived in 1802 with a land grant from the government of Spain. After the Louisiana territory became the property of the United States and after the organization of the parish, more settlers began to enter the area and communities began to form.

During the administration of Gov. Alexander Mouton, Jackson Parish was created by Act 38 on February 27, 1845, by combining territory from Ouachita, Union, and Claiborne Parishes. The boundaries were fixed by Act 179 of 1846. The parish was named in honor of Pres. Andrew Jackson, hero of the Battle of New Orleans and seventh president of the United States. He died June 8, 1845.

Jackson Parish, located almost in the center of the northern half of the state, is primarily forest. The parish is in the heart of a rich pine belt and is part of what is known as the "Hill Parishes." The land is rolling hills with creek bottoms and springs. When the first settlers came, they found a vast wilderness filled with wild game for food as well as soil and a climate that would produce the crops necessary to feed themselves and any livestock. They found land that would produce the southern staple—cotton, a cash crop.

The people drawn to the Hill Parishes by the offer of cheap farmland represented many ethnic groups, but it was the Scotch-Irish who proved to be the driving force of the parishes. These people were hard-working and had strong faith that they would succeed in a new land. When they came, one important institution they brought with them was a strong Protestant religion. The overwhelming majority were Baptists, while Methodists and Presbyterians made up the remainder of the population. Catholicism was mainly in south Louisiana, which was dominated by the French population, though there were a few Catholic churches in north Louisiana before the Civil War. Organized religion was introduced to the area in 1821, and in 1841, the Louisiana Baptist Convention was organized in nearby Bienville Parish.

By act of legislature in 1846 (Act 173), Vernon became the seat of Jackson Parish. Vernon was never a large town, but it was centrally located in the parish. According to the 1850 census, there were over 5,000 people living in Jackson Parish. As settlers from the East moved in, little communities appeared everywhere. The men and women who traveled so far for cheap farmland found themselves faced with treacherous waterways and densely packed forests. The land had an overabundance of timber. The trees that once grew in the parish were large; one tree could take a week and an entire community to cut down and move.

The presidential election of 1860 was an emotional one, and its outcome proved to be a matter of life and death. When the votes were counted, Jackson Parish had given strong support to the Southern Democrat John Breckinridge. The voters of the South could not stop the tide however, and Abraham Lincoln was elected president. Louisiana held its convention on January 23, 1861; three days later, the state withdrew from the Union.

Many families in Jackson Parish were divided by the Civil War and found one son fighting for the South and another for the North. During the war, Louisiana sent 56,000 troops to fight. Nine thousand stayed in home defense units, and when it was over, 15,000 men were lost. The war caused hardship in the communities. During this time, it did little good to grow cotton to sell. Cotton was ginned and taken by wagon to creeks and bayous that flowed in the Red and Ouachita Rivers, then transported to the textile mills of the Atlantic seaboard. However, the Union fleet controlled the Mississippi River and much of the Red and Ouachita Rivers, so the cotton could go no further than a gin or storehouse. Many farmers also found their produce being used as forage for the horses and mules of the armies that passed through the areas. With the loss of fathers, husbands, and sons, the families left behind struggled with little food and no one to work the fields.

The struggles did not end with the war. Reconstruction brought its own set of troubles. Men who came back from the war found farms devastated and could not afford to pay laborers to help work the fields. The newly freed slaves had no money and no land themselves. It was then that sharecropping and share-renting methods began to appear.

In 1892, the railroad made its way into the parish. It was constructed 12 miles north of Vernon, which began to see its population dwindle as people were drawn to the railroad and the new towns near it. Railroads could be the life or death of a town. The Tremont Lumber Company saw potential in the timber of Jackson Parish and built a railroad south, creating the town of Eros in late 1899. It wanted to continue the line south through the community of Dalley, but because of the lack of interest, the company decided to curve the railroad through some of the land it owned, and the town of Chatham was formed.

By this time, the Southern Arkansas Railroad, later know as the Rock Island Railroad, had already come to the Macedonia community, soon to be named Jonesboro. Several saw mills were already in the area and timber was becoming a big industry. The saw mills at Eros and Chatham continued for almost 30 years, until the company depleted the area's timber.

Timber was the reason the Davis brothers left their operations in Arkansas and bought land in Jackson Parish and started the town of Ansley. They built their own railroad to service their mill and town. At the same time, Quitman began growing because it too was on the railroad. Timber is what brought major industry to Hodge. The mill there has changed names many times but has become the lifeblood of the parish, even to this day.

The parish struggled during the Depression. Food and money were on everyone's minds. Towns saw farms abandoned and left to grow back into forests. Lumber companies took advantage of this and bought acres of land. Not long after the Depression, World War II came and many young men left to fight. Schools all over the parish began to close as enrollment dropped. Three school systems strengthened and remain in the area to this day: Quitman, Jonesboro-Hodge, and Weston.

The parish has had its ups and downs through the years, but it is a proud parish with many citizens wanting to preserve the history of their own towns. It was through these people that this book was made possible. This is not a comprehensive history, but I hope it will pique your curiosity about the events and people mentioned, encouraging you to delve deeper into the intriguing history of Jackson Parish.

# *One*

# Jackson Parish Courthouses

The Vernon townsite was formed in June 1845. Two villages wished to be the location of the parish seat; however, Vernon was centrally located in the parish and most convenient to the majority, so by Act 173 in 1846, it was chosen the parish seat. A small log courthouse was immediately built to represent Vernon's authority, and then a two-story frame structure was erected for expansion; it was said to have been impressive, with wide halls extending through the entire building. This served the parish until January 1878, when the courthouse burned; very few records were saved. The courthouse was set on fire by a prisoner who was sentenced to 10 years and did not want to be prosecuted. Court was held for the next six years in churches and sometimes in schools. The third and last courthouse was paid for by private subscription and dedicated in 1884.

William B. McDonald was a parish representative to the state legislature. He was consistently trying to get a bill passed to move the courthouse. At that time, Vernon's population had dropped to 75 inhabitants. His opinion, that the parish seat should be moved to a settlement where railroads and sawmills could build, cost him his life, as he was killed while preparing to go to the legislature. He did not live to see the bill passed. In 1884 and 1904, as well as 1908, bills for the removal of the parish seat from Vernon were introduced and defeated. In 1910, the legislature passed Act 67, allowing for the relocation of the seat to a place as close to the center of the parish as possible.

The first election was held February 7, 1911, between Chatham, Center, Jonesboro, Quitman, and Weston. When the votes were counted, it was determined that Chatham and Jonesboro would be in a runoff. The final vote for the parish seat was held on March 14, 1911. The decision between the two towns was strongly contested, as the votes proved when they were counted and the police jury declared Jonesboro the winner. Chatham was angry at the loss, and the courthouse was packed up and moved to Jonesboro immediately. The loss of the parish seat was the end of Vernon.

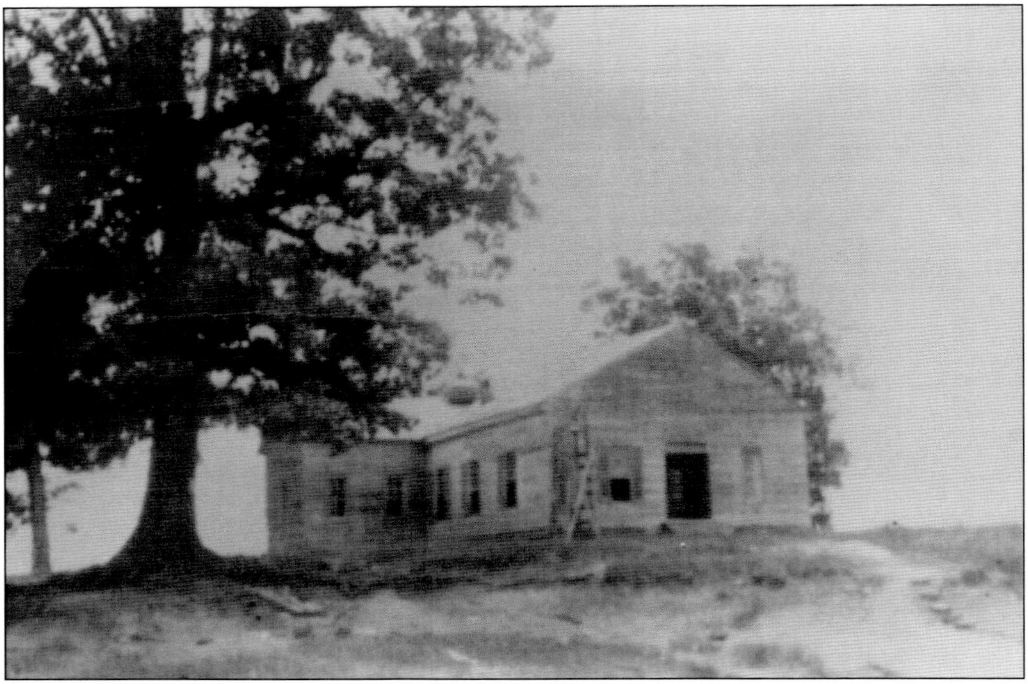

The third and last courthouse built in Vernon was a single-story structure dedicated in 1884. In 1878, a fire destroyed the second courthouse, along with almost all its documents. It would take 12 years of hard work to sort it all out and re-document everything lost by hand. The people of Vernon decided against a tax to raise money for a new courthouse. The new building was constructed with money from private subscriptions. (Courtesy of T.L. Colvin estate.)

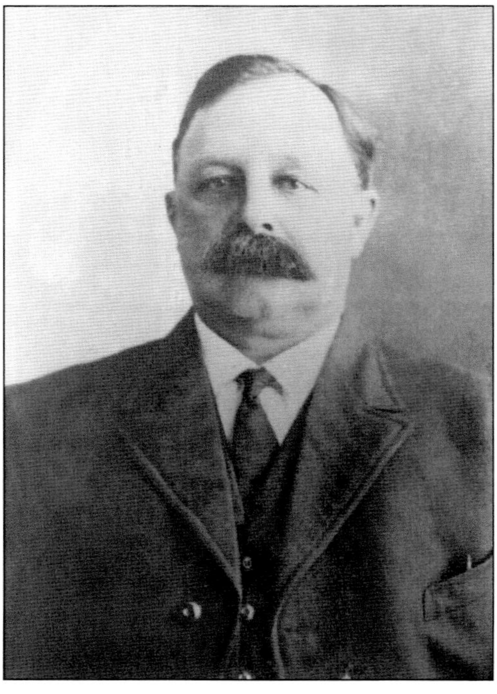

Jonesboro was eventually declared the parish seat. That night, all available wagons and buggies were sent to Vernon, and Sheriff William Jonathan "Bill" McBride (pictured), along with clerk L.W. Ramsey, quickly packed all the records and took them south to the sheriff's father's house. When the "Posse," as it was described by the sheriff's nephew, Woodrow McBride, arrived from Chatham, they saw they were outnumbered. Realizing there was nothing they could do, they returned to Chatham, leaving the "stolen" parish seat in Jonesboro. McBride became sheriff in 1908 and left office in 1916. He was a business owner until he became sheriff and was involved in local affairs until his death in 1947. (Courtesy of the Jackson Parish Sheriff's Office.)

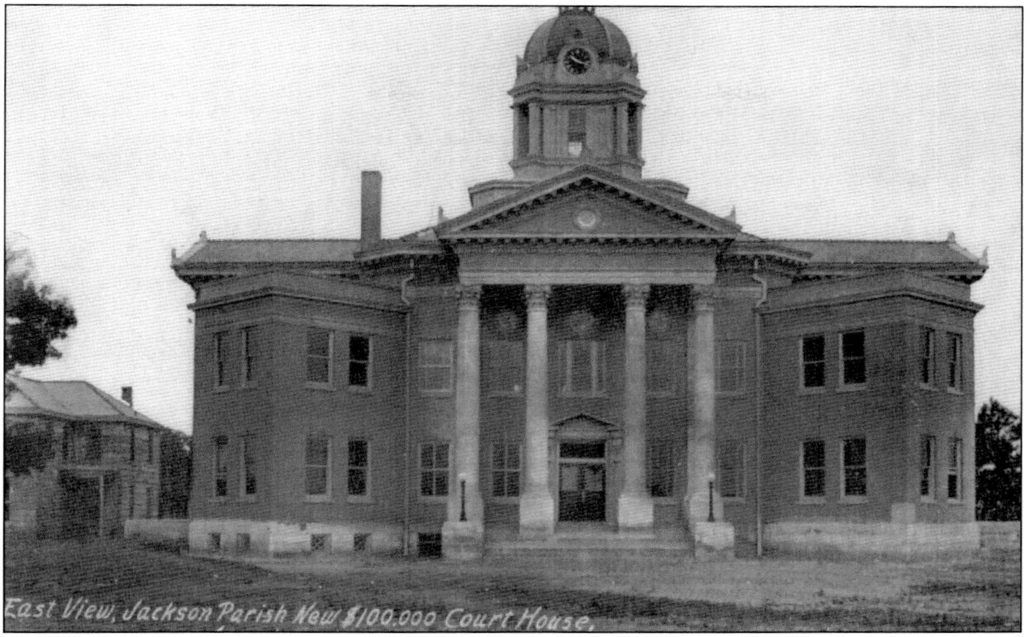


This postcard boasts of the cost of the newly built courthouse in Jonesboro. On May 22, 1913, the *Jackson Independent* printed an article titled "Courthouse Completed." According to it, the dome was made of copper, and the main roof was slate. The courthouse, with its reinforced-concrete construction and strong foundation, was expected to endure for ages. There were three main entrances, with one placed on the side of the building opening to the east and covered by a beautiful Corinthian portico. The interior of the building was finished in harmony with the exterior. (Courtesy of Jackson Parish Museum.)

The courthouse dedication was a joyous day, as this large crowd shows. The courthouse was constructed on a block of land owned by the town known as Courthouse Square. The day Jonesboro won the parish seat, whistles and church bells could be heard ringing loud and clear. Dedicating the courthouse was an exciting day, as this gave Jonesboro authority. It became the center of progress in the parish. (Courtesy of Jackson Parish Museum.)

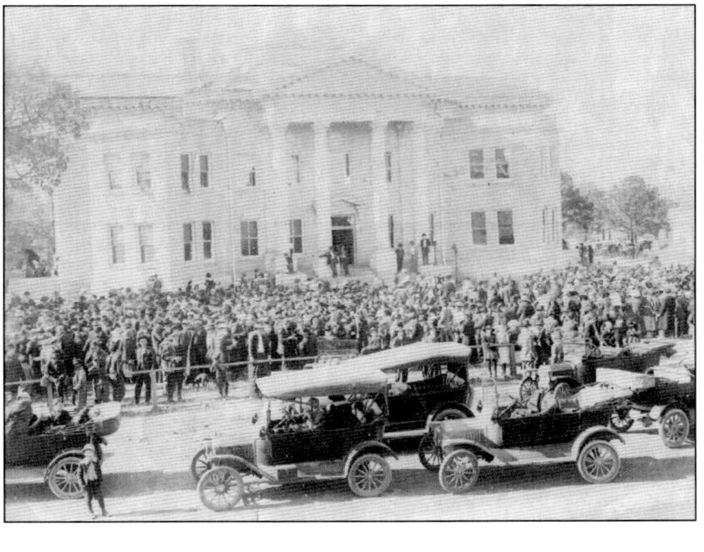

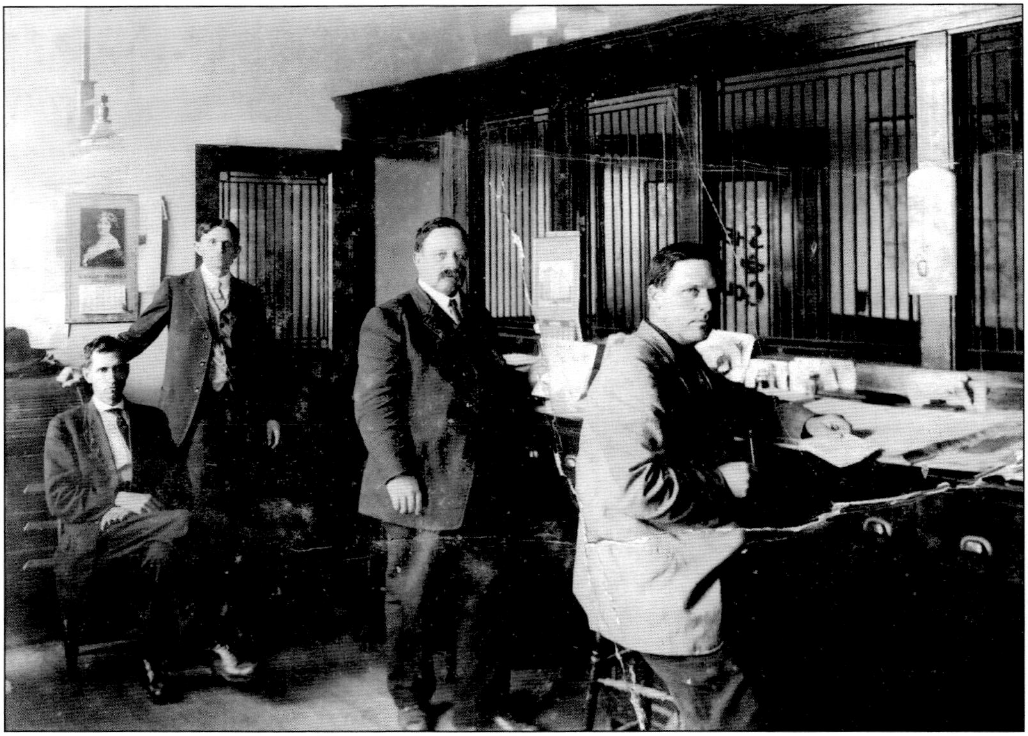

In April 1920, inside the courthouse sheriff's office and clerk of court's office, men pause in their work to pose for a photograph. Dr. W.S. Jones was sheriff from 1916 to 1924. From left to right are William Jefferson Hammon, L.W. Ramsey, Bill McBride, and Jesse David McBride. (Courtesy of Jackson Parish Library.)

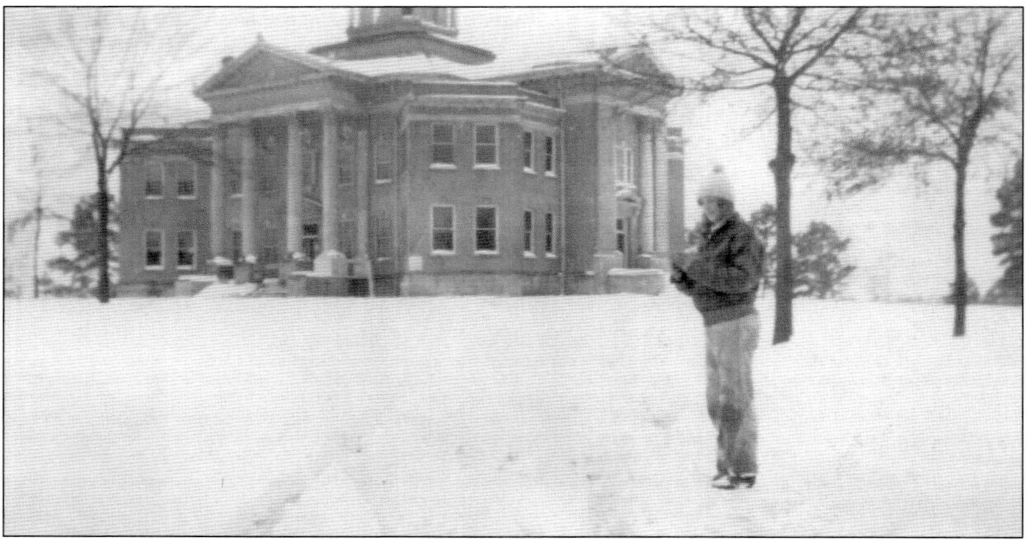

This beautiful snowy day in Jonesboro in 1927 was captured by Pauline Mitchell Brumley. The courthouse, seen from Main Street, shows its beautiful portico on the front, along with young trees that are still growing. The woman building a snowball was playing in the snow with several friends when this picture was taken. (Courtesy of Ronnie Brumley Spillers.)

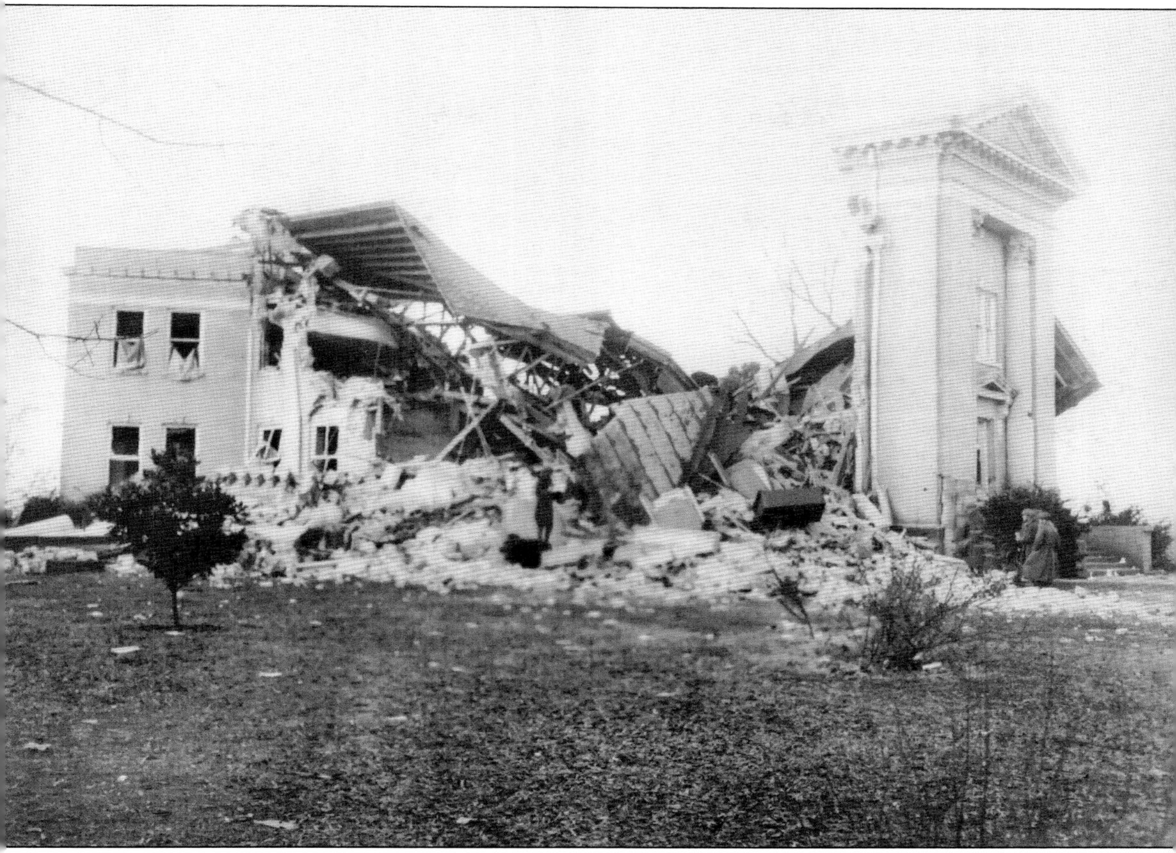

On January 16, 1936, at 8:30 p.m., the courthouse that the town of Jonesboro was so proud of was blown to pieces by a mysterious explosion. There were many theories as to where the explosion came from; however, it is believed that it occurred in the basement from a gas leak. Thankfully, all records were retrieved. There were five people in the building at the time, but W. Luther Barnes was the only one killed in the explosion. Jack McCain died the next day while working to clear the debris when a wall of cement and brick fell on him. (Courtesy of Jackson Parish Museum.)

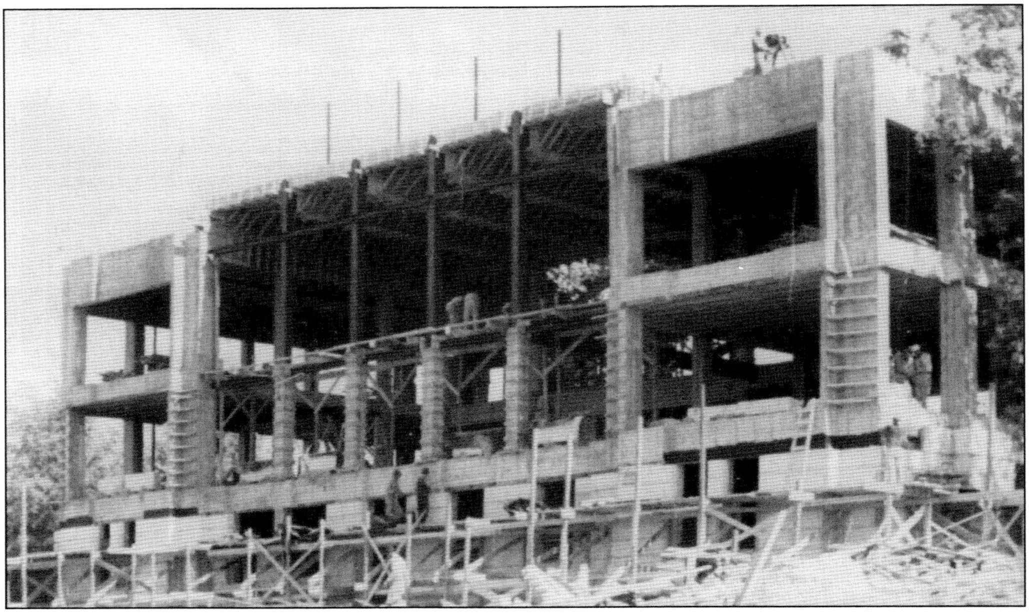

After the explosion, Jonesboro found itself in need of another courthouse. Work on a bigger, more modern courthouse began in December 1936 after the police jury issued a bond for its share of the cost of construction. The building, said to be the last word in beauty of architecture at the time, was completed exactly one year later, and in January 1938, parish officials moved in. An escape-proof jail is situated on top of the building and can be reached by a private elevator through the sheriff's office. In later years, a fire escape was built onto the structure's west side. Presently, the jailhouse is no longer in use. (Both, courtesy of the T.L. Calvin estate.)

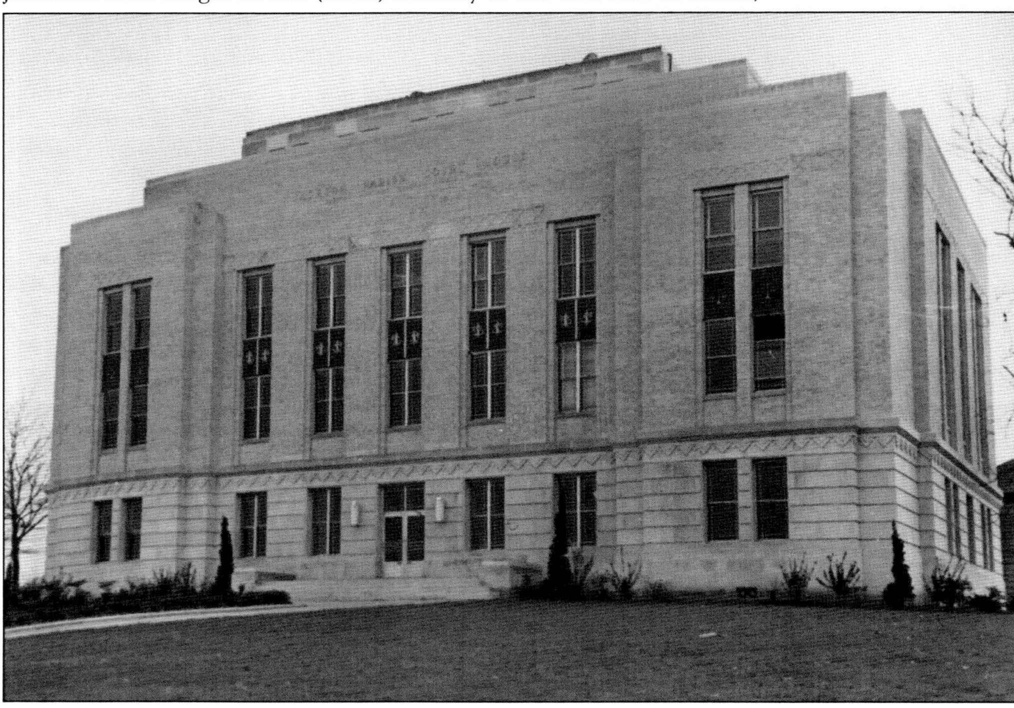

# *Two*

# North Central and Eastern Communities

Vernon is in the north central part of Jackson Parish. It is uncertain exactly when Vernon was settled or how it was named, though it is widely believed to have been named for a family that lived there. In 1846, Vernon was approved as the parish seat and incorporated as a town in 1859. Vernon was not a large town. It had seven roads leading in, which indicated its importance to the residents of the parish. It was the courthouse town and chief trading center for a large area. The railroad passed 12 miles north of Vernon, drawing businesses away. It remained the seat of the parish government for 66 years. By 1892, only 75 people were living in the area, and Vernon's decline was imminent when the parish seat was moved to Jonesboro in 1911.

The Tremont Lumber Company decided to expand its operations, and the company built a railroad south. Mary Nash Collins suggested the name of the new post office be Eros in 1898, after the Eros asteroid discovered by Carl Gustov Witt. Eros, situated in the eastern part of the parish, became a thriving town with three hotels, a company commissary, three doctors, a drugstore, three churches, a jail, a bank, and its own telephone exchange and newspaper. At one time, the population boasted over 1,000 residents; the first high school there had over 600 students. In 1911, a fire broke out at the Tremont mill, and the company rebuilt. Then, in 1920, a tornado destroyed the entire town and the mill with it. The town decided to rebuild and Tremont once again rebuilt. Sadly, six years later, another fire decimated the mill, and Tremont decided to close. This caused the town of Eros to eventually close.

Tremont wanted to expand its operations with another mill and a train through Dalley; however, no one from Dalley showed up to the town meeting except for Dr. Samuel Wilder. The representative from Tremont offered the doctor a job and first pick of lots in a new town. Tremont decided to build the railroad, and Chathamville was founded. The post office was named Avard. The name was changed to Chatham in 1906.

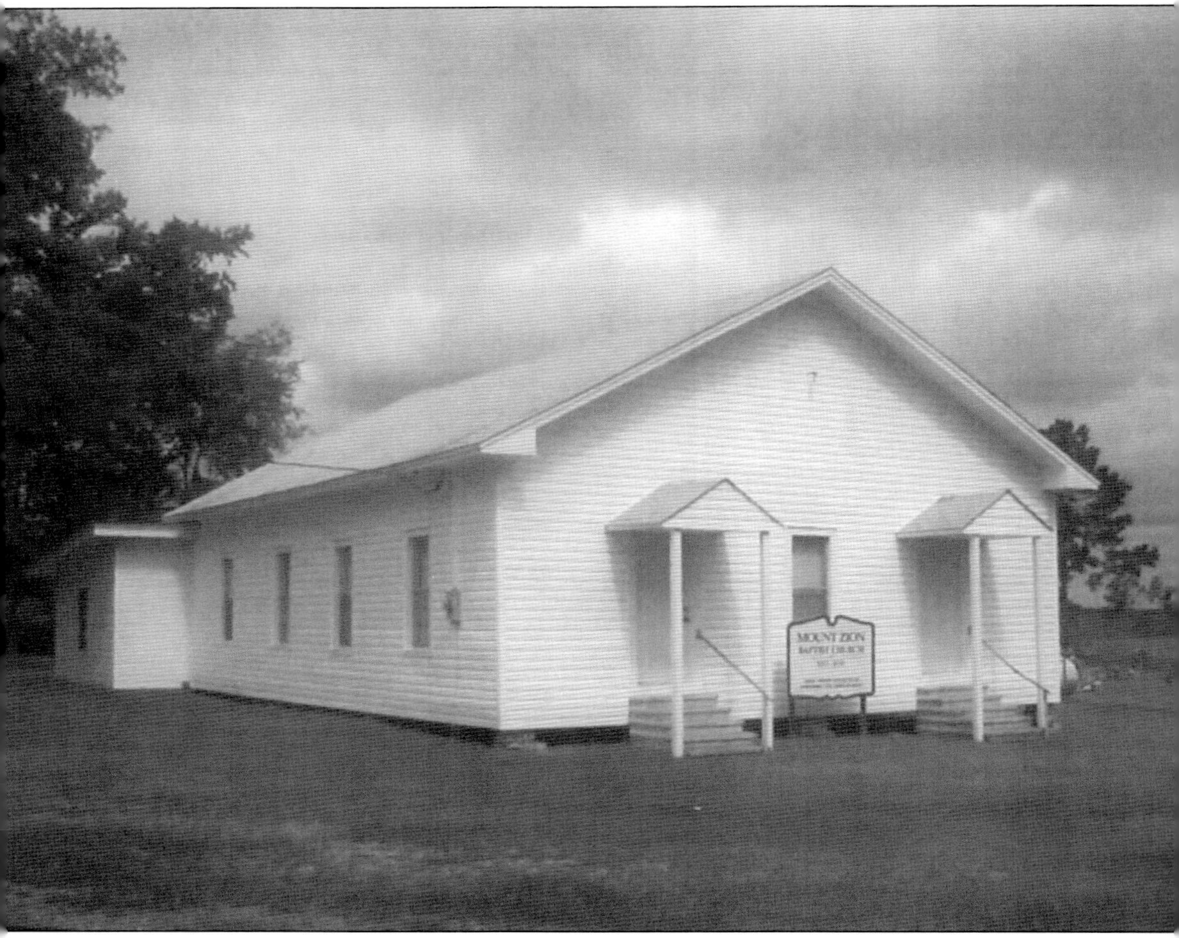


On September 10, 1842, Jacob Hickman and J. Newman met in the home of Irwin and Frances Scarborough to organize a church. They continued to meet in the Scarboroughs' home until a small log structure with wooden shutters was built in 1843, and Mt. Zion Baptist Church was created. The second church building was erected around 1851. This church, which still stands today, has been remodeled by the addition of a fellowship hall. Sunday school rooms were partitioned off from part of the auditorium. The original columns, hand cut by Warren Willis, are still inside the church. The cemetery is located next to the church, and after years of neglect, it has been restored to honor the faithful members who are buried there. Mt. Zion still holds services to this day. (Courtesy of Nella Robison.)

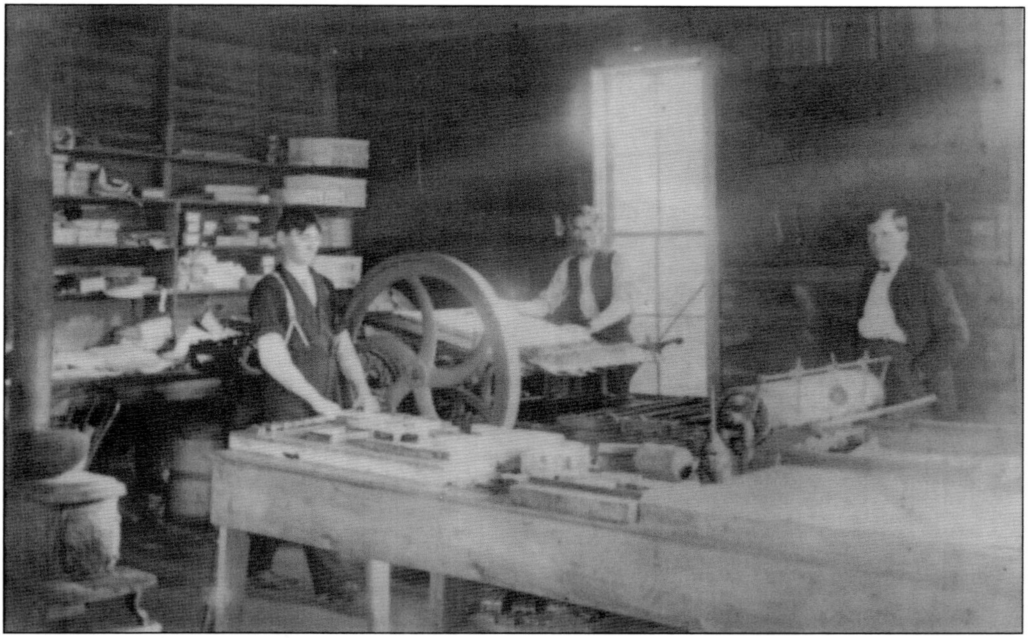

The *Jackson Independent* was established in 1892 by Warren E. Bush after he bought a newspaper plant in Vernon. This image most likely shows the entire staff that worked in Vernon, after it was bought by Jesse David McBride in 1902. The man at right is McBride, and the other two are unidentified. McBride sold the newspaper back to Bush in 1906, and Bush continued to produce the paper until he sold it to A.H. Colvin Sr. in 1908. The newspaper is still published to this day. (Courtesy of the Jackson Parish Museum.)

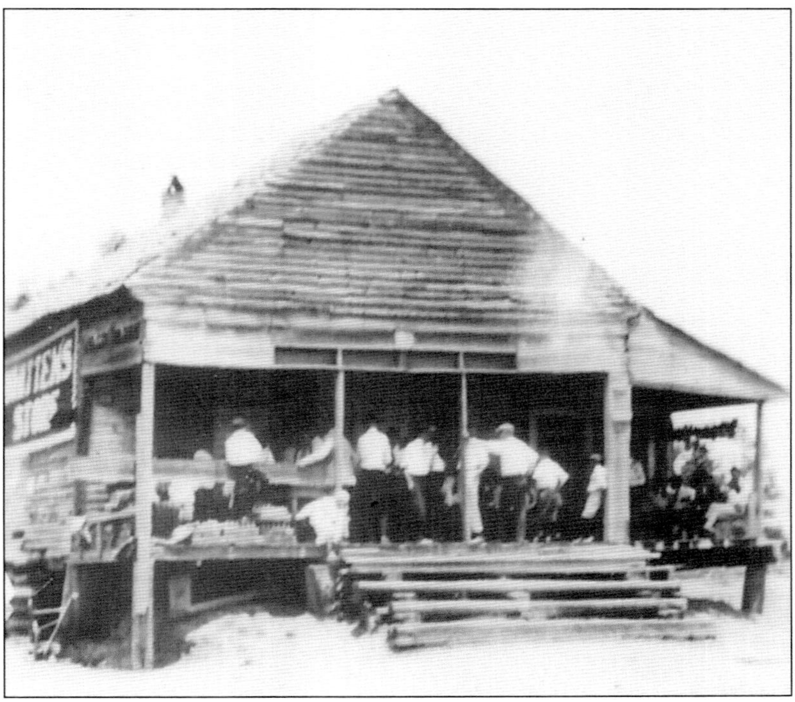

There were a number of stores located in Vernon. Some store owners around 1860 included M.B. Kidd and brother W.C. Ashley, Davis and Sholar, Samuel and Cann, William Lewis, Lloyd and Ives, and Charlie Whitten. For a time, Charlie Whitten was postmaster and operated the post office in his store in 1915. (Courtesy of Kay Barr.)

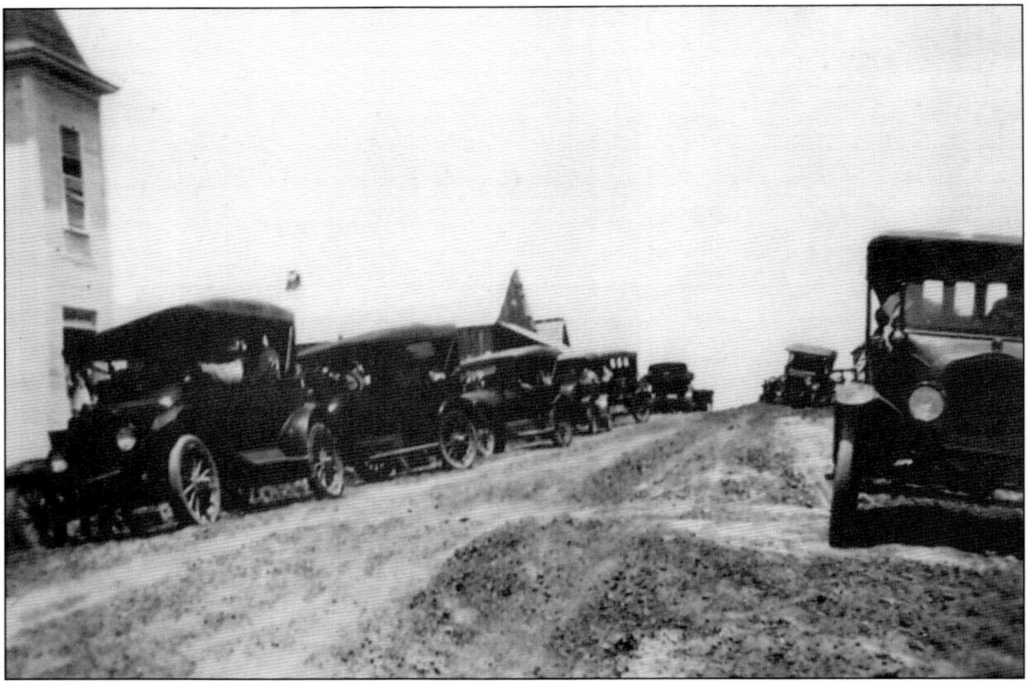

Vernon had seven roads that led into it, proving the importance of the town in its day. The main road was located just east of the present-day Vernon Baptist Church. During the height of Vernon's day as parish seat, the town was full of activity. The courthouse square was not only surrounded by homes, but also doctors' offices, lawyers' offices, merchandise stores, a post office, and several saloons. There were several schools, a jail, three newspapers, several churches, and even a stagecoach station. The area outside of the town was mainly farm and timberland, which supported the town. After losing the parish seat, Vernon continued to struggle to keep the town alive. As schools closed and businesses moved to larger towns on the railroad, Vernon closed with them. (Both, courtesy of Kay Barr.)

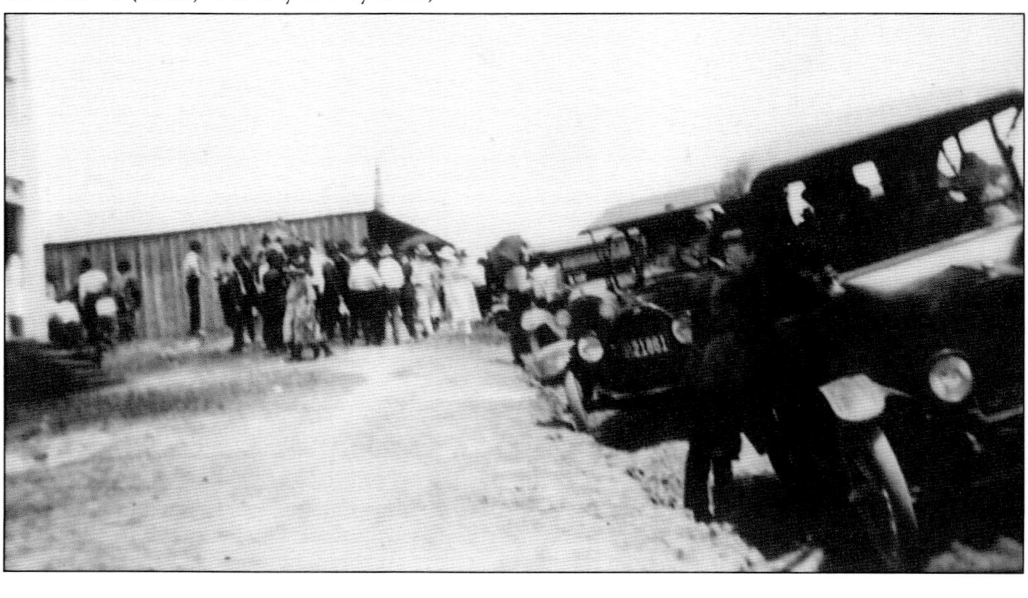

Rosana Puckett became postmaster in 1918, and the post office was moved to her store, which faced what is now Highway 146. The store was small and attached to her house. She closed the store in the 1950s, and the Wainwright store, across the highway from Archie Barr's store, became the post office. The postmaster at that time was Maggie Wainwright, who served until 1964, when the post office was closed and moved from the town. Rasberry Gay and James Calvin Edminston were farmers in Vernon who liked to visit the store daily. (Courtesy of Kay Barr.)

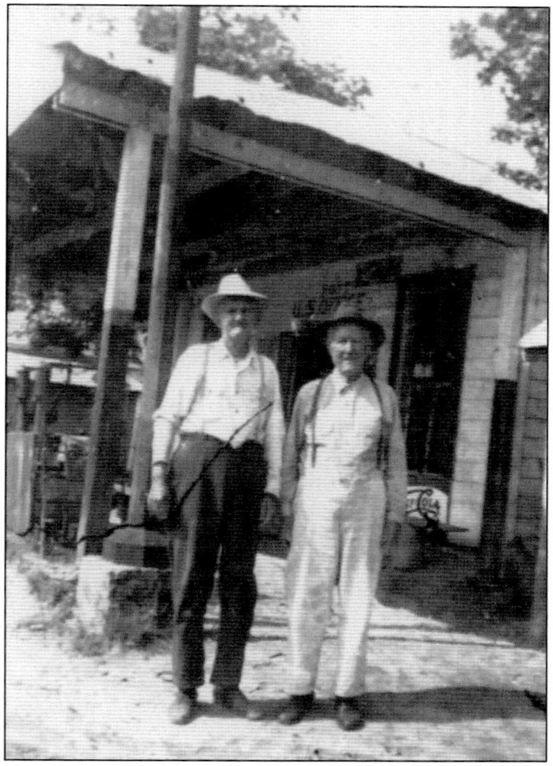

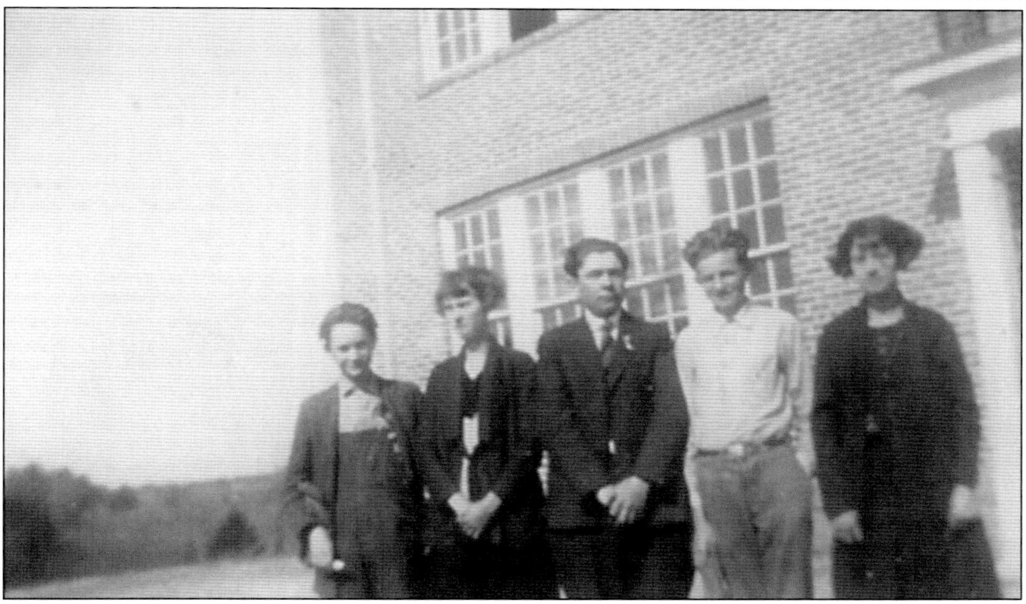

The Vernon school was built off the northwest corner of the town square and was a redbrick building. It started as an elementary school, and later, grades above seventh were added in 1910. By 1918, they employed two teachers, one of whom was Rivers Barr, seen here at center. By 1943, the enrollment was 43 students, and the school was consolidated with Chatham. (Courtesy of Kay Barr.)

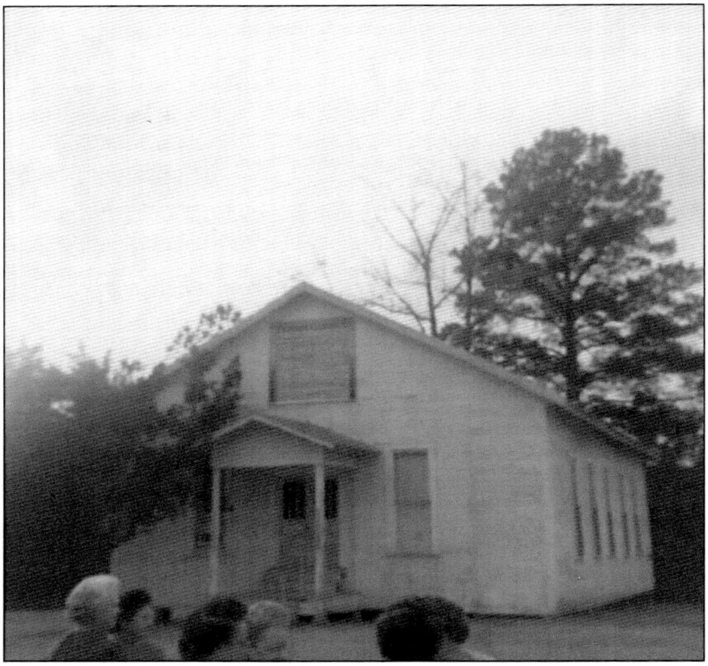

Vernon Baptist Church was established in 1910, and the congregants started by meeting in the old courthouse until 1914, when a building for church use was erected. The wood frame church was located to the southwest of the courthouse square. This place is now the Vernon Baptist Church Cemetery. In 1968, a new church was erected, and the old building was still used by the church until the late 1980s, when structural issues required its removal. (Courtesy of Kay Barr.)

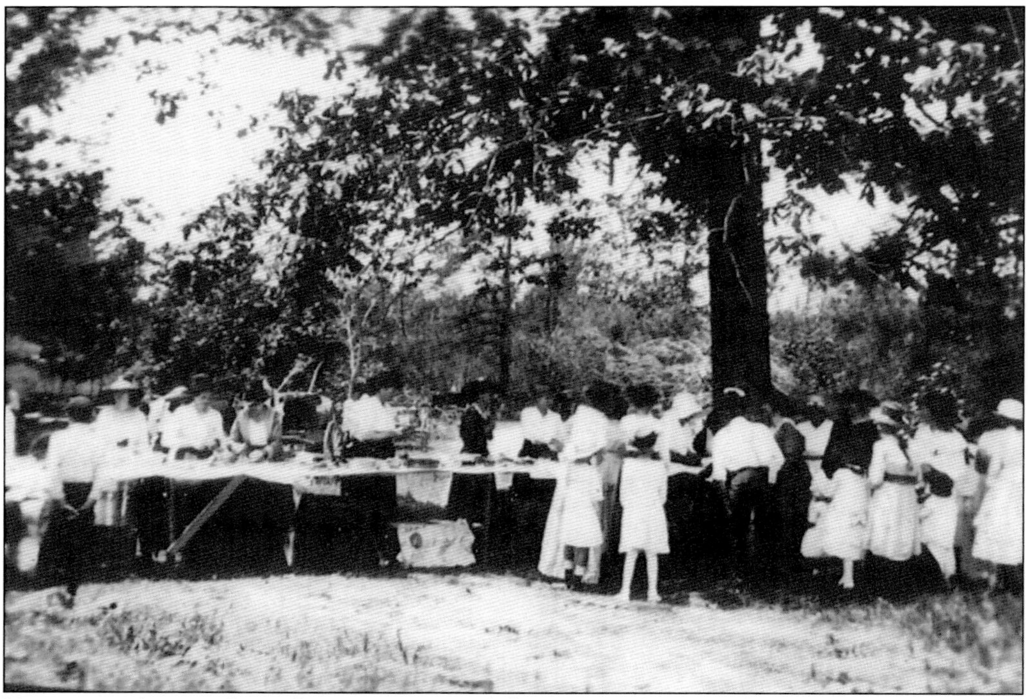

Vernon was known for its homecomings and dinners on the grounds since the beginnings of the town. Often, all of the area's churches came together for these homecomings. There were several churches in Vernon during its heyday; now, only the Vernon Baptist Church remains. The location of the current cemetery, just west of the church, used to be a busy street. (Courtesy of Kay Barr.)

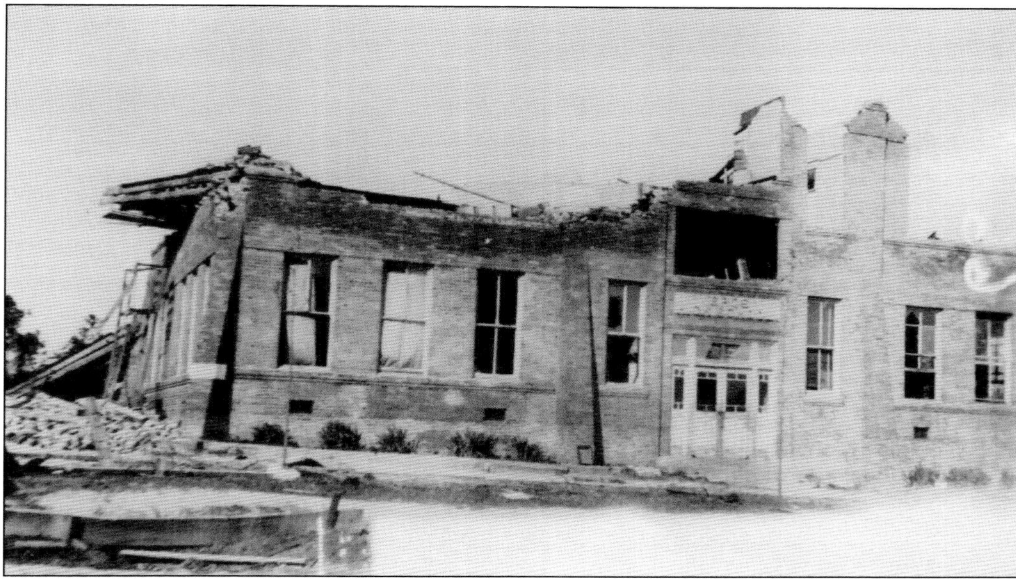

On April 8, 1920, a tornado tore through Eros, destroying everything in its path. It was said that in moments, the town the Tremont Lumber Company founded was no more. Miraculously, not one person was killed. Several were buried in debris, some badly cut and bruised, but everyone survived. Even the high school was destroyed, as seen in the photograph above. The people of Eros chose not to give up, and rebuilt. Only six years later, the mill that keep the town alive closed and Eros as a boom town closed with it. (Both, courtesy of the T.L. Colvin estate.)

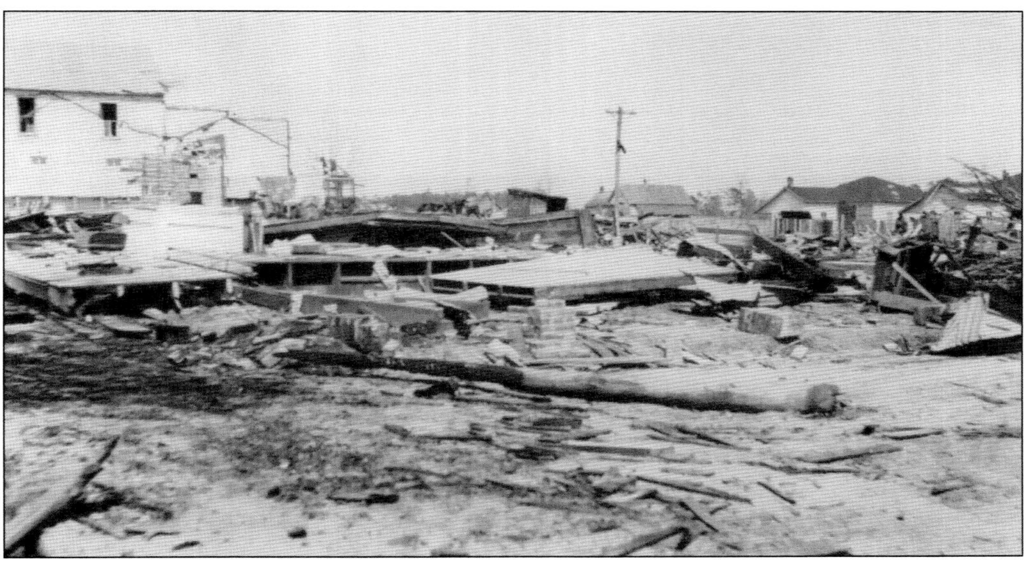

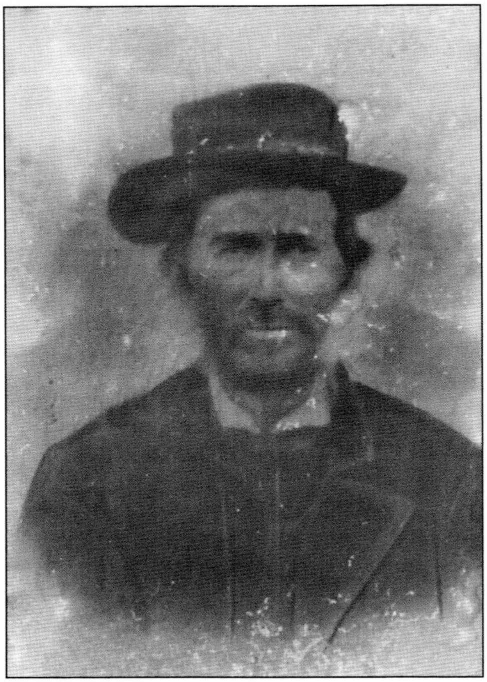

One of the first known settlers to Jackson Parish was Jesse Wyatt. He and his wife, Elizabeth Hagler, came by packhorse from Catahoula Parish in 1815. Supposedly, Wyatt traded a keg of gunpowder to the local Indians to purchase land in Dalley. Born in 1777 in Kentucky, he was buried along with several family members and slaves in a little cemetery just west of Chatham in 1835. (Courtesy of the T.L. Colvin estate.)

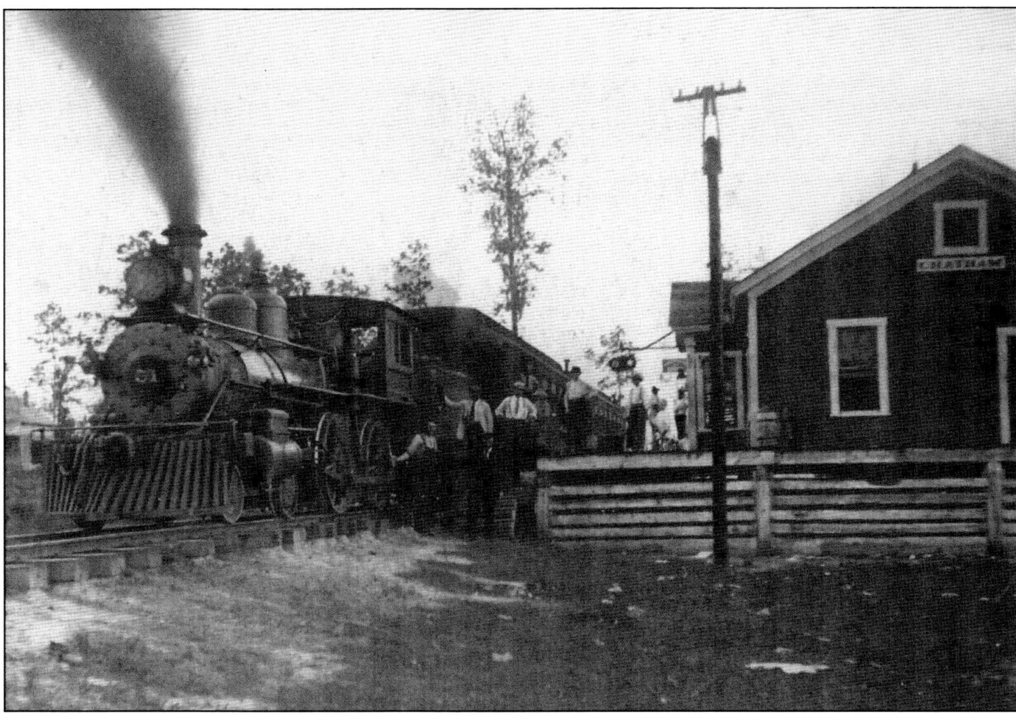

In 1905, the town of Chathamville was surveyed by Sam Collins, who worked for the Tremont Lumber Company. On July 4, 1905, serving as an official representative of Tremont, Collins stood on the depot loading platform and auctioned off town lots. People came from miles around to participate in the auction. (Courtesy of Ronnie Brumley Spillers.)

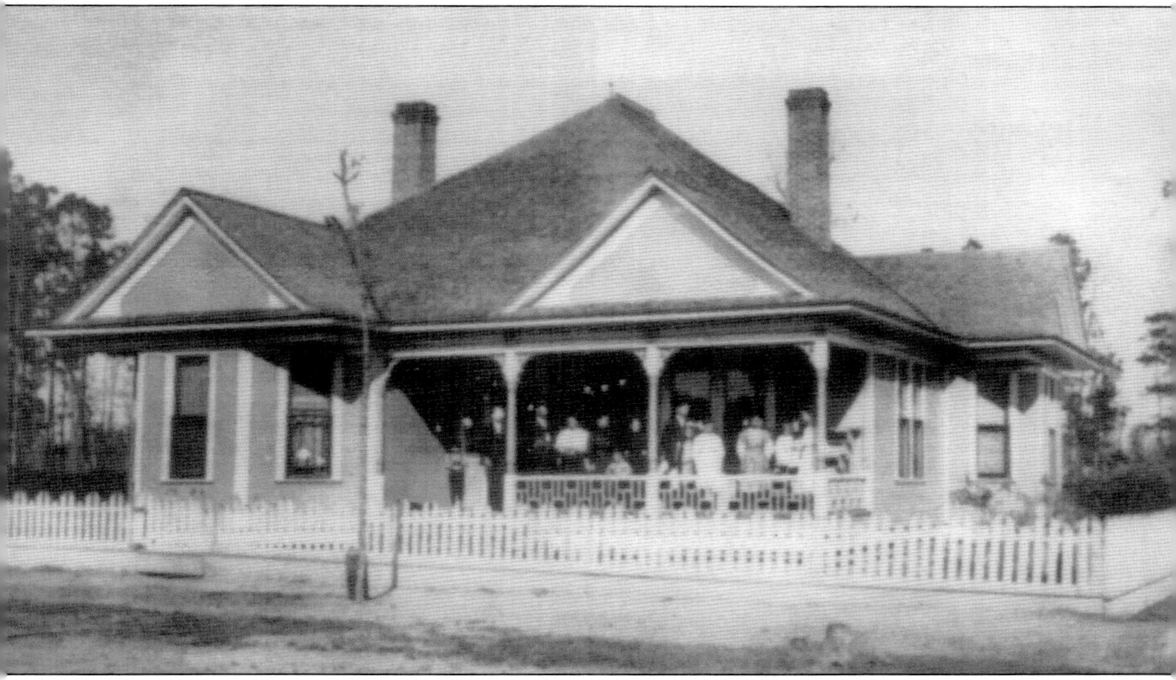

Dr. Sam Wilder was hired as the Tremont Lumber Company doctor and was given first choice of lots in the new town of Chatham. In 1904, he built this home and served as a company doctor for about 20 years. He also owned and operated a mercantile business. The Wilder house still stands today and is listed in the National Register of Historic Places. (Courtesy of Ronnie Brumley Spillers.)

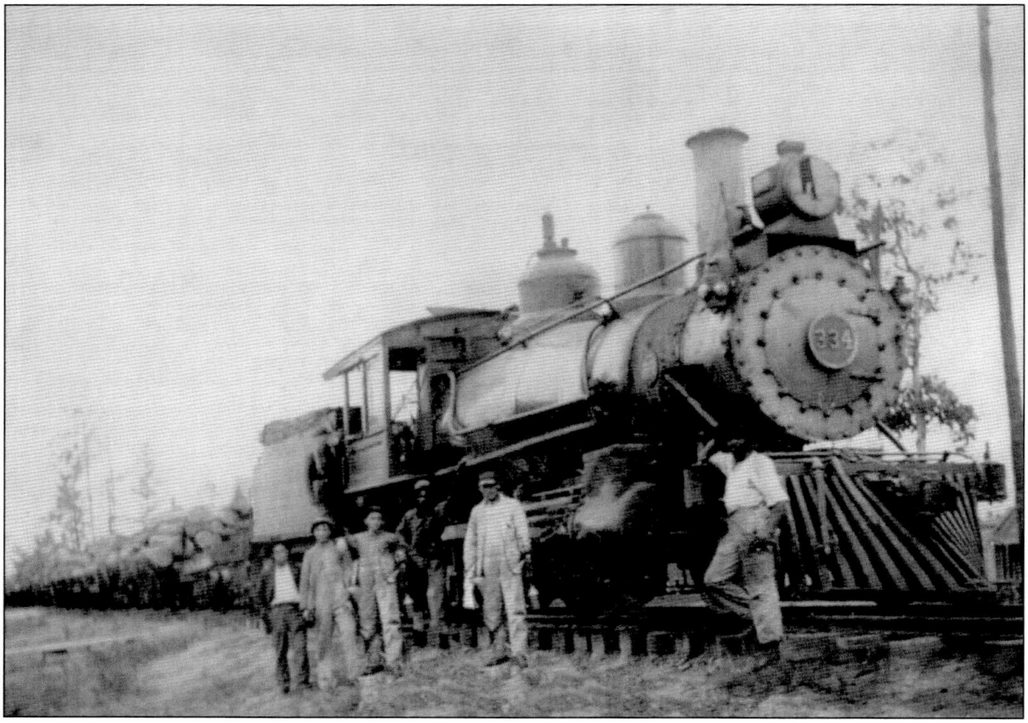

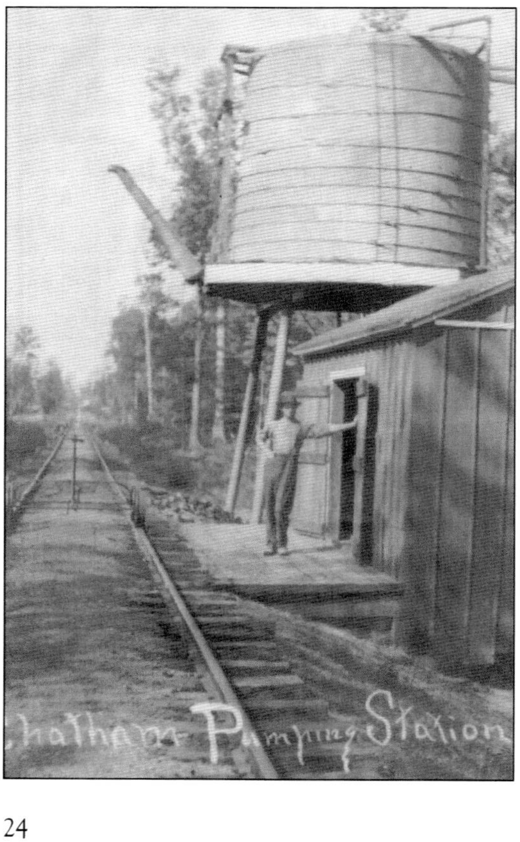


This is a log train in Chatham around 1912. Log trains serviced several mills in the area. The first was a stave mill that produced the narrow strips of wood that make up the sides of barrels, which were vital for the transportation of goods. Stave mills were frequently established in areas where timber was being harvested to take advantage of the easy availability of needed resources. (Courtesy of Ronnie Brumley Spillers.)

In the early 1900s, small locomotives fueled with wood supplied steam power to cranes, which were used to hoist logs onto railcars. Chatham built a pumping station for the trains to fill with water as they came into town or left. At one time, Chatham had four trains passing through the town in one day. (Courtesy of Ronnie Brumley Spillers.)

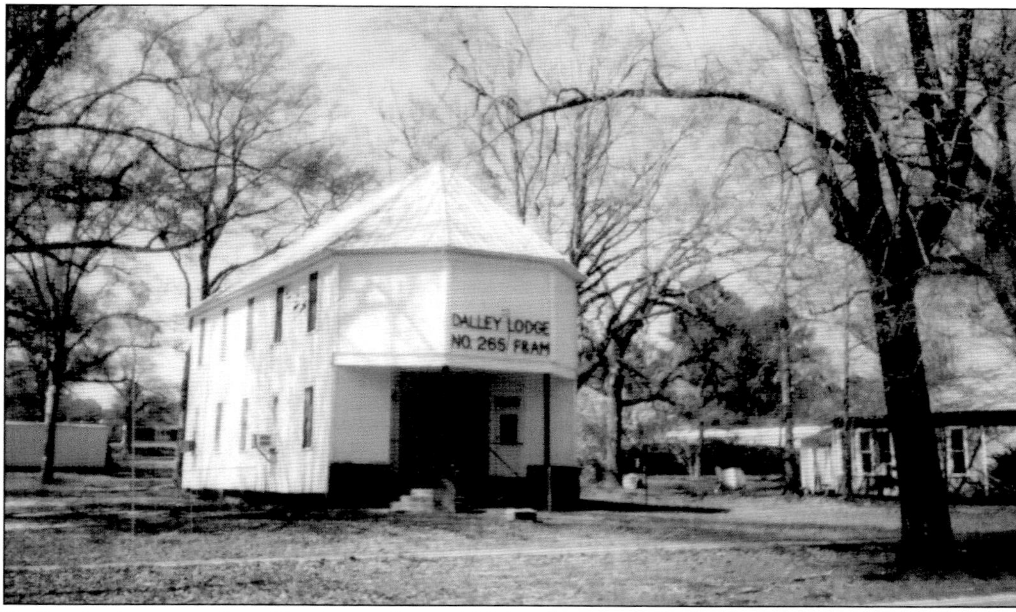


Dalley Lodge moved to Chathamville in 1906 and met in the upper floor of Forney and Roy Barnes until 1913, when a fire destroyed the building. A proposition was put forth to build, and Dalley Lodge and Woodmen of the World made a joint land purchase; the Woodmen agreed to build the first floor, and the masons constructed the second floor. The building was completed in 1914 and still stands today. (Courtesy of Ronnie Brumley Spillers.)

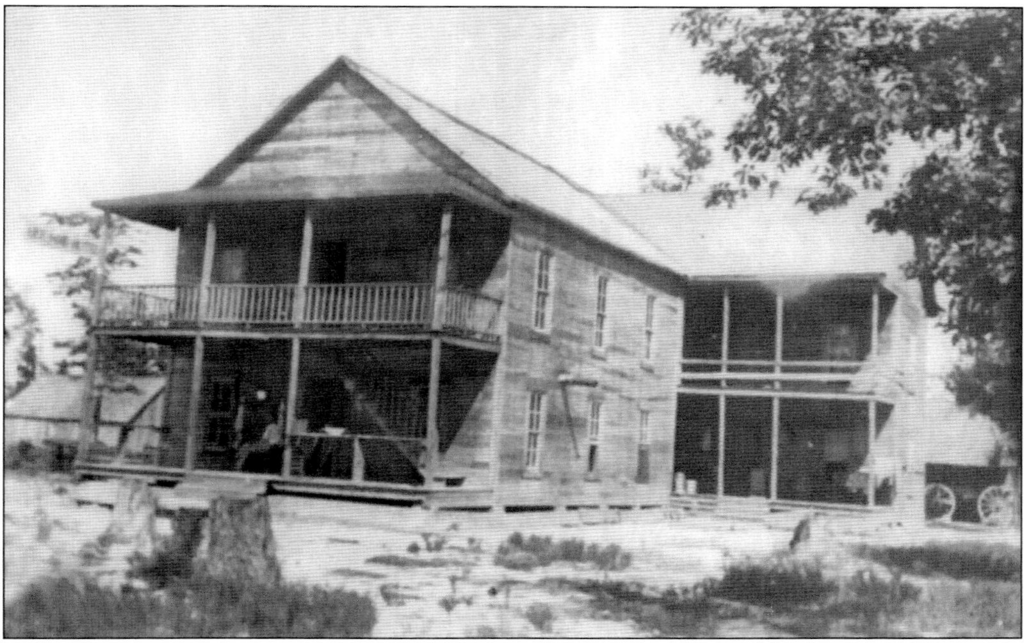

The Honey Bee hotel was constructed about 1908 by Oscar Stanford. It was a two-story building containing 25 to 30 rooms. The hotel was located on the corner of Johnson and First Streets. Its business mainly came from travelers and locals who stopped in for meals. (Courtesy of Ronnie Brumley Spillers.)

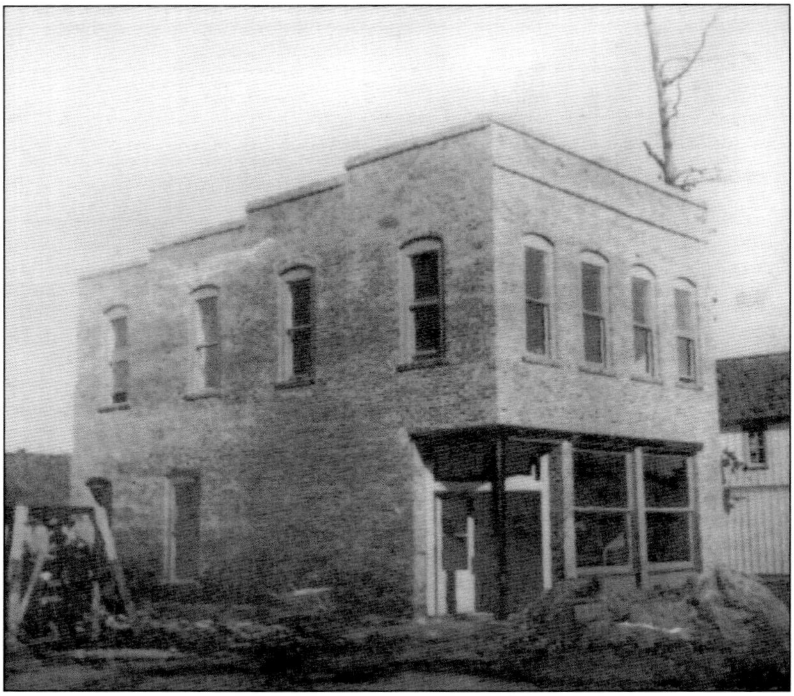

The Peoples Bank, chartered in 1907, was a two-man operation. It was a two-story building, and the second story held the telephone exchange service. The second floor was also once used by thieves in robbing the bank. They broke through the floor into the vault, and the bank did not know they had even been robbed until someone went into the vault. (Courtesy of Ronnie Brumley Spillers.)

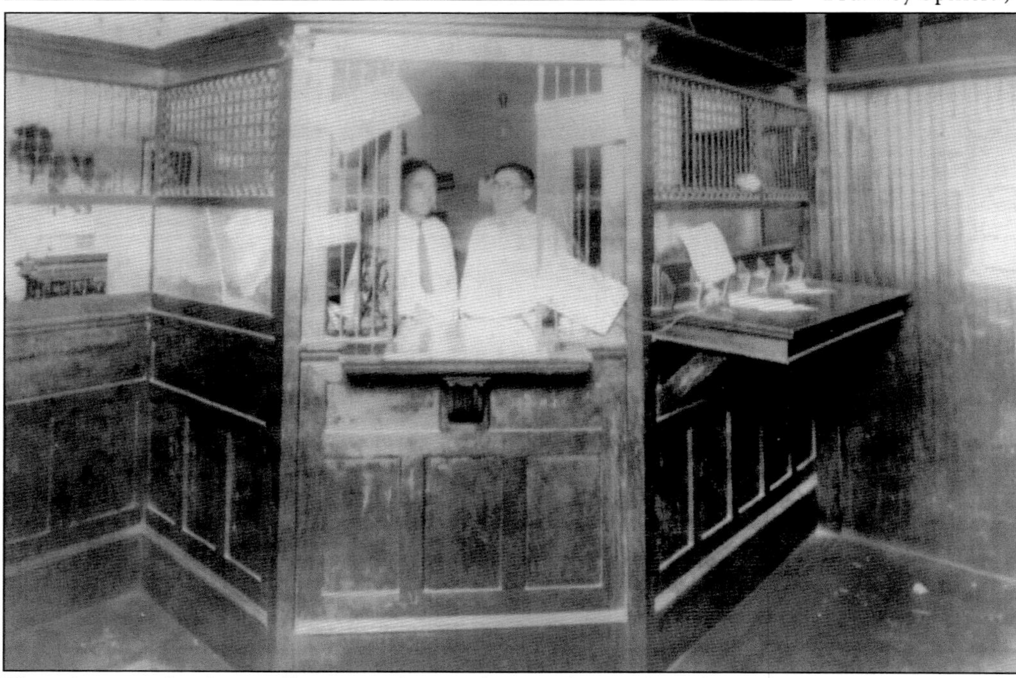

This photograph of two tellers was taken at the Peoples Bank in the 1930s. The entrance of the bank was constructed in the corner of the building on Highway 4. The top floor was later removed and remodeled. Later, it was moved from Highway 4 two blocks north on Highway 34, and a drive-through was added. The bank still serves the community and has recently been completely remodeled. (Courtesy of Ronnie Brumley Spillers.)

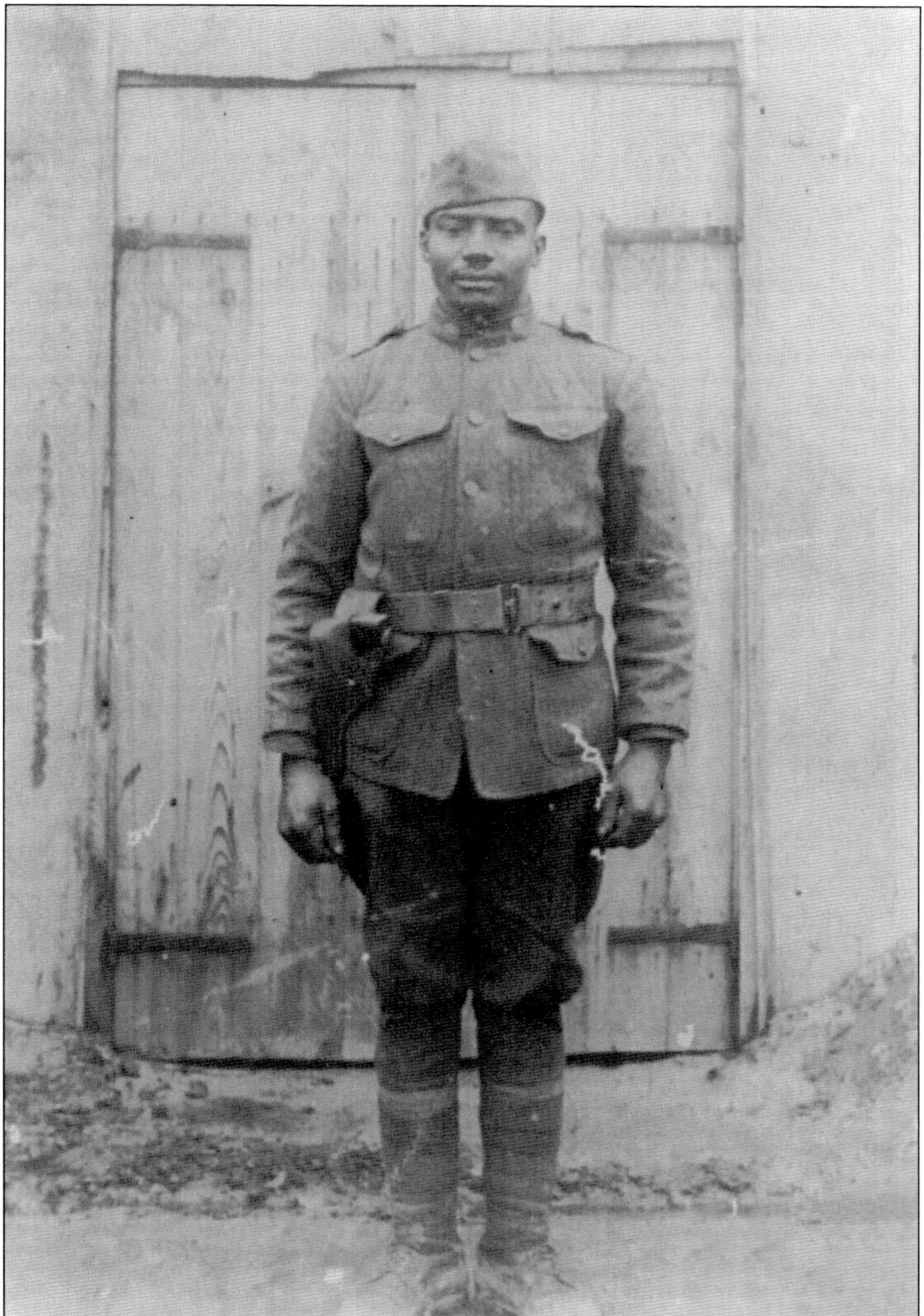

Alva Jackson West fought in World War I. During this time, the United States armed forces remained segregated. However, many black Americans eagerly joined the Allied cause following America's entry into the war. By November 1918, over 350,000 black Americans had served with the American Expeditionary Force. West returned from the war and lived the remainder of his life in Chatham. He is buried in Saint Clair Cemetery on highway 146. (Courtesy of Eddie Ruth Wyatt.)

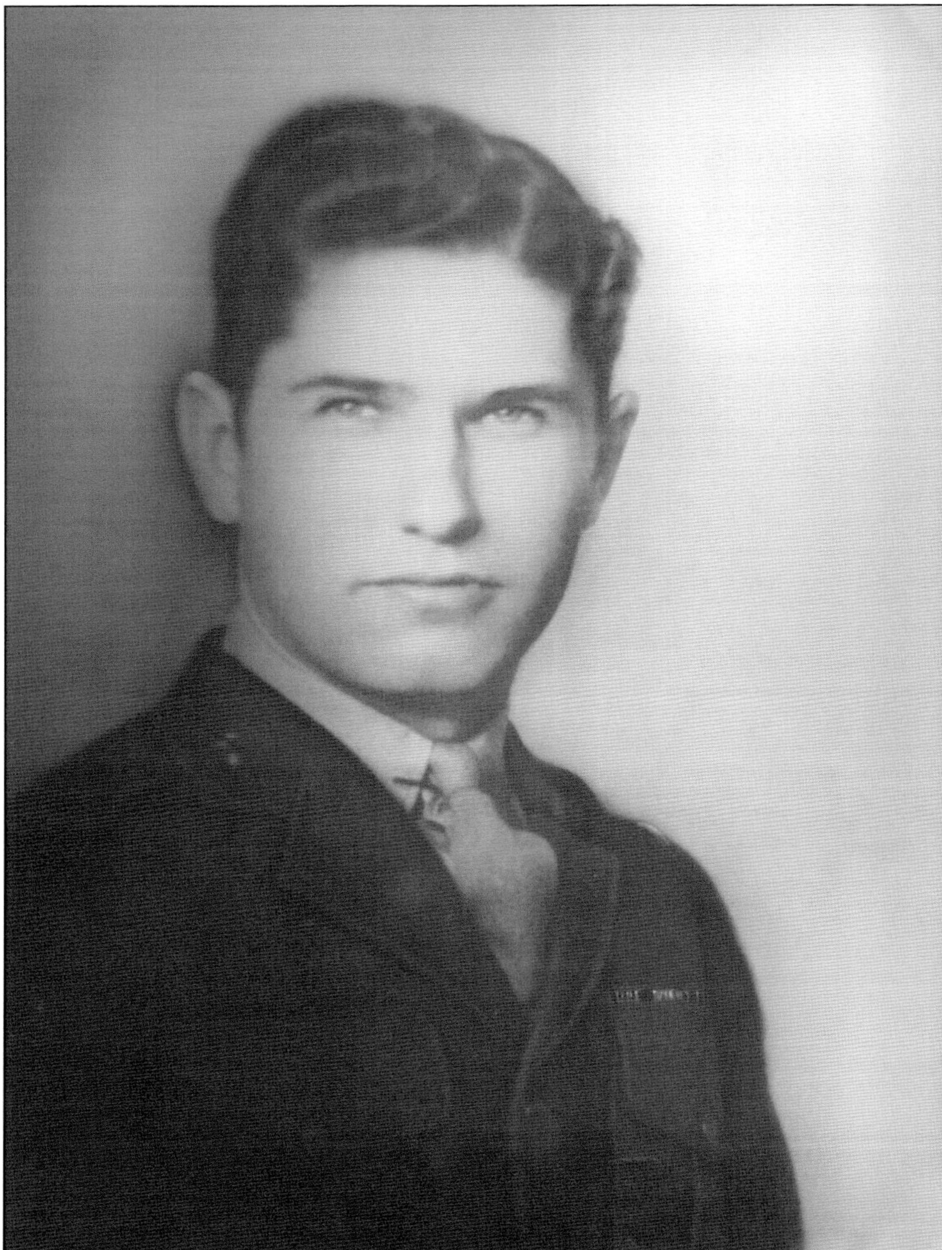

Harvel Moore was one of Jackson Parish's most decorated war heroes. Moore graduated from Chatham High School in 1938 and immediately enlisted in the Marines. He went overseas and died during the Battle of Tarawa, which took place from November 20 to November 23, 1943, at Tarawa Atoll in the Gilbert Islands. Nearly 6,400 Japanese, Koreans, and Americans died in the battle, mostly on and around the small island of Betio. Moore's body was never sent home. He was decorated with the Silver Star, Purple Heart, Presidential Unit American Defense Service Medal, Pacific Campaign Medal, World War II Victory Medal, and a citation with ribbon bar and two stars. (Courtesy of Herman Lenard.)

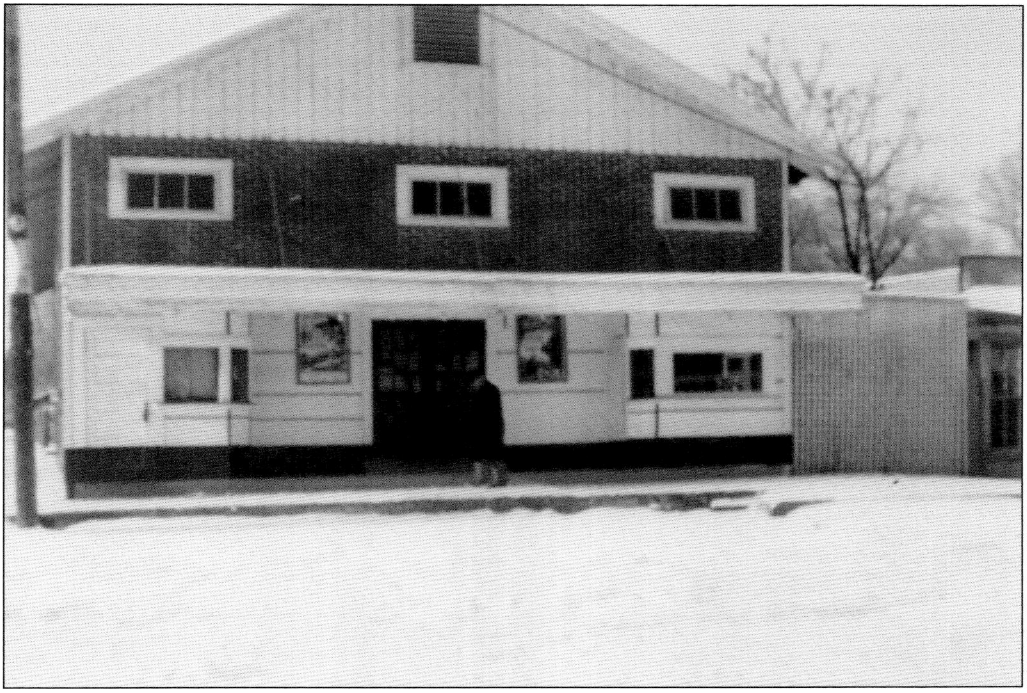

Chatham's first and only movie theater was built in 1939 by O.E. and Pauline Mitchell Brumley. There was only one screen, with upper and lower viewing balconies. The windows in the front of the building were used as a ticket window on the left and for selling popcorn and coke, the only choices for snacks, on the right. (Courtesy of Ronnie Brumley Spillers.)

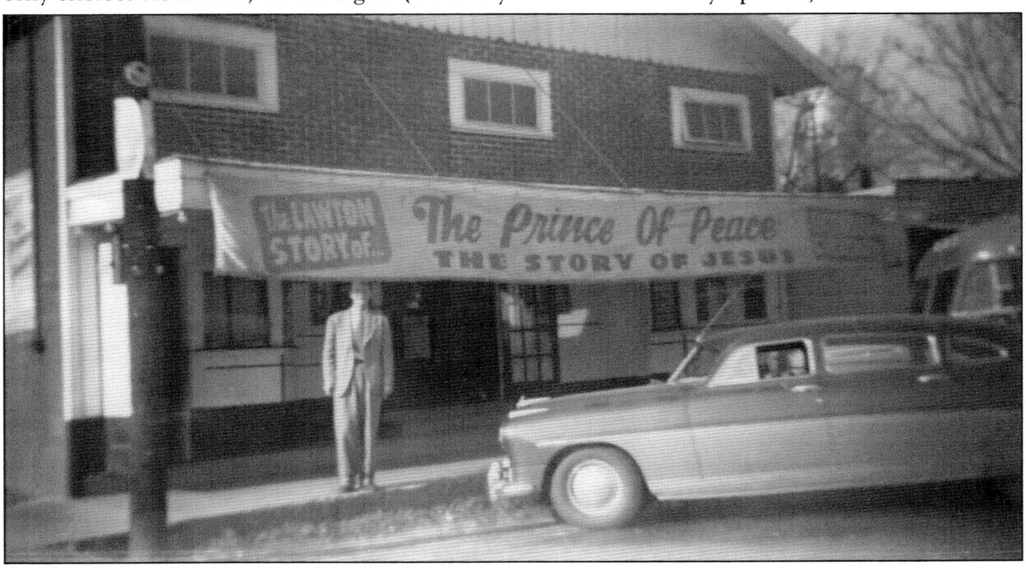


In 1948, the short film *The Prince of Peace* was released. It came to Chatham and the town closed its school and bused children to the theater to see it. By the late 1950s, television came to individual homes and the theater began to see a decline in business. The Brumleys decided to convert the building into a café. They sold shortly after the remodel. (Courtesy of Ronnie Brumley Spillers.)

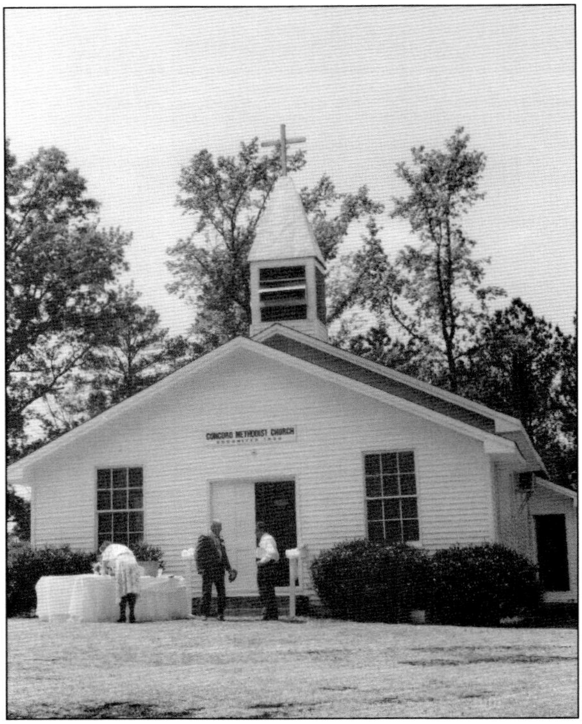


The Concord Church was established in 1890, just east of Chatham. James Barnes donated land with specific instructions that it be used for a church, which would also serve as a school and cemetery. This is the third church building on this site, erected in 1976. Soon after, a social hall and bell tower were added. (Courtesy of Sandy Waits.)

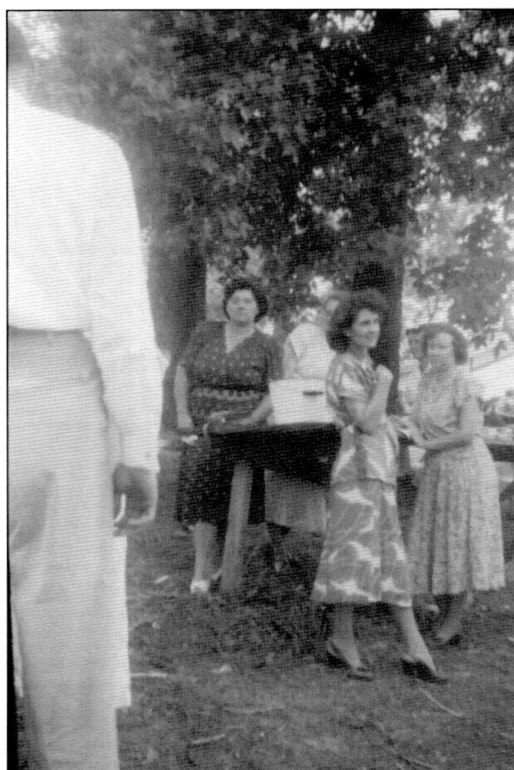

Homecomings and dinner on the grounds were part of the church community and were typically held once a year. Former preachers were often invited to speak, and meals were served on the grounds. These events were used to bring back distant family and friends for a weekend get-together. They would also include a visit to the cemetery. (Courtesy of Sandy Waits.)

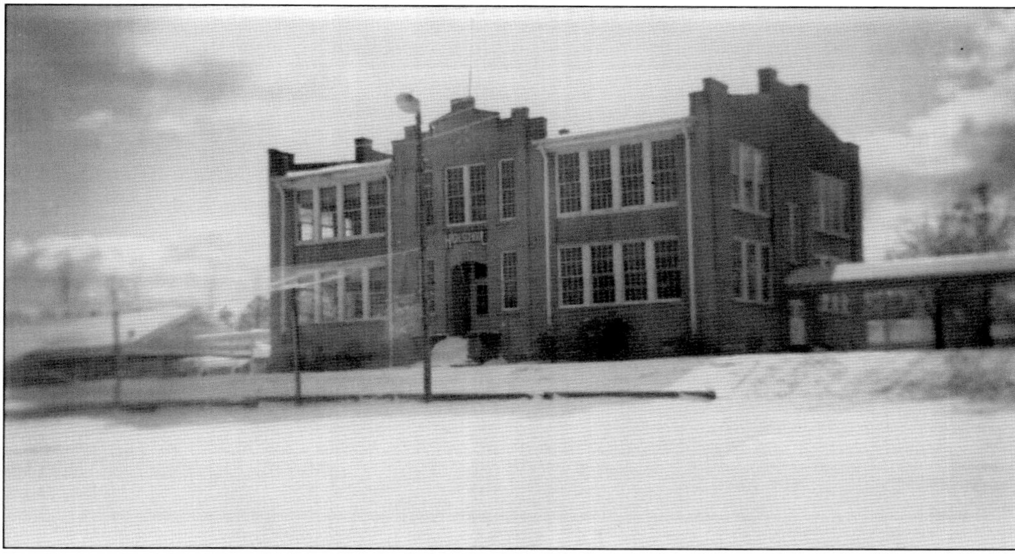

Chatham school started as a two-story frame building in 1906. Tremont Lumber Company donated 10 acres to the school board for a new building, and the first high school was built in 1917. Chatham became an accredited high school in 1920. Money ran out in December 1920, so the school had to close, but it reopened in September 1921. A new school needed to be built, especially with the consolidation of the surrounding schools. The 1931–1932 high school sessions began with a new structure for classes, and the 1917 building was used as an elementary. Chatham was consolidated into Jasper Henderson School in 2000. These buildings were recently torn down, and the Jackson Parish Library at Chatham was erected in its place. (Both, courtesy of Ronnie Brumley Spillers.)

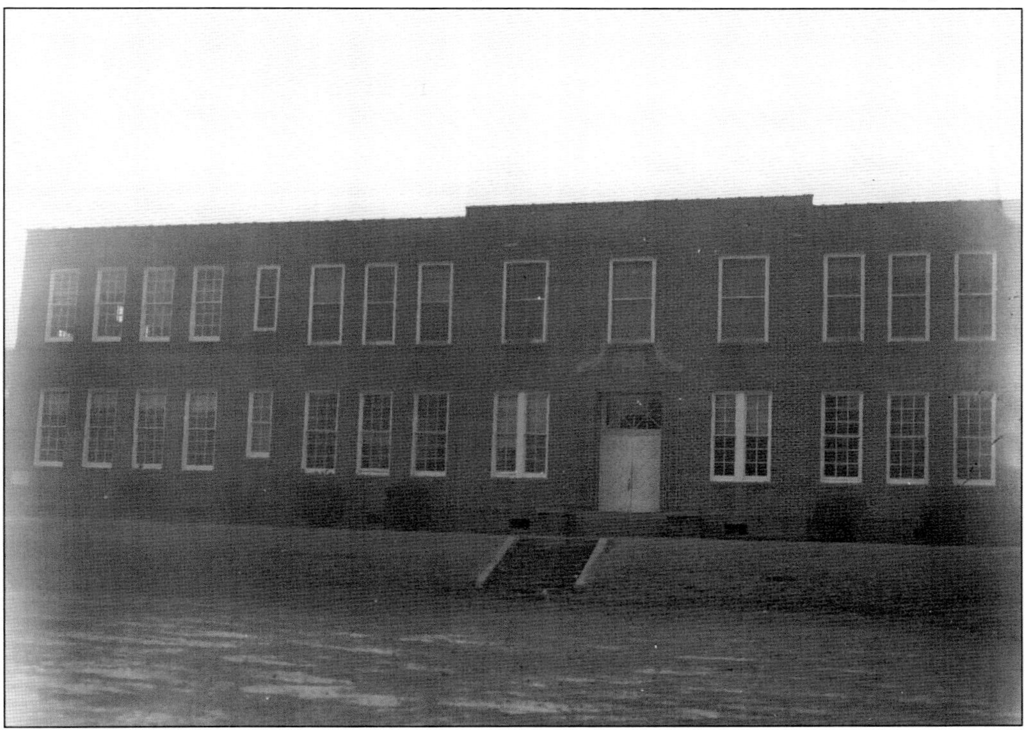

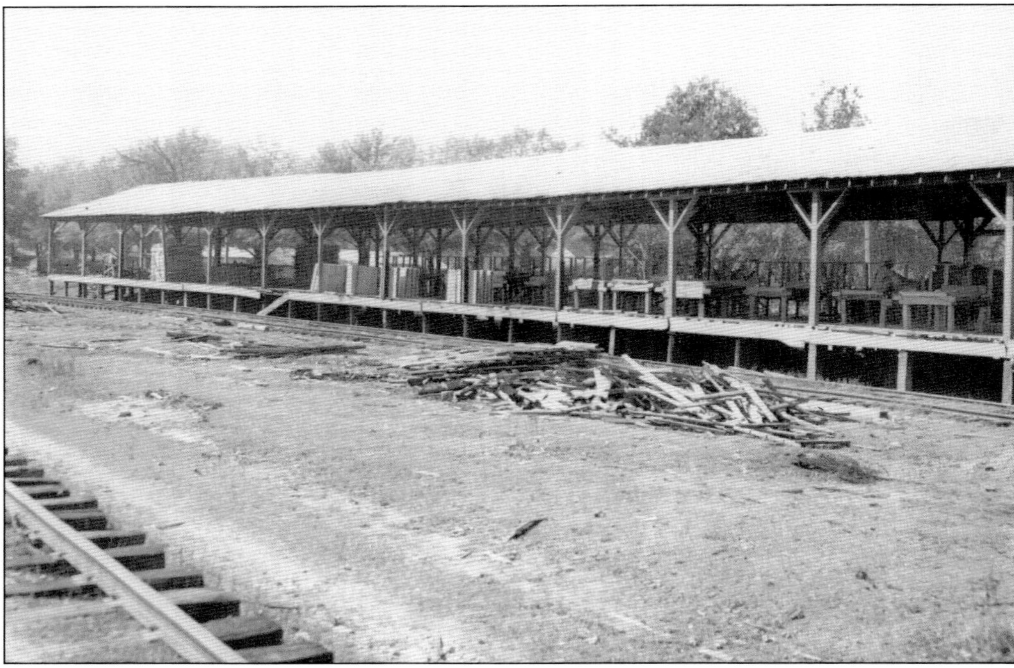

In the 1930s, the Tremont Lumber Company saw potential in truck farming and constructed a produce shed that was used for packing and loading locally grown tomatoes and potatoes. It was built about 100 yards from the depot towards Winfield. During the harvest season of 1938, Chatham shipped 60 carloads of tomatoes and 17 cars of potatoes. This production ceased in 1946. (Courtesy of Ronnie Brumley Spillers.)

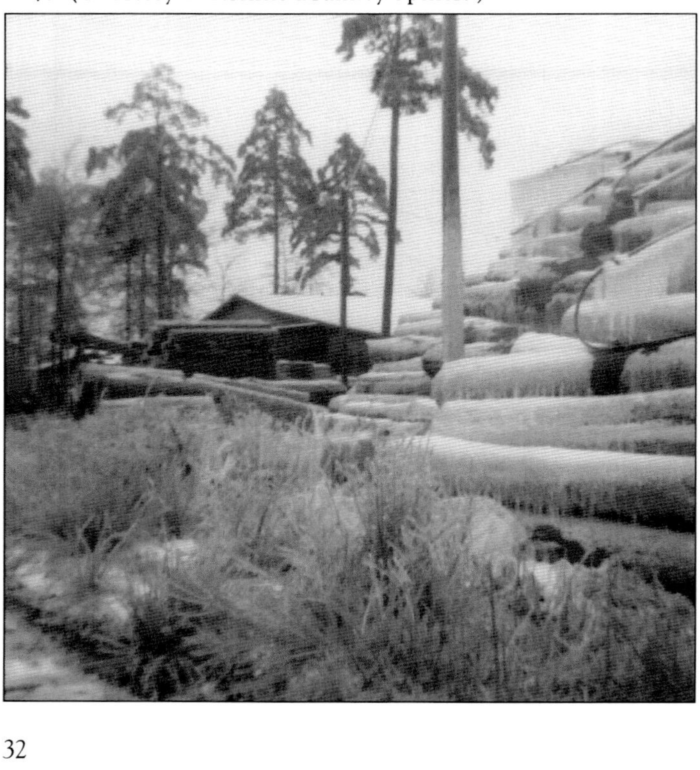

Winfred L. "W.L." Browder opened his first mill in 1938 and ran it for three years before World War II. Browder joined the service and served until 1945. He decided to build another mill in Chatham, and the W.L. Browder Lumber Company was established in 1947. In the mid-1960s, he switched to cutting oak logs for flooring and gum logs for furniture frames. Browder retired in 1983, and the mill shut down in 1989. (Courtesy of Ronnie Brumley Spillers.)

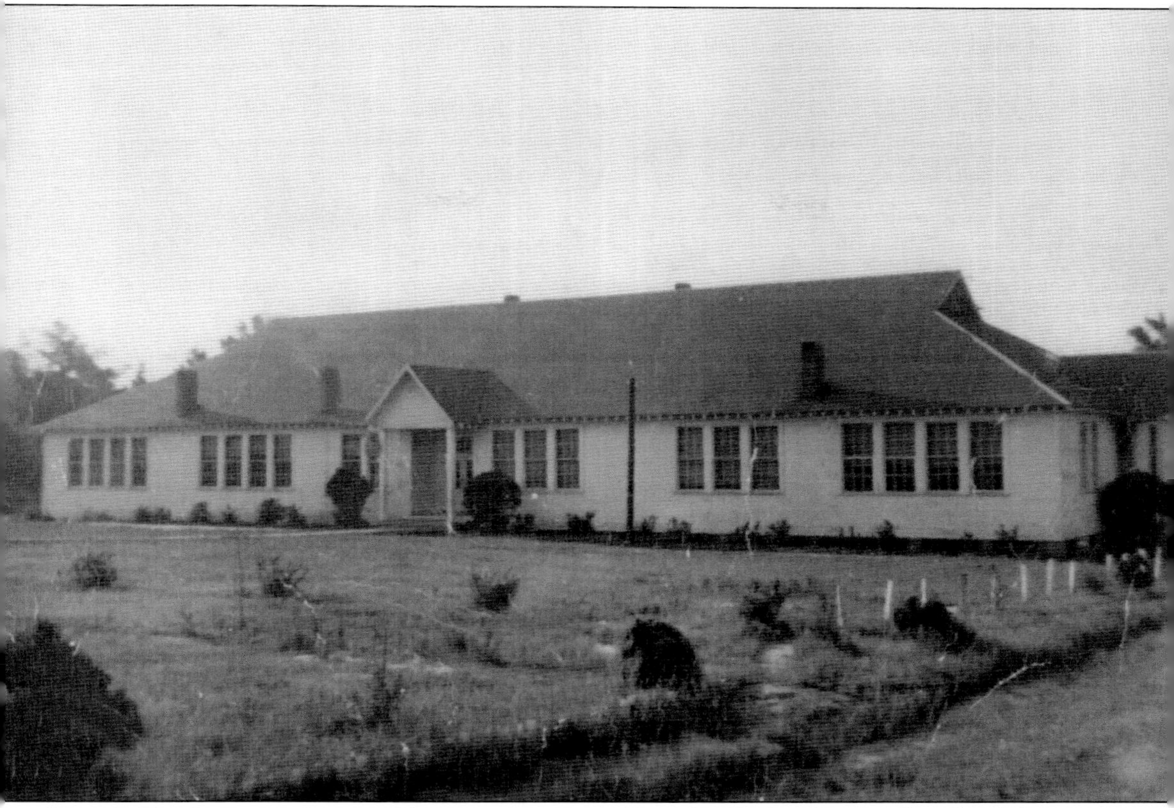

Jasper P. Henderson was born in Clay, Louisiana, in 1863. He had little education but this did not deter his ambition. He owned horses, hogs, a car, and 635 acres in Chatham. After Pine Grove closed, there were no schools for six years. So, he prepared his land with a building and went to the school board to offer the use of it. The board approved, and several sessions were carried out by various teachers. Henderson then offered the deed to six acres of his land to the school board to build a high school. They again accepted, and Chatham Colored High School was built. In April 1949, the board decided to honor Henderson by changing the name of the school to Jasper Henderson Elementary. A brick building replaced the original structure in 1955. Chatham High School was consolidated into Jasper Henderson Elementary, and it became Chatham–Jasper Henderson High School. (Courtesy of Eddie Ruth Wyatt.)

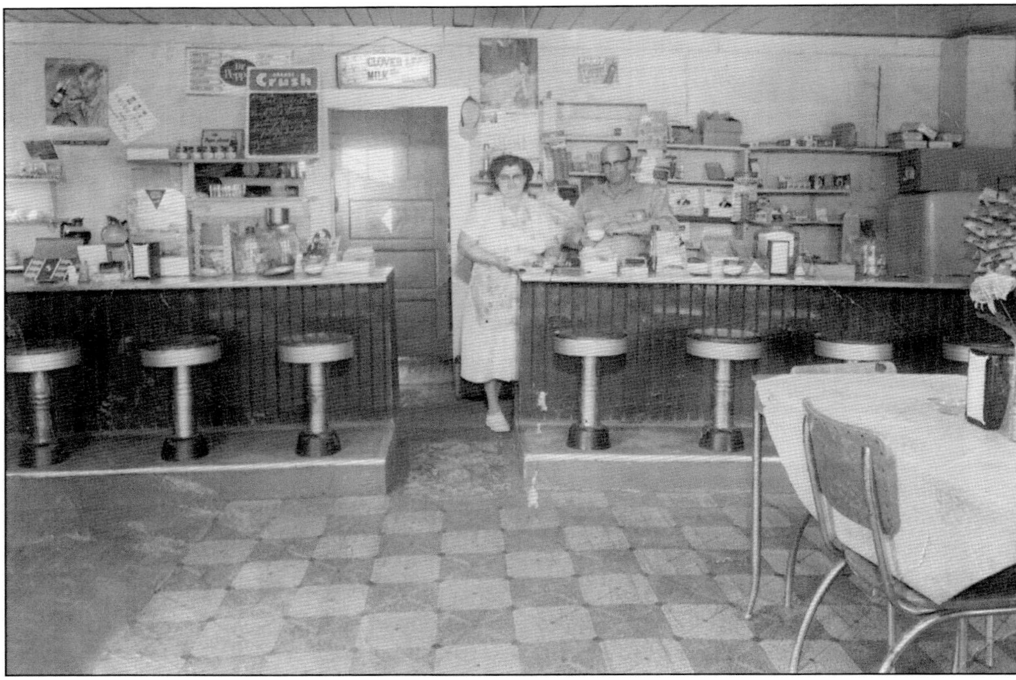


The Hiway Café was run by Joel Napoleon "Poly" Roberts and his wife, Una Miller Roberts. It was one of two cafés open in Chatham at the time. The Roberts owned and operated this café on Highway 4 until 1972, when Poly passed away and the business closed. (Courtesy of Sandy Waits.)

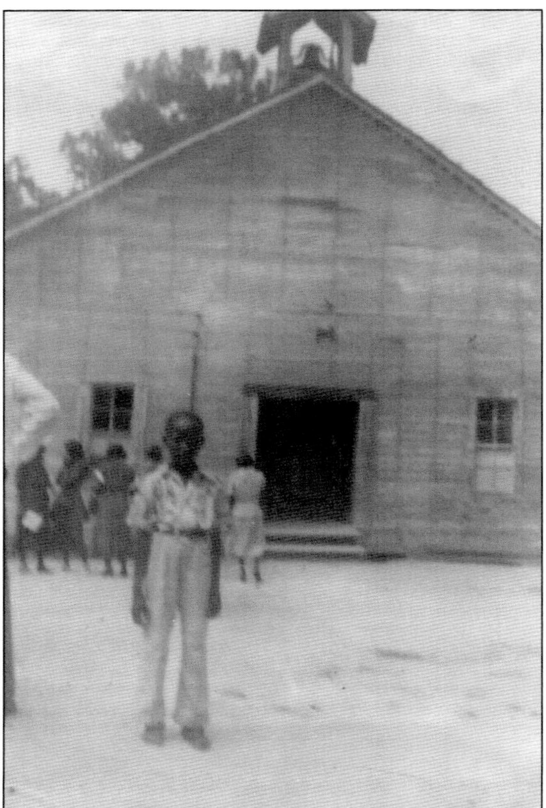

Mount Mariah Baptist Church's earliest recorded deed is dated October 19, 1894. In 1960, forty acres of land that belonged to Mount Mariah School were redeemed and deeded to Mount Mariah Missionary Baptist Church. The church is located north of Vernon. It has been rebuilt and is still in use today. (Courtesy of Eddie Ruth Wyatt.)

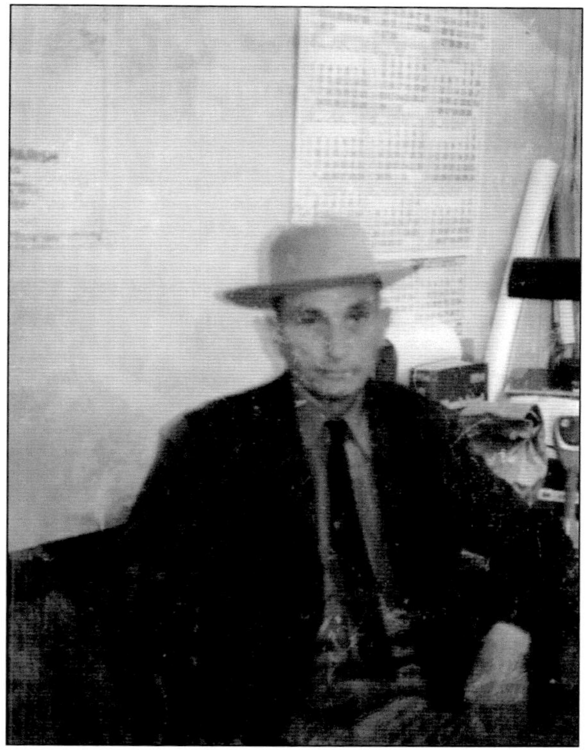

Murphy R. "Murph" Tolar was born in Jackson Parish, and his grandfather and great grandfather, who came from Mississippi, both owned land in the Weston community near the present-day Weston High School. Murph became marshal of the town of Chatham in July 1931. He then became deputy sheriff in May 1932. Murph and his son Jimmy began raising and training bloodhounds for use in the search for criminals through the dense woods and for hunters who got lost in the woods. Murph retired in 1964 and was given honorary status as deputy sheriff. (Both, courtesy of Jimmy Tolar.)

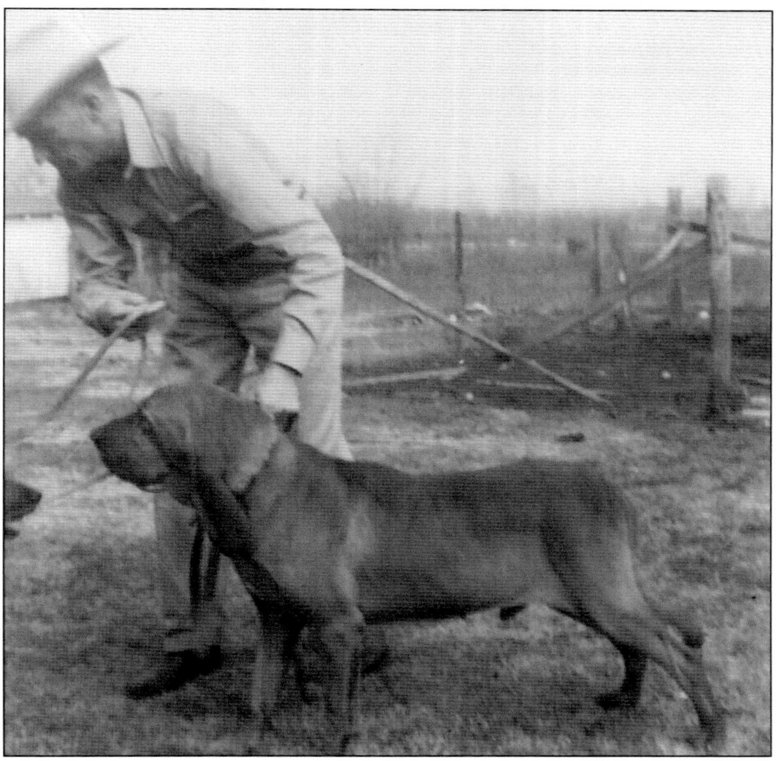

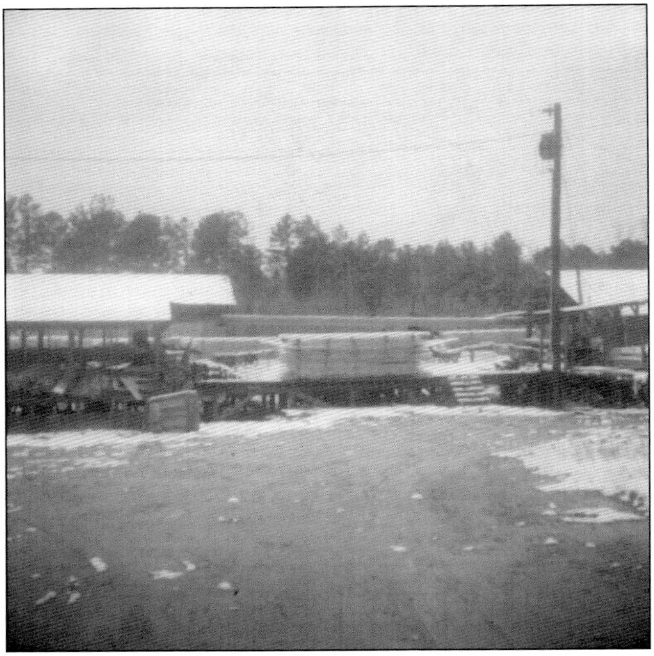

Walter T. Roberts came to Louisiana from Mississippi in the 1880s and bought land southeast of Chatham near the Jackson Parish and Winn Parish boundary. In 1889, Roberts saw potential in the timber of the area and decided to build a mill, to create a better life for his family. Roberts's Mill began production, lasting almost 82 years before closing. (Courtesy of Sonda Roberts Womack.)

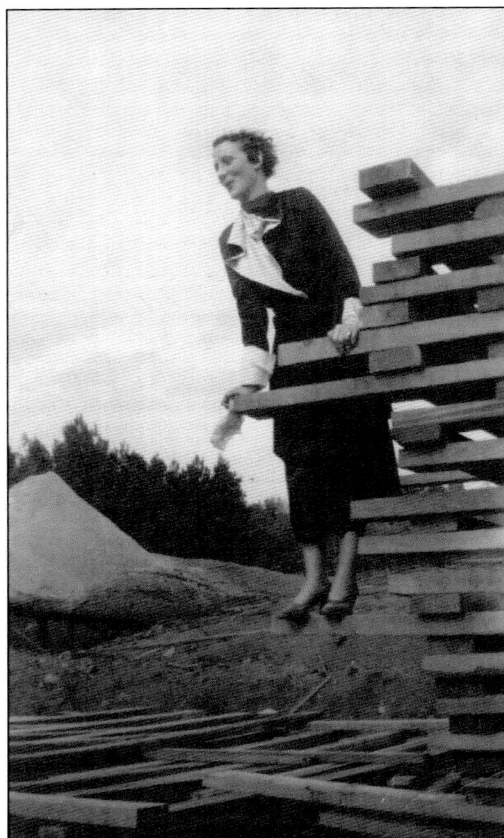

In the late 1930s, Walter T. Roberts's sons Willie and Nathan took over the mill. Willie hired men from Chatham and furnished transportation for them. In the mid-1950s, Willie bought out Nathan. In the 1960s, Willie's sons took over the mill and ran it until 1971. The family remembers the years of children playing at the mill; Aline Johnson Roberts, seen here, enjoyed playing at the mill as well. (Courtesy of Sonda Roberts Womack.)

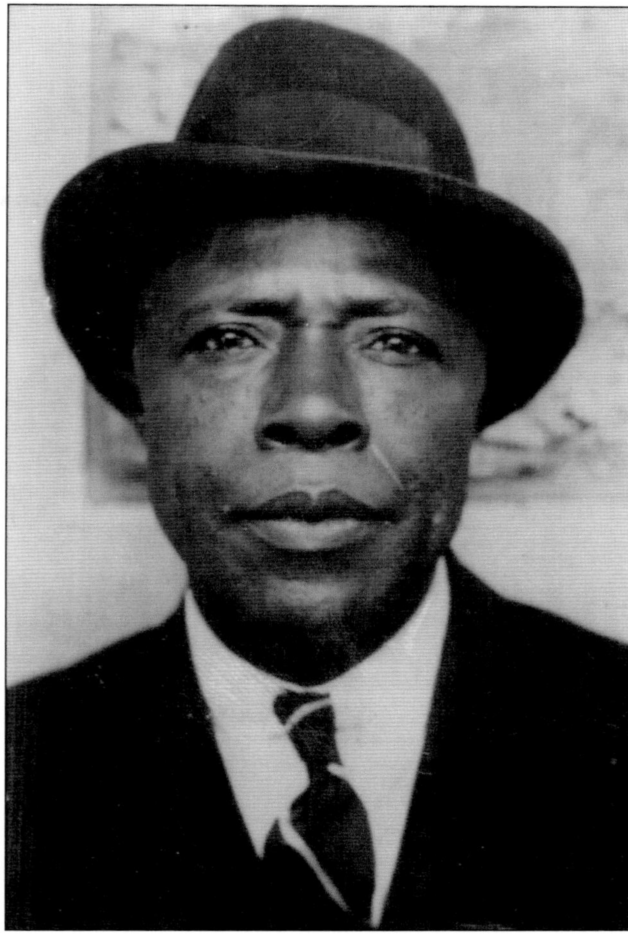

Rev. Lawrence Caesar Sr. was born in 1885 in Dodson, Louisiana, and moved to Jonesboro. He pastored at several Methodist churches, including Asberry Baptist Church. Reverend Caesar traveled to pastor these churches but continued to live in Jonesboro. When he died in 1957, he was carried back to Dodson to be buried. (Courtesy of Eddie Ruth Wyatt.)

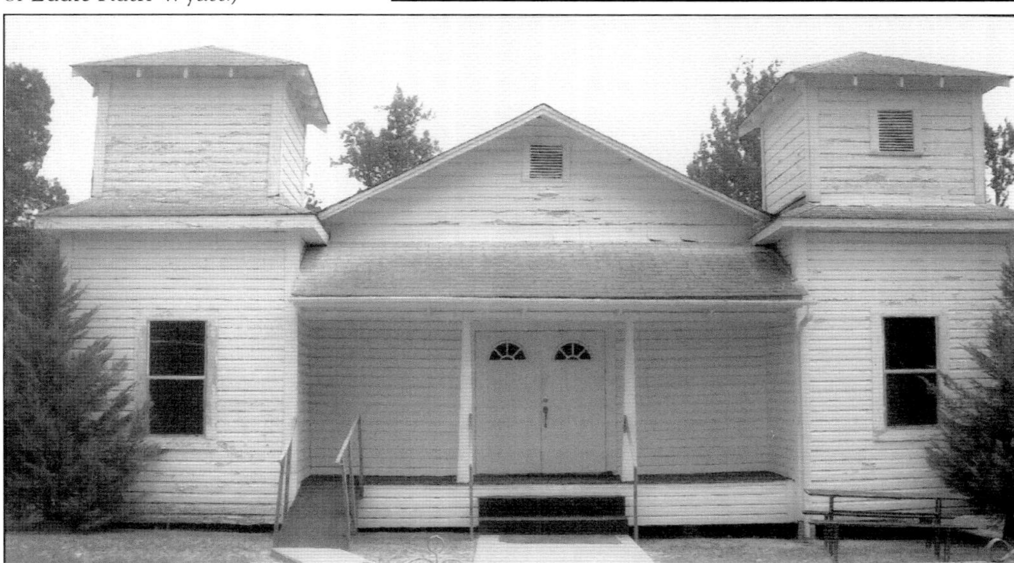

Asberry Baptist Church was organized in 1868, just a few miles north of Chatham on Highway 4. The church, school, and graveyard were on three acres of land in 1905. The second building was erected on the site of the original small church in 1944. It served its congregation until it was torn down and replaced with a new building in 2014. (Courtesy of Eddie Ruth Wyatt.)

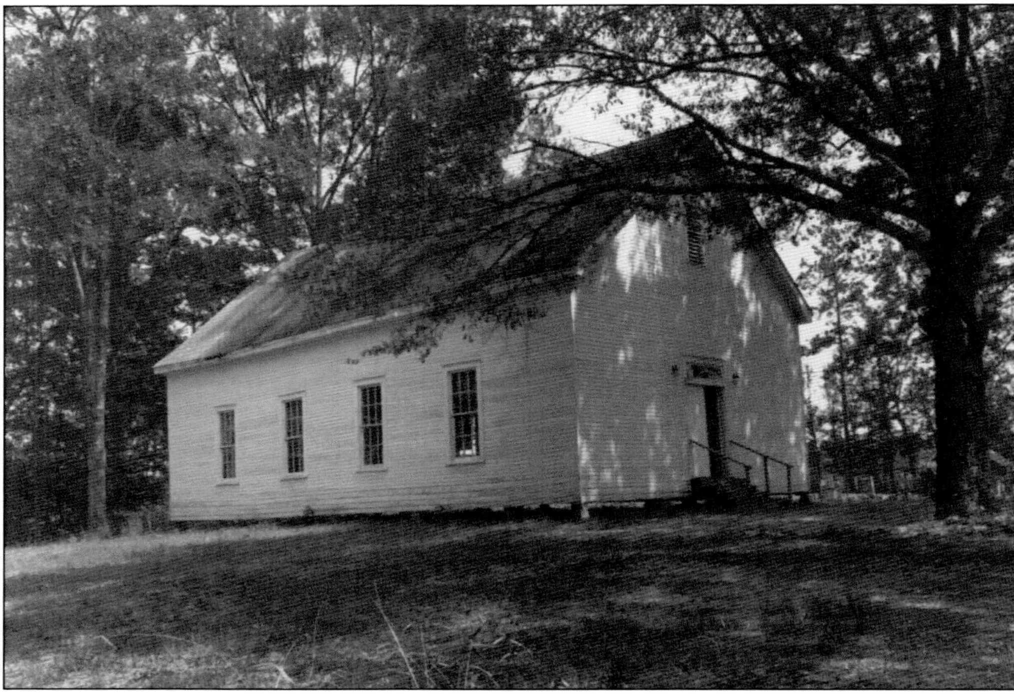

Brooklyn Methodist Church, established in 1838, was a small log structure. In 1902, descendants of the early settlers who founded the church erected a large one-room building that still stands today. Inside the church are the original pine wood seats from 1891. School was held in the church until 1904, when a small building was constructed and used for 18 years. Then it was consolidated with Chatham High School. After the Depression, many of the members began attending the more convenient First Methodist Church, located in the town of Chatham. In 1939, Brooklyn discontinued regular services. Because of its historic value, it has been preserved by the people of the community. Once a year, during the second week of September, the doors are opened for a homecoming revival. (Both, courtesy of Ronnie Brumley Spillers.)

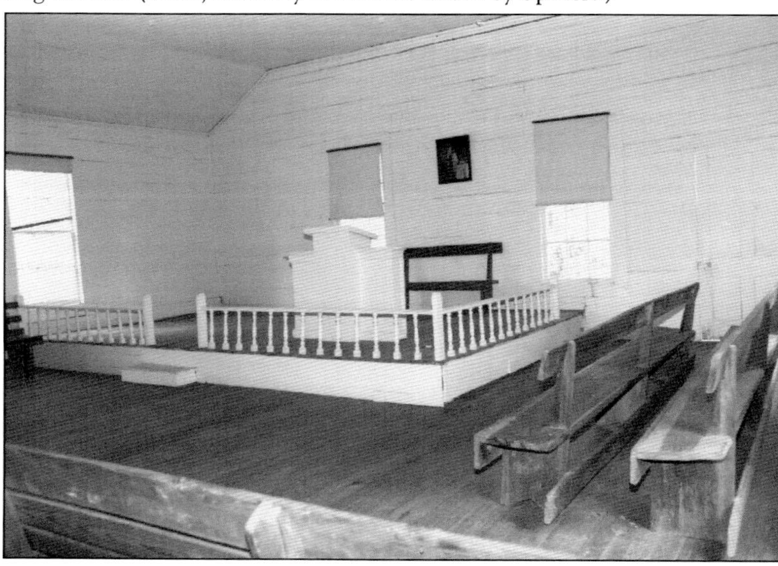

# *Three*

# South Central Communities

As pioneers crossed the country looking for new land, many stopped in Louisiana and stayed. Many areas of southeast Jackson Parish saw small communities being built. The Ebenezer community was established when a group of pioneers came to the area in the 1840s. As homes were built, the need for a church became paramount. This group held services in one of the homes until a church could be built, and in late 1849, the congregation had their church. A school became a necessity, and one was started around the 1890s. The little community thrived until the school was closed, and most residents moved into Weston or Chatham for work and school.

No one is sure exactly when the community of Weston began or how it was named, but a public school was started in 1882 in an area called Rock Springs. As the population grew, so did the need for a large school; after moving a little farther south, the school reopened for a short time and was then moved again to its present site. Weston was a thriving town with a store, churches in the area, and even a post office. It currently has one of the three remaining high schools in the parish. One convenience store, along with a few churches, is all that still stands in the community.

In the late 1840s, more settlers from Mississippi traveled into Louisiana and decided to stay, buying land and creating the Walker community. By 1918, it was decided that land and a house would be bought in this area to consolidate the other small schools into one large school. This was a successful endeavor until enrollment dropped in the 1940s and the school was closed, causing students to go to Jonesboro and Weston.

The small schools of Midway and Stovall were closed and consolidated into the Walker School. The Midway community stayed strong. Its church still stands today and is used on a regular basis. Stovall had thriving businesses, and many people from the surrounding communities traveled to get supplies and mail there. J.J. and George Stovall ran the businesses, and after J.J. left the area for Dodson in 1902, George had the post office moved into his home near Weston, which led to the closing of the town of Stovall.

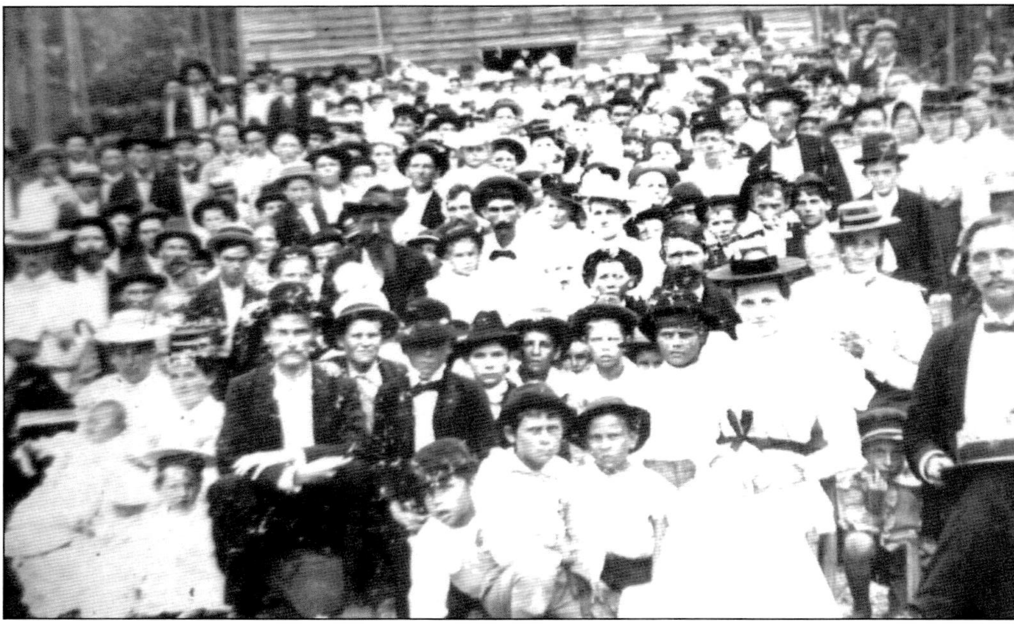

Midway Baptist Church was established in October 1896, and the first services were held in the Anders schoolhouse. Services were the first Saturday of the month. This is a picture of the entire congregation, showing only a glimpse of the second building, a two-story church, in the background. In 1900, A.G. Anders donated two acres of land for a church. The deed was recorded in 1905. (Courtesy of Patricia Maddox.)

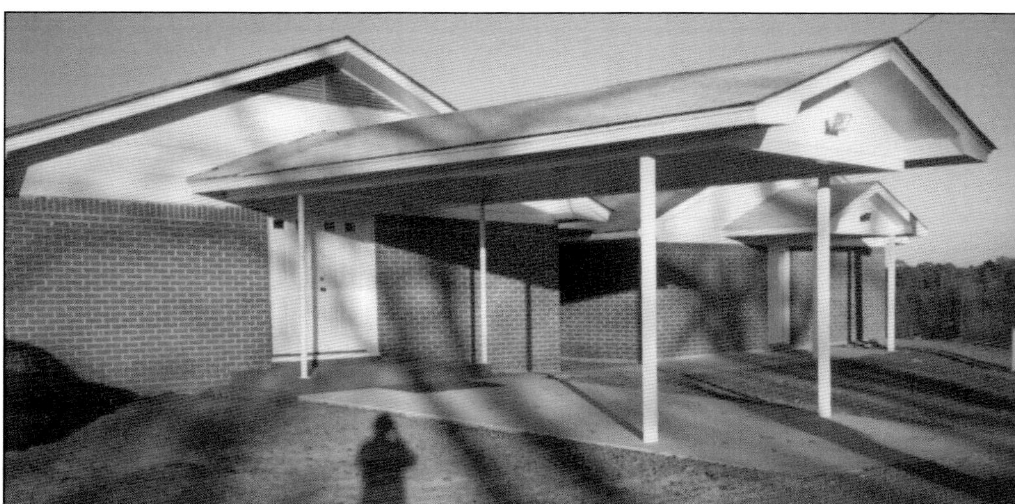

Midway started as a one-room church that was also a school and was later consolidated into the Walker School in 1918. A second building was erected after the first burned. A third wooden building was constructed, and the second one was moved. Then a fourth, larger structure with better facilities was built. This brick building was erected in the 1960s; later, a fellowship hall was added. (Courtesy of Lucille Anderson.)

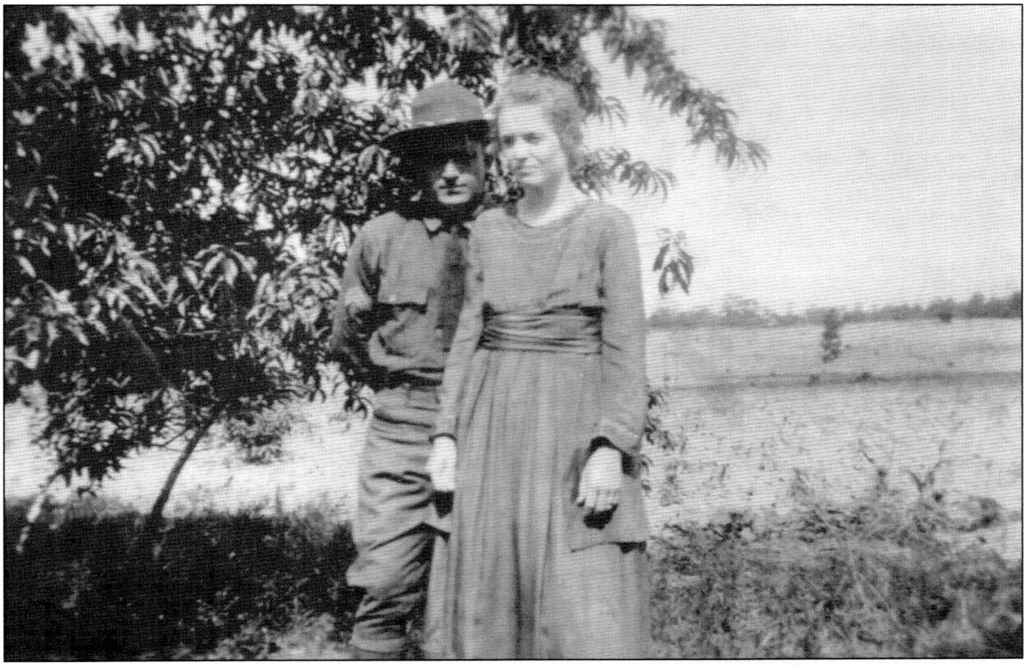

Around 1917, Henry Posey McBride posed in his World War I uniform only a few months after his marriage. He served from September 18, 1917, to April 24, 1919. Posey, as he was called, taught in the 1930s at Jonesboro-Hodge High School. He then served from 1940 to 1948 as deputy sheriff of Jackson Parish, and in 1948 was elected as sheriff and served until 1952. (Courtesy of the McBride family collection.)

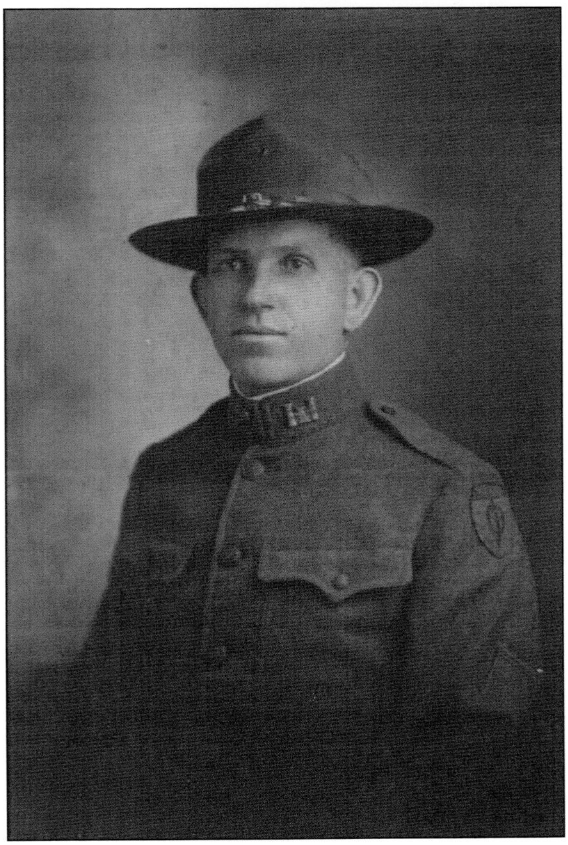

Benjamin Luther Avery registered for service in World War I on June 5, 1917, and was honorably discharged on March 21, 1919. He, along with many other young men from Jackson Parish, joined the war effort. This left many families without the help of their sons and husbands. The Weston community, along with the surrounding towns, lost many of its children to the war. (Courtesy of Glen Nash.)

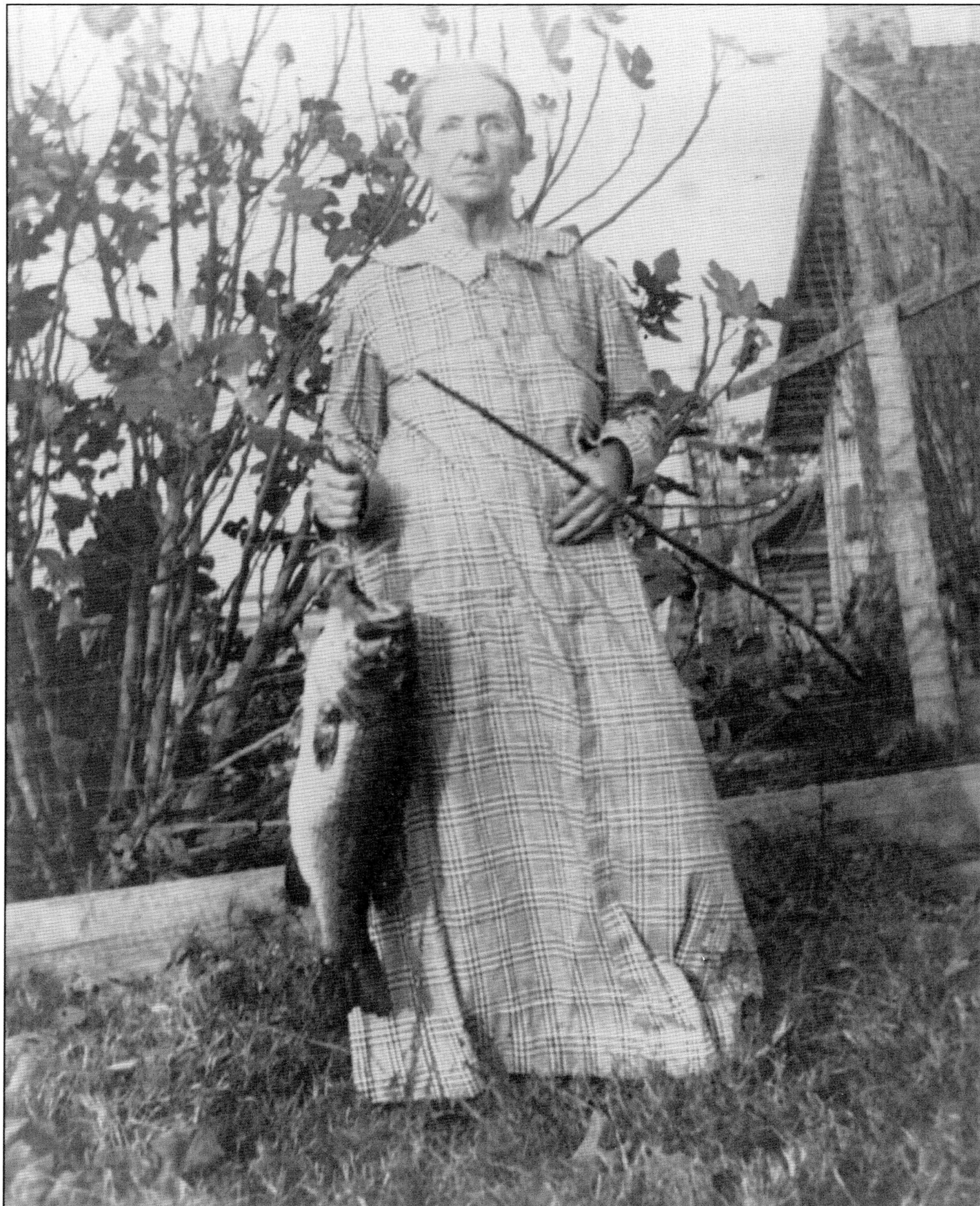

Martha "Babe" Walsworth, pictured around 1920 at age 70, shows off her large bass catch from a deep hole on Caney Creek in the Weston community. Cane poles, like the one she used, often took weeks to months to dry out. If a slight bend began to form, the pole had to be weighted and straightened to cure correctly, so it could handle the weight of a fish. (Courtesy of Johnny Culpepper.)

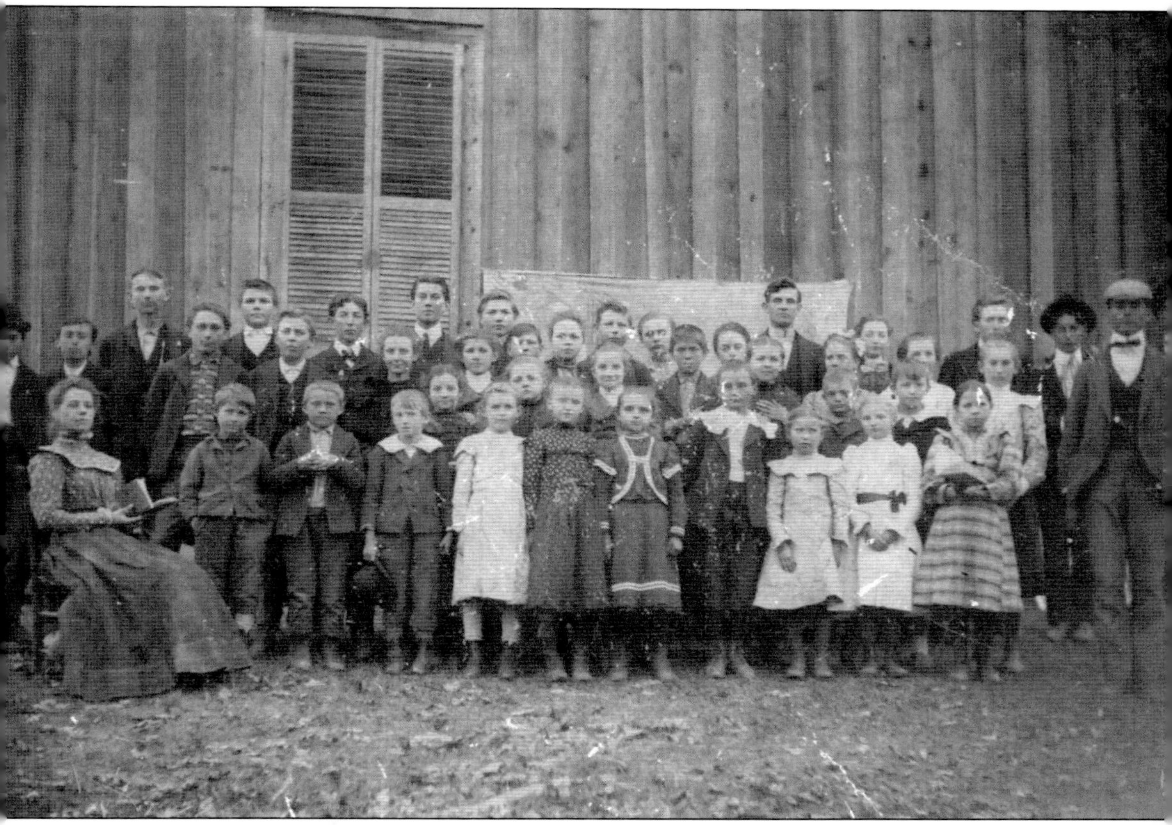

The school held in the Ebenezer church began in the late 1800s and had two teachers by 1918. In the late 1840s, a little group of pioneers settled there, and Ebenezer Missionary Baptist Church was organized in August 1850. Attendance was sometimes poor due to bad travel conditions and limited modes of travel. In the late 1800s, school and church were held in this building, which was located where the cemetery is now. This school was closed and consolidated with Weston because of low enrollment. (Courtesy of Glen Nash.)

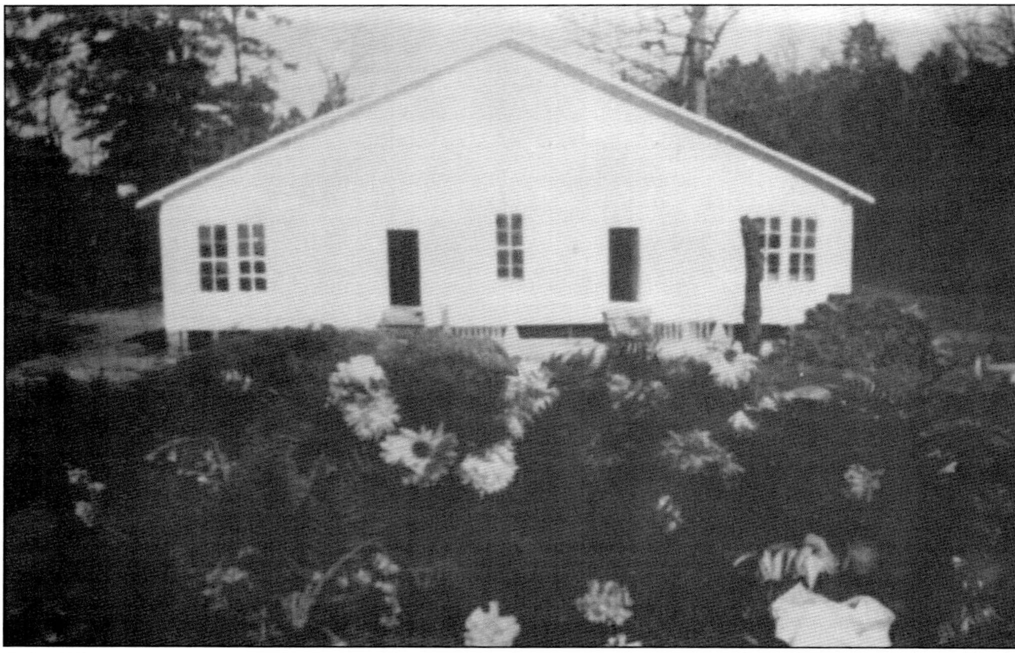

A building committee was appointed to erect a new church for Ebenezer in 1903, and in 1904, it was finished. In 1921, the church began to lean, and poles were used to correct this and fix the windows. Around 1926, the church was enlarged, and double windows were added to each side. In 1933, the old school building was obtained from the school board and used to build Sunday school rooms. (Courtesy of Ebenezer Baptist Church.)

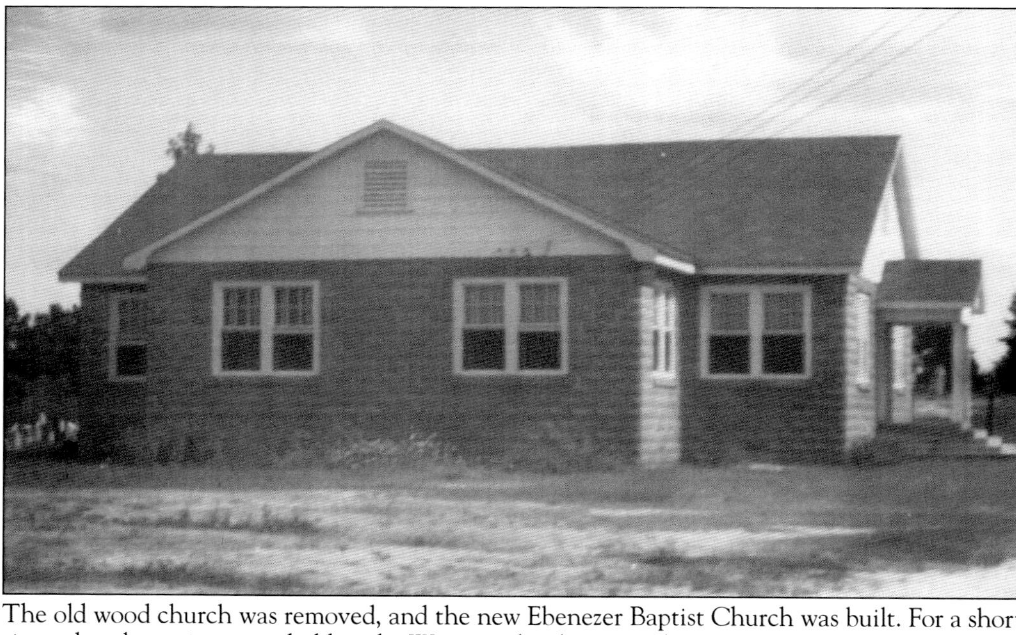

The old wood church was removed, and the new Ebenezer Baptist Church was built. For a short time, church services were held in the Weston school gym, and on June 22, 1947, the first service was held in the new building. On August 28, 1949, the 100-year celebration and dedication of the new building and pastor's home was held. (Courtesy of Ebenezer Baptist Church.)

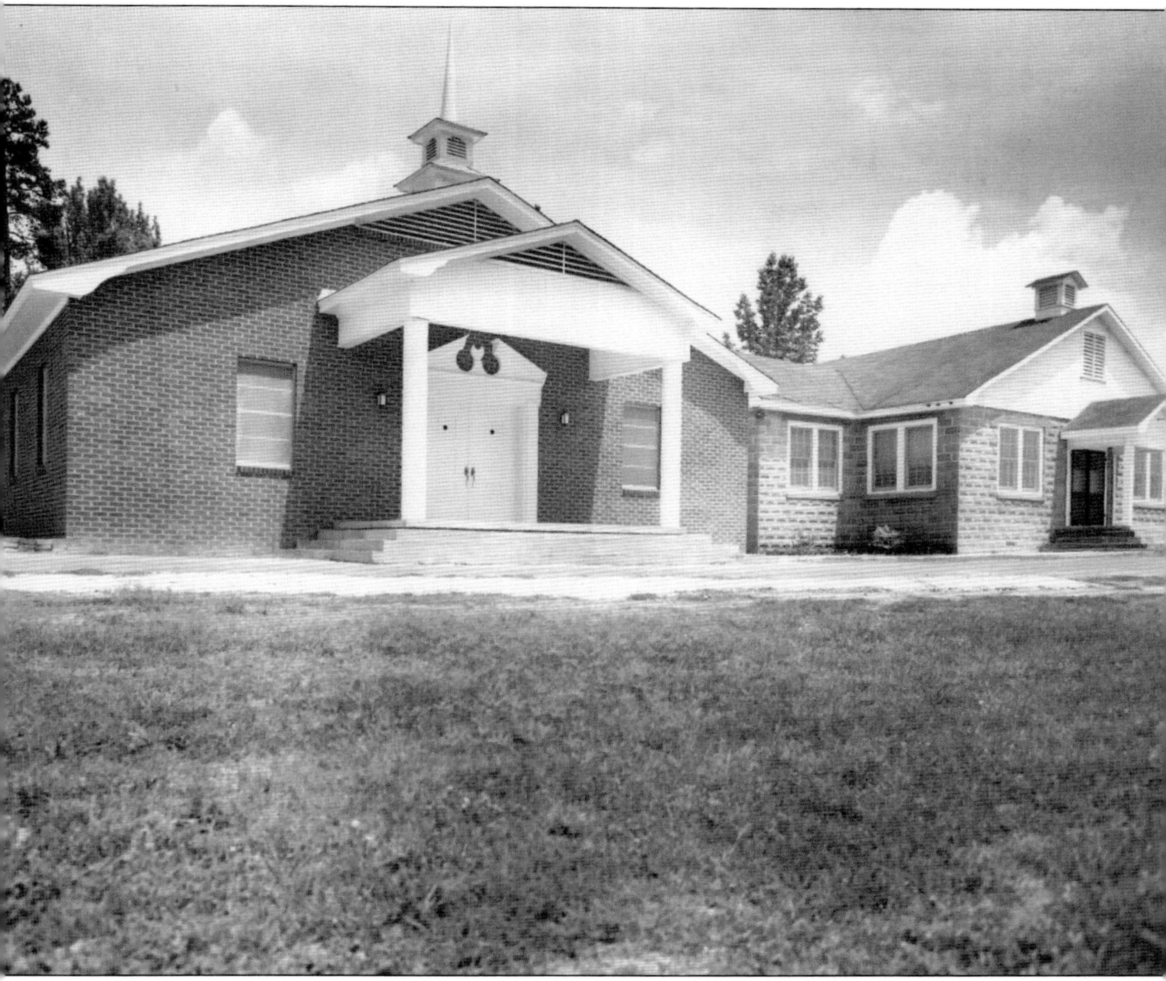

In 1958, a new church was built. The auditorium was of brick veneer and measured 44 by 70 feet. There were four rooms, with two at the front and two in the back. The front had a vestibule closed off by doors. A breezeway with a concrete walkway was built to connect the old building to the new one. In 2004, the old auditorium was torn down, and the Family Life Center was built, complete with a library, offices for staff, a kitchen, and rooms for Sunday school. The two connected buildings were set up for use by the youth. (Courtesy of Ebenezer Baptist Church.)

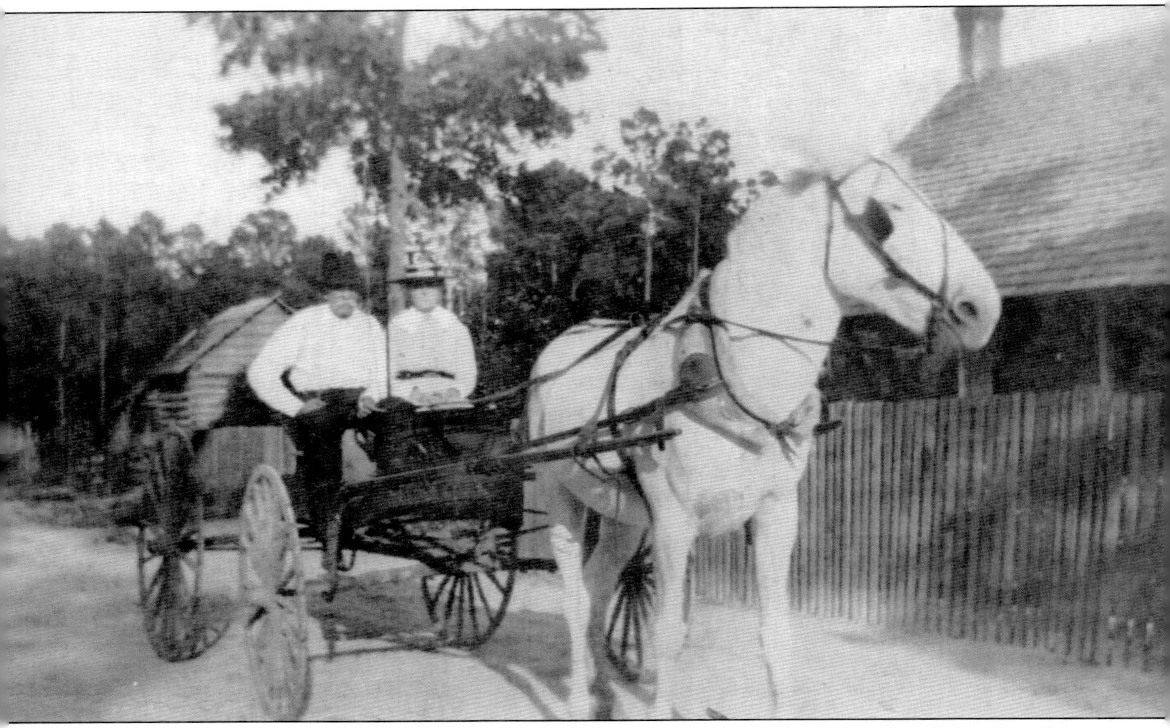

Modes of transportation in and around the Weston community consisted mainly of walking or riding a horse or a horse-drawn buggy. Here, L.D. Avery and his wife, Viola, are in their buggy, ready for church. Avery was appointed as a deacon to Ebenezer Baptist Church in 1883 and served on the building committee board in 1903. (Courtesy of Glen Nash.)

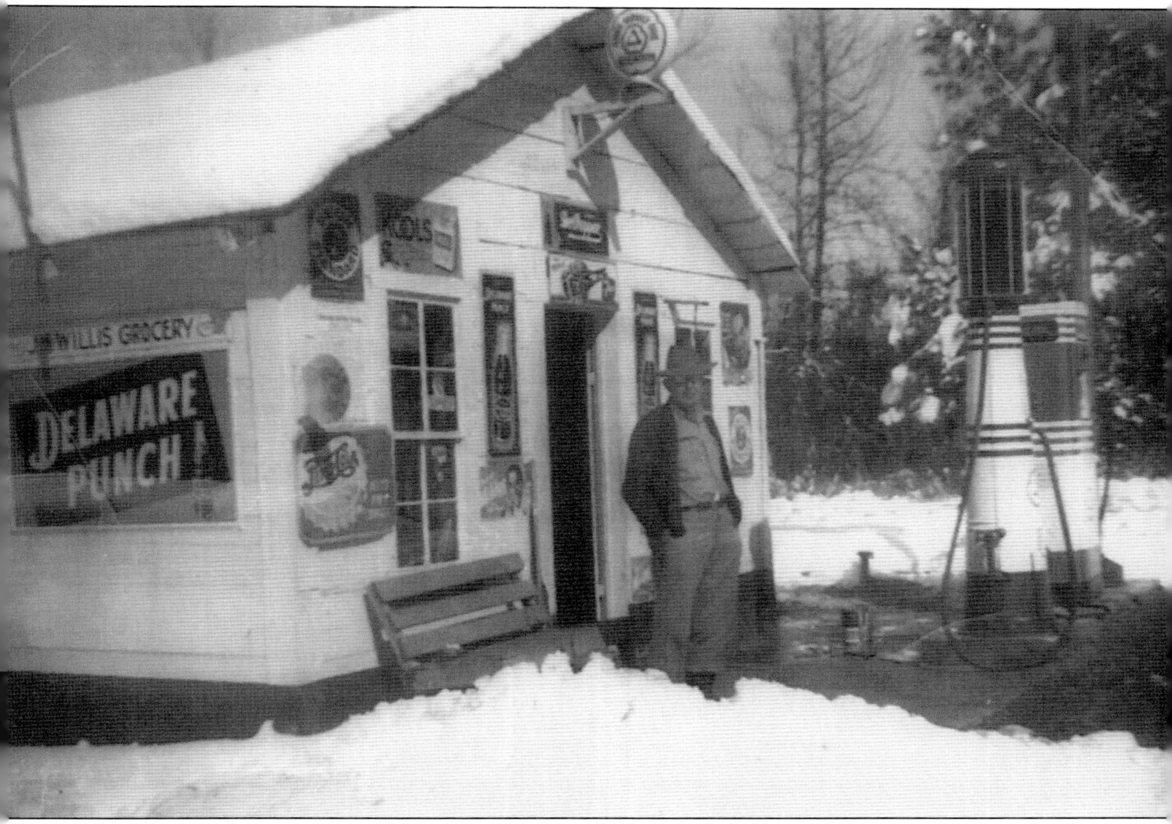


Martin Willis was born and raised in Jackson Parish. He was a farmer but decided to open a little store on the Corner of Ebenezer Church Road and Highway 4. He sold the business and then bought it back. He allowed for charging in a credit book for the locals who got paid once a month. Willis kept the store open until he retired in the early 1960s. (Courtesy of Yvonne Peel.)

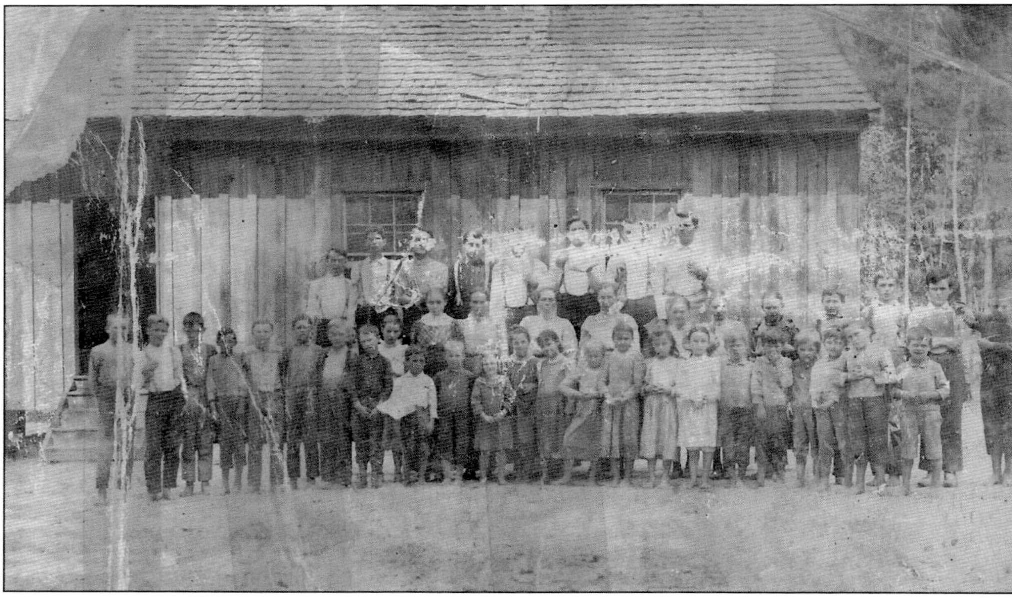

In this 1892 photograph, Stovall Community School trustees, teachers, and pupils stand in front of the Stovall School, located on the old Winnfield Vernon Road. Professor Wailes was principal of the school. Schools in the parish were often given subscriptions by the families of students able to pay something to send their children to school. This school closed, and children were sent to Walker school in 1918. (Courtesy of the George Walker family.)

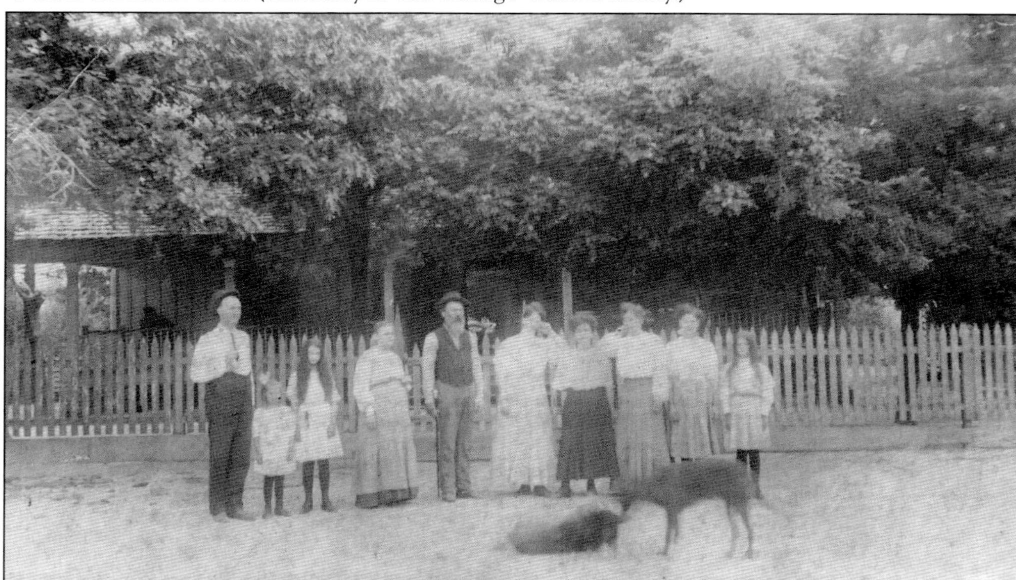

In the 1890s, Stovall was a prosperous farming area, located about seven miles north of Dodson. Stovall had two general stores, two cotton gins, and a post office. J.J. and George Stovall each had a store and gin, and J.J. was postmaster. In this 1904 photograph, Jeremiah Jackson Stovall is on the left, the bearded man at center is George Samuel Stovall, and to his right is George's wife Sally Maddox Pyburn. Their daughters pictured are Hazel, Josie, Ella, Mary Elizabeth, Mae, Willie, and Eva. (Courtesy of Ellen Walker Stephenson.)

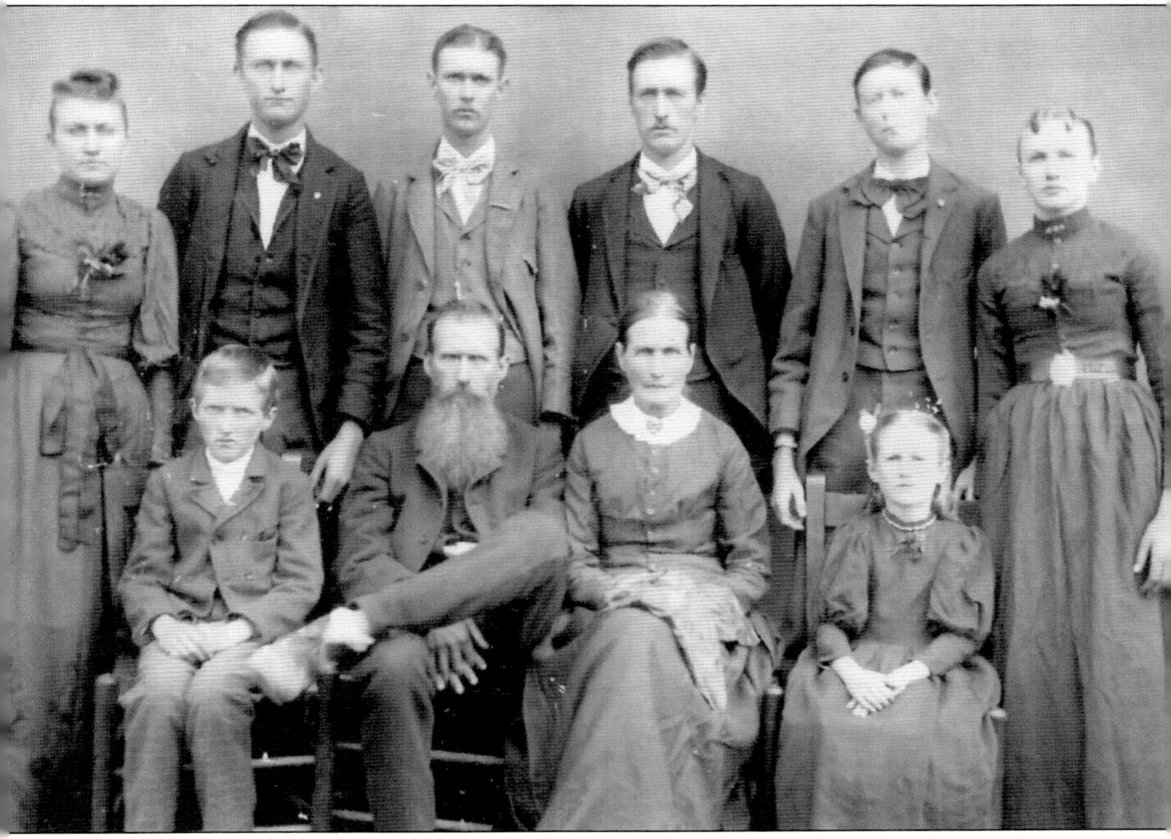

Thomas Walker's father, Lafayette Sanders Walker, left Mississippi with plans of settling in Texas. However, as he and his family made their way into Louisiana, they became friends with the Wyatt family, who sold them land. Sanders Walker bought more land, as did Thomas, and thus began the Walker community. There were no stores in this area, and electricity did not come until the 1950s. The Thomas Walker family, pictured here in 1895, is made up of, from left to right, (first row) Joel Jefferson, Thomas, Rebecca (Reed), and Novella; (second row) Emma Louella, William Thomas, Sanders Milford, Franklin, Ira Eugene, and Maggie Josetta. (Courtesy of Ellen Walker Stephenson.)

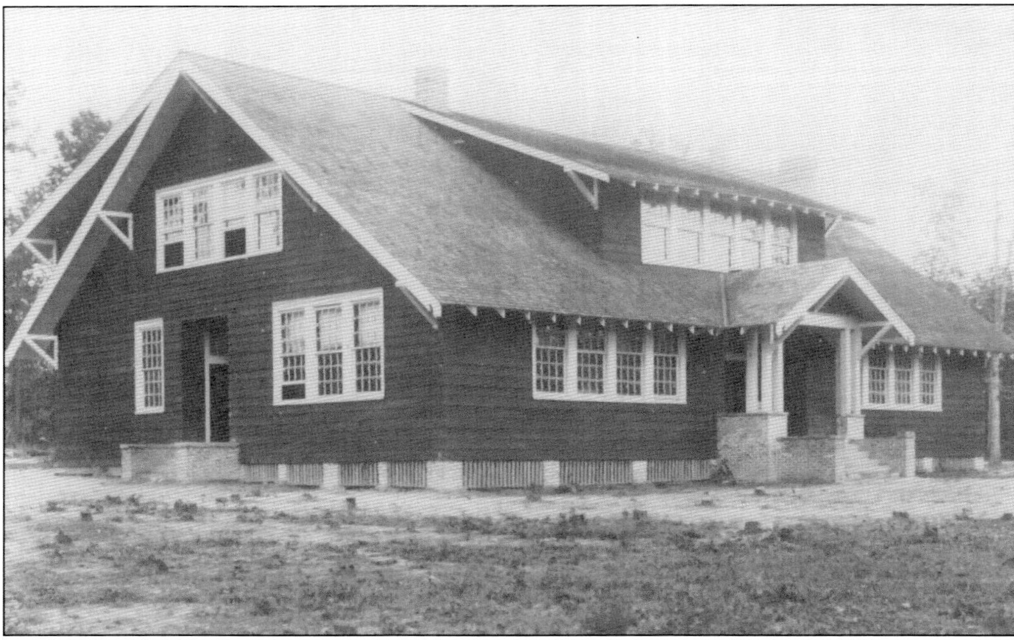

Most families in Jackson Parish lived in the country and farmed for a living. These communities would have a one- or two-room building constructed for a school, which usually doubled as a church. The parish superintendent of schools at the time was R.L. Dickerson, who proposed to consolidate the schools of Boatner, Midway, and Stovall. This proposal was accepted, and the school board bought a house and 40 acres in the Walker community. A large two-story building that contained seven classrooms, a library, and an auditorium was built, and classes started immediately in December 1918. The first graduating class was 1922. In the 1923 photograph below, students play a game during recess. This school operated until the high school closed in 1944 due to low enrollment, and the grammar school closed in 1952. (Above, courtesy of the Luther Walker family; below, courtesy of Ellen Walker Stephenson.)

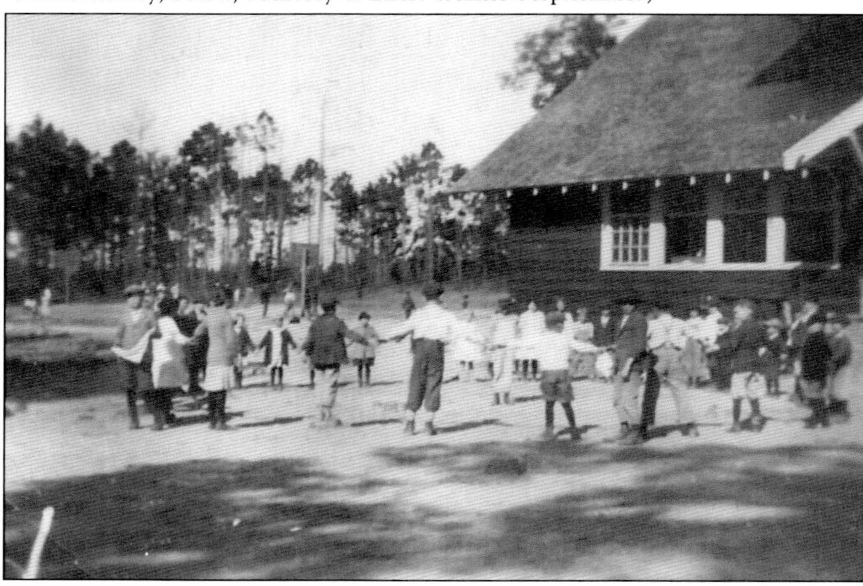

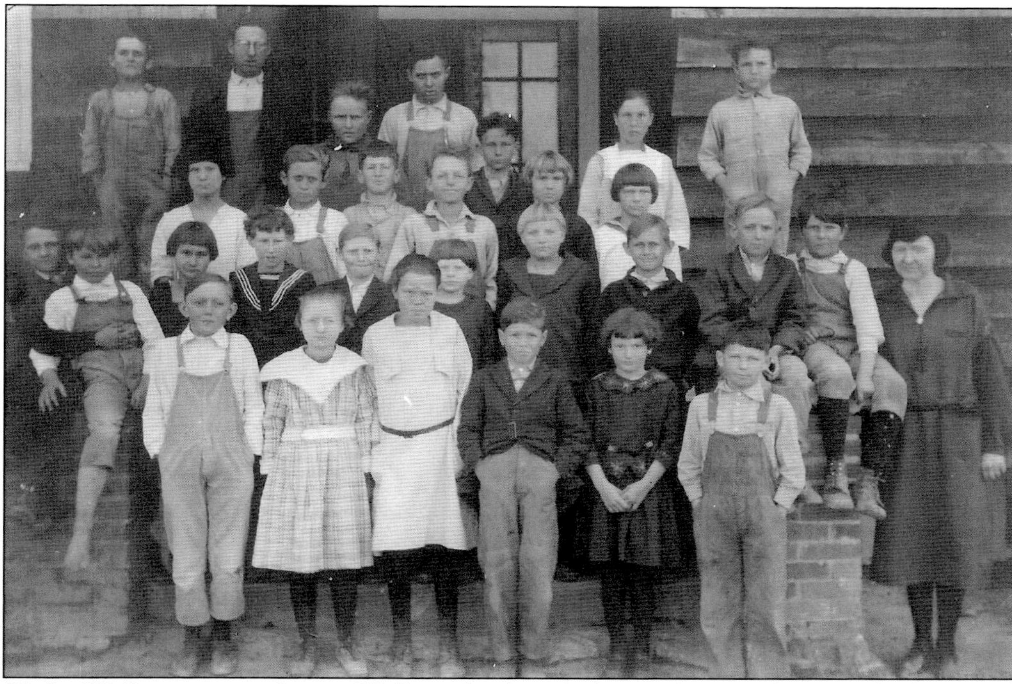

Gladys Walker was a student at Walker school, and after graduating, she came back to teach until the school closed. Pictured is the class of 1922, along with Gladys Walker (at far right), who collected many photographs from the Walker school era showing a thriving school. The Walker community consisted of the school and a church across the street. The members of the community went to Weston or Stovall for supplies. (Courtesy of Ellen Walker Stephenson.)

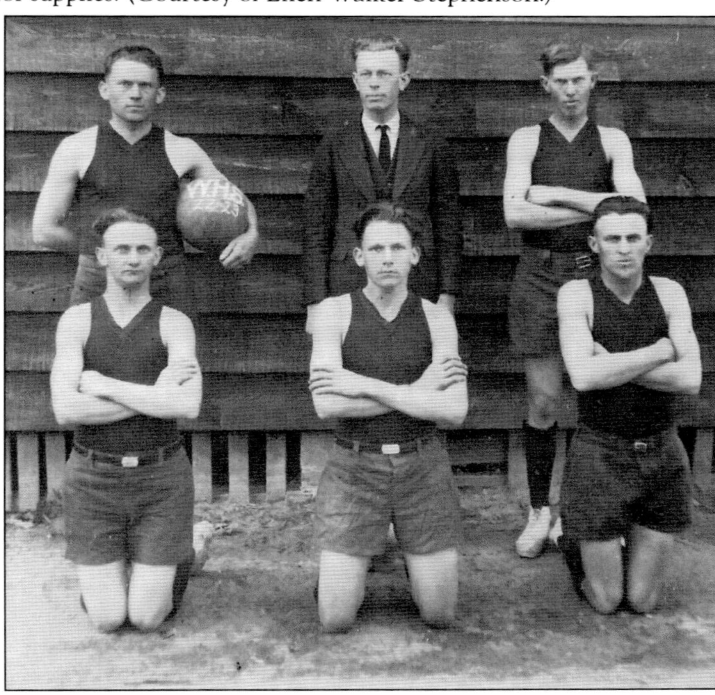

Pictured here is the 1922–1923 Walker school basketball team. They are, from left to right, (first row) cousins Elmo Walker, Carlos Walker, and Mose Moffett; (second row) Dewey Walker, coach and principal Alton Alford, and Marshall Chappell. There was also a girl's basketball team, and the school had a dirt court on which to practice. The team said it was an adjustment to play against teams that had an indoor court. (Courtesy of Ellen Walker Stephenson.)

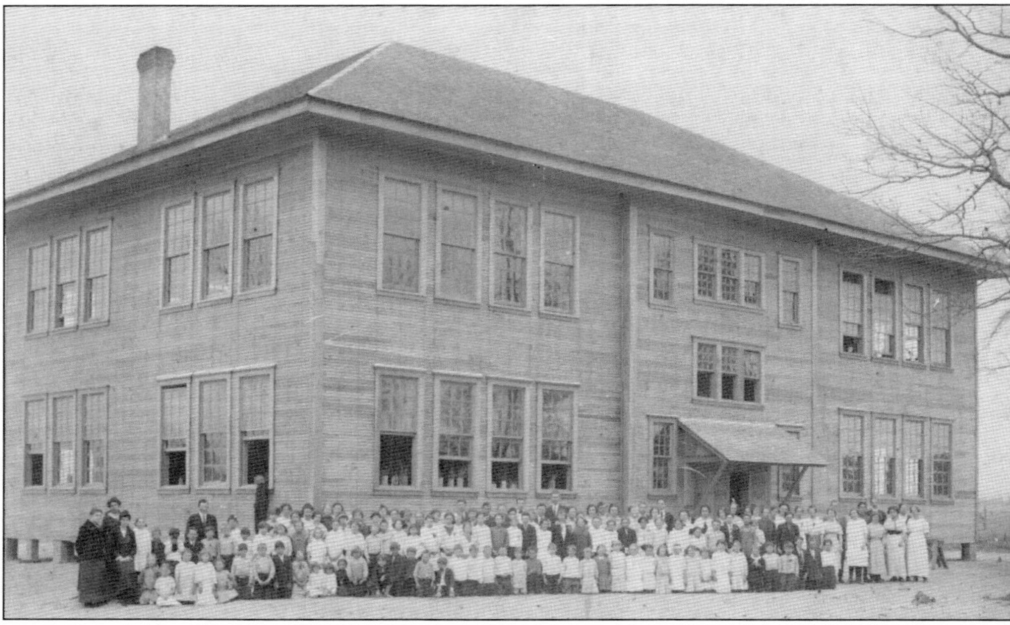

There was a need for a school in the Weston community, and in 1882, a public school was established in a one-room log cabin. In 1883, the school was moved to Rock Springs, a mile west of the previous site, and continued there until 1890. That year, the community moved a little farther south to its current site and erected a two-story building. This structure, built in 1914, was completely destroyed by fire one year later. (Courtesy of Weston High School.)

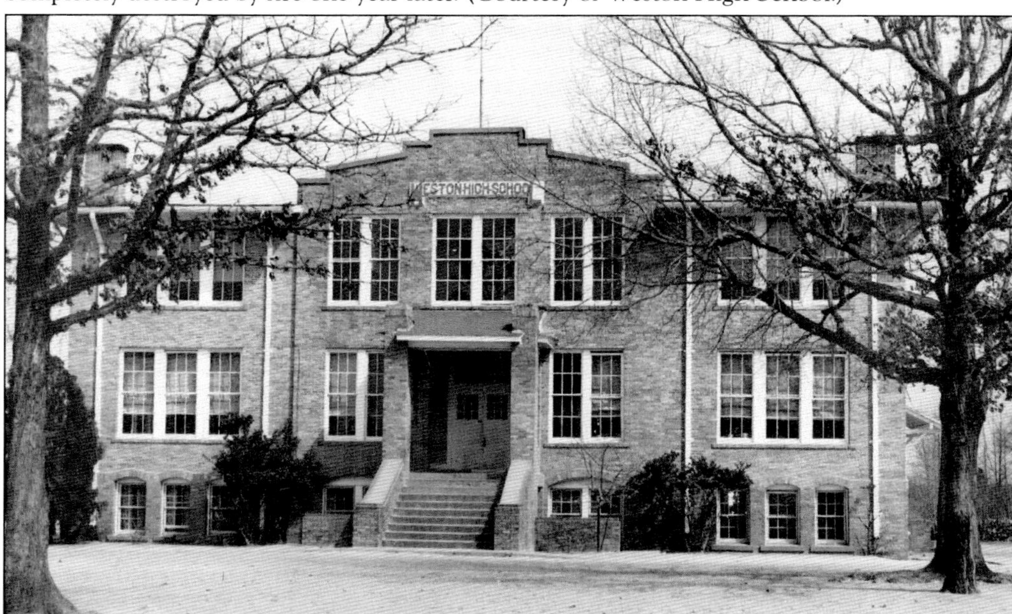


In 1916, a new three-story building was constructed to replace the old school. The year 1918 marked the first commencement of Weston High School, with two graduates. In 1937, a bond was issued to erect a gymnasium, the first in the parish. In the 1940s the smaller schools began to close, and the Weston student population began to grow. (Courtesy of Weston High School.)

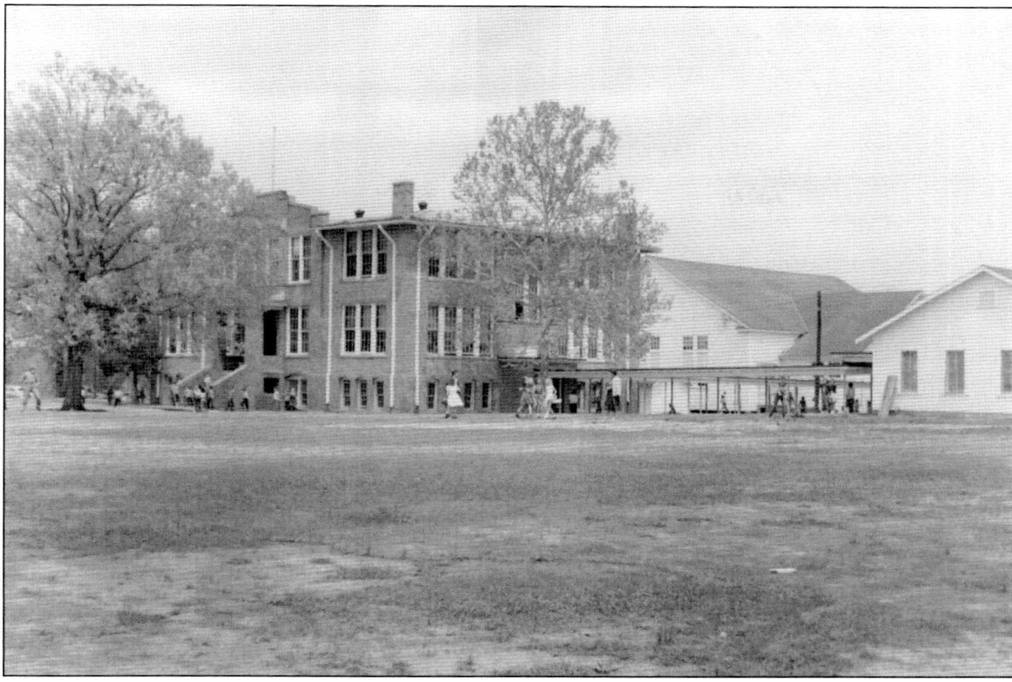

By 1955, an agriculture building had been constructed, along with a cafeteria. In 1958, two business classes were added to the curriculum, and during the 1960s and 1970s, there were many changes made in administration along with new facilities and new programs, and integration. Since the old three-story building was torn down and a new structure was erected in its place, the school has been remodeled. (Both, courtesy of Weston High School.)

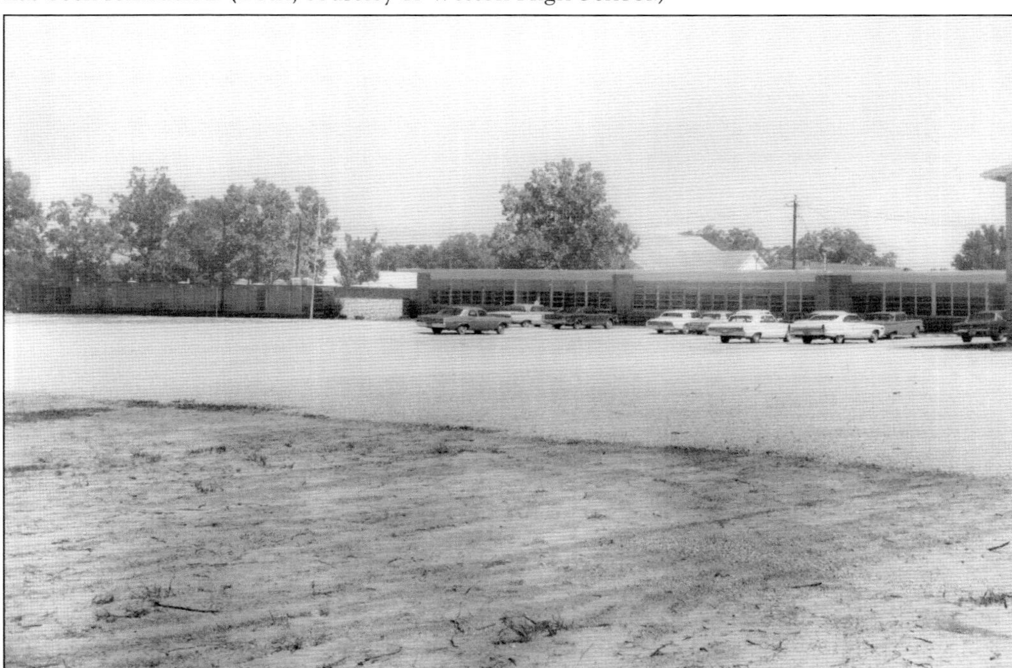

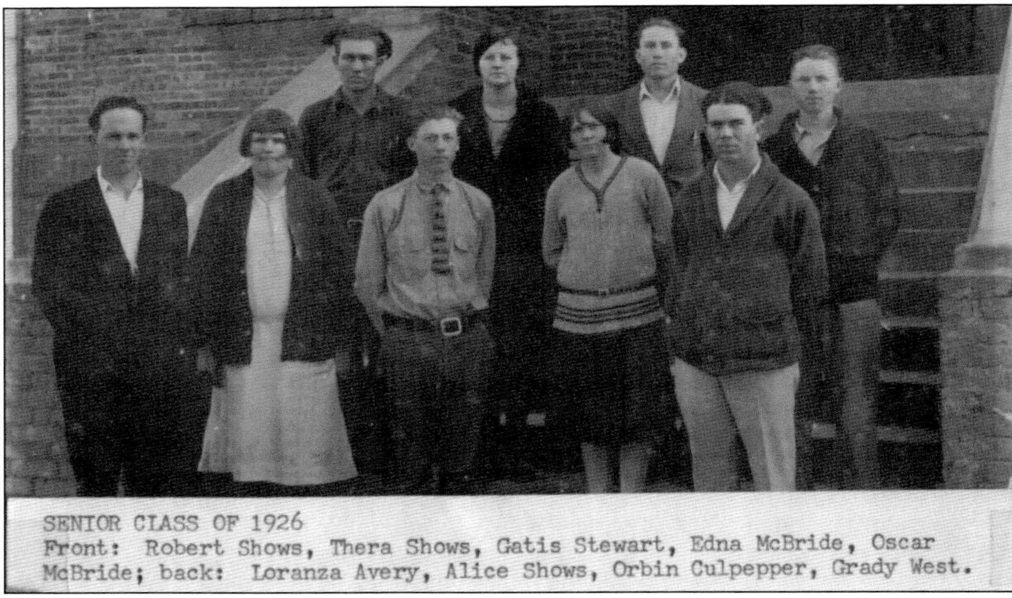


The main hall of the high school building proudly displays photographs of every individual who has graduated from Weston High School since 1918. Though many graduates have moved away, many have come back to become teachers, principals, and community leaders. Weston has since changed again, adding more buildings and more students. This is one of the three remaining schools in the parish. Seen here are the graduates of 1926–1927. (Above, courtesy of Glen Nash; below, courtesy of Paula Smith.)

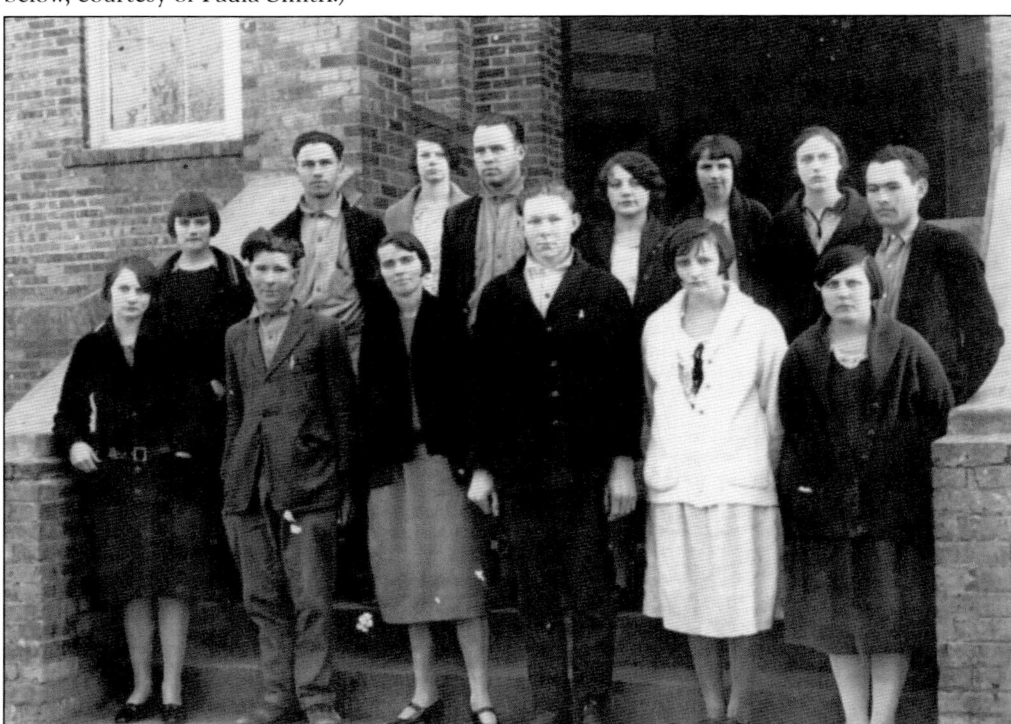

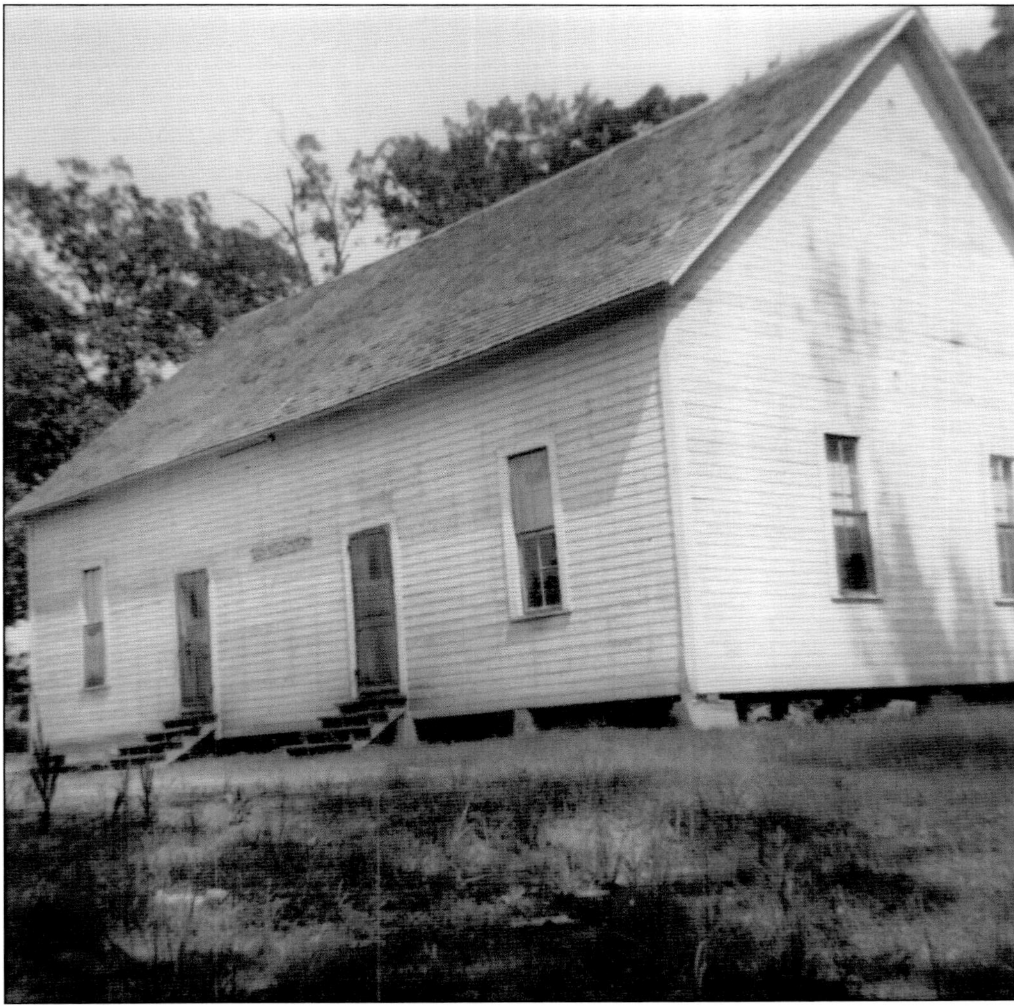
Zions Rest Baptist Church, located off of Gladway Road about two miles from Weston, was organized in 1851 as Pilgrim's Rest Baptist Church. In 1857, the name was changed to Zions Rest Primitive Baptist Church. At some point, the name was again changed to Zion Hill Baptist Church and moved to Springhill. By 1870, the name had been changed back to Zions Rest Baptist Church, and in 1890, John Stewart donated two acres of land for a church. Along with a cemetery, it still stands to this day. The cemetery is well cared for, and many descendants of James L. McBride who came to Louisiana in the mid-1850s are buried there. (Courtesy of the McBride family collection.)

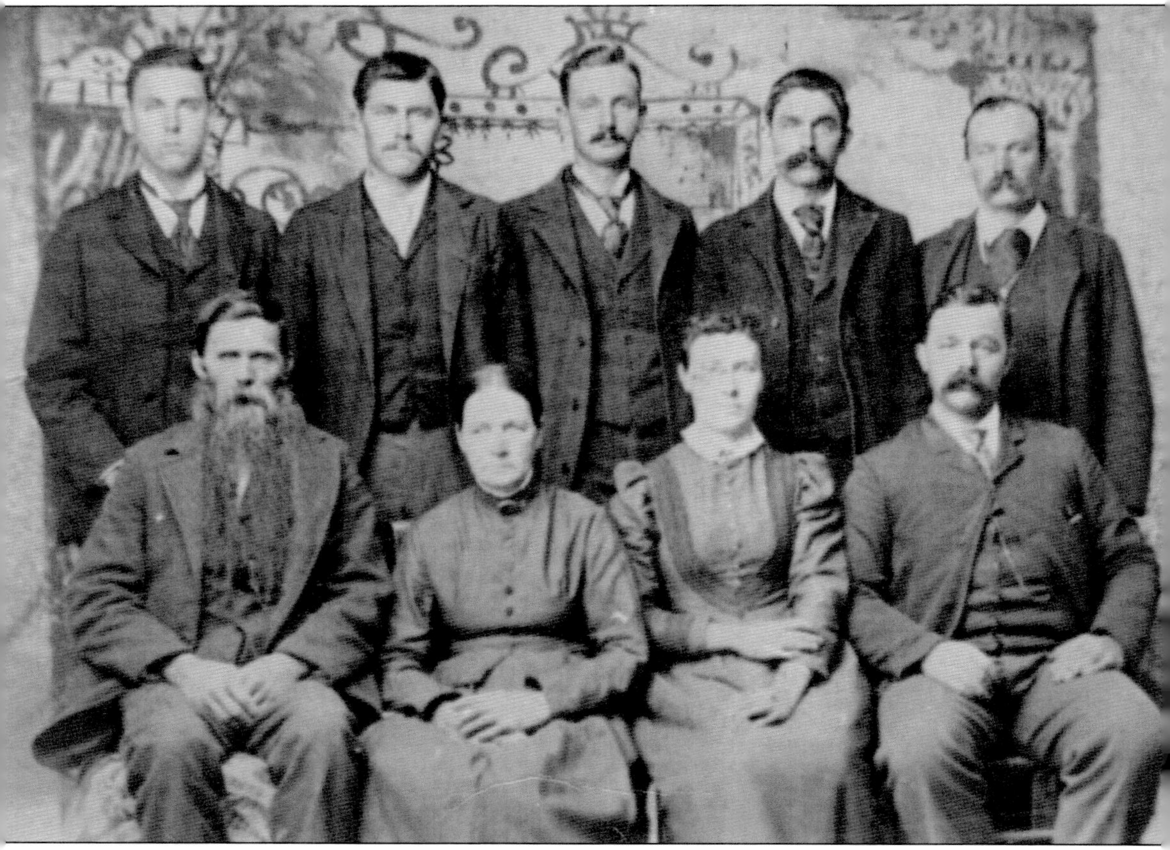

Pictured from left to right are (first row) Jesse Edward McBride, a Civil War soldier who owned a store near the Weston high school; Lucinda Hatcher, who married Jesse while he was in Kentucky during the war; Martha Ann, the wife of William Stewart, who owned a brickyard; and William Jonathan, a sheriff and store owner; (second row) Jesse David, a newspaperman and clerk of court; Stephen Daniel, a farmer and police juror; Charles Franklin, deputy sheriff and mayor of Jonesboro; James Louis, a general store owner who also operated a post office; and John Thomas, a school board member who sponsored the Parish Farm Bureau. (Courtesy of the McBride family collection.)

# *Four*

# JONESBORO

In 1860, Joseph Jones moved to Macedonia and bought property. Two log cabins were soon built, and at the location of one of these cabins, several graves were found. Because of this, Jones put aside four square acres for a public cemetery and a church—the Macedonia Baptist Church.
In the summer of 1900, the Arkansas Southern Railroad came into Macedonia. Around July 1900, a Mr. Cargile bought 160 acres for the future site of a sawmill and a town. One block of this land, the area of highest elevation, was designated a public square and given to the town; it later became Courthouse Square. Surveying for the future town began, and the layout of the streets, avenues, and blocks was completed by December of the same year.

On January 10, 1901, the first passenger train came to town, bringing people from as far away as Cargile and Arkadelphia, Arkansas. On this rainy day, the community gathered as lots were sold, and the town began to grow. On January 16, 1901, Macedonia became Jonesboro and was confirmed by the US Post Office. On September 4, 1901, Gov. William Wright Heard signed documents creating the village of Jonesboro.

The population began increasing, and when it reached 1,000 or more inhabitants, the mayor petitioned the governor for a change in status from village to town. On May 14, 1903, Governor Heard declared the village now the town of Jonesboro.

Eight years later, in a hard fight against Chatham, Jonesboro became the parish seat in March 1911. The block of land Cargile donated was given to the police jury, and work on the courthouse began. It was finished in 1912. In 1936, the courthouse was destroyed by an explosion, and the construction of a new courthouse was started in 1937 and finished in 1938.

Progress began to slow. By 1929, all mills were shut down, except the mill in Hodge. In recent years, the Highway 167 bypass was built, and chain restaurants and stores have popped up around it. However, Jonesboro still loses many of its youth to bigger cities and further education. It has become one of the little towns of Louisiana that struggles to stay alive.

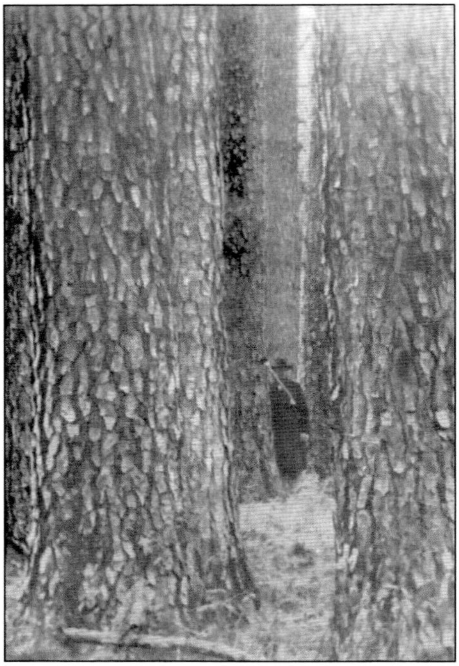

After Jackson Parish was formed, settlers began coming into the area to buy cheap land. They were greeted by large towering pine trees that hindered immediate farming. It could take a week to remove a single tree and longer to clear enough space to build a home and remove enough trees to allow sun to reach plant crops. It was because of these trees that some pioneering men came into the parish and began making a living on the forests that were once such a hindrance to settlers. (Courtesy of the *Jackson Independent*.)

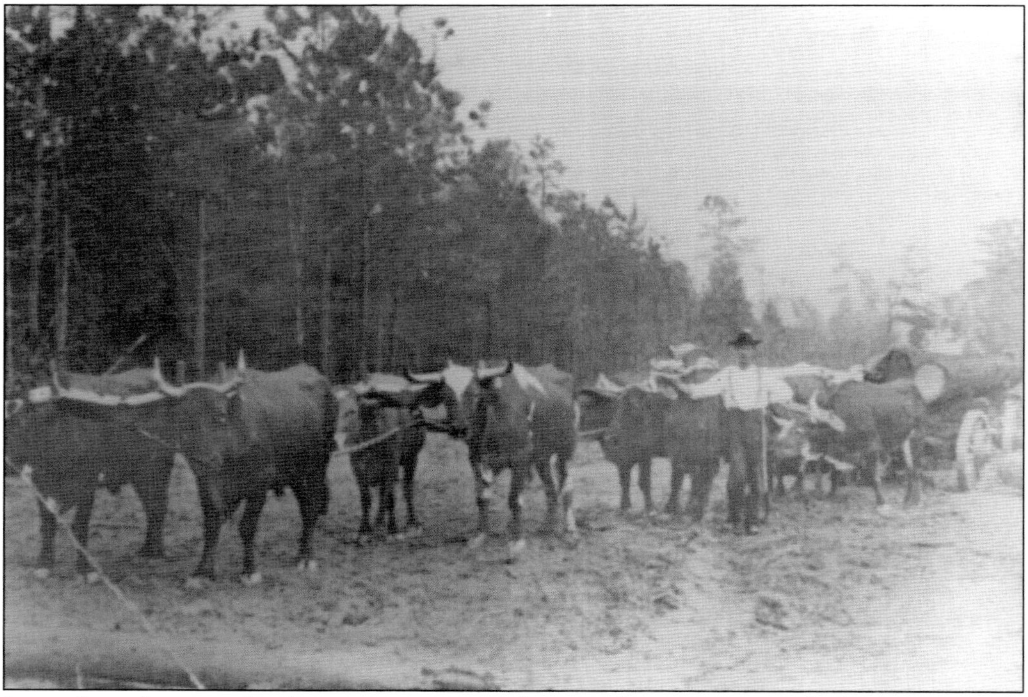

It usually took teams of eight or more oxen to pull one to three cut trees in the late 1800s. Roads were almost nonexistent, and if it rained, most roads were impassable. Soft ground made it hard to move trees to the sawmill, and the oxen were worked hard. The oxen were the only way trees could be hauled out of the woods, especially before the trains and skidders came. (Courtesy of the Jackson Parish Museum.)

Richard Henry Jones was elected sheriff in November 1876 and was killed in January 1891 while transferring a prisoner. It has been told that the town of Jonesboro was named after him because he was an honest man and well liked by the people of the parish. (Courtesy of the *Jackson Independent*.)

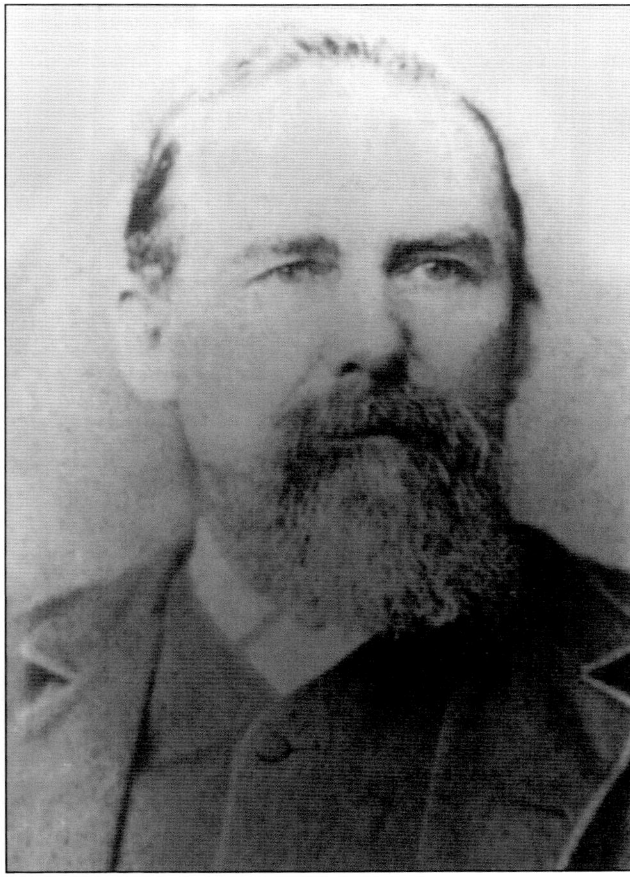

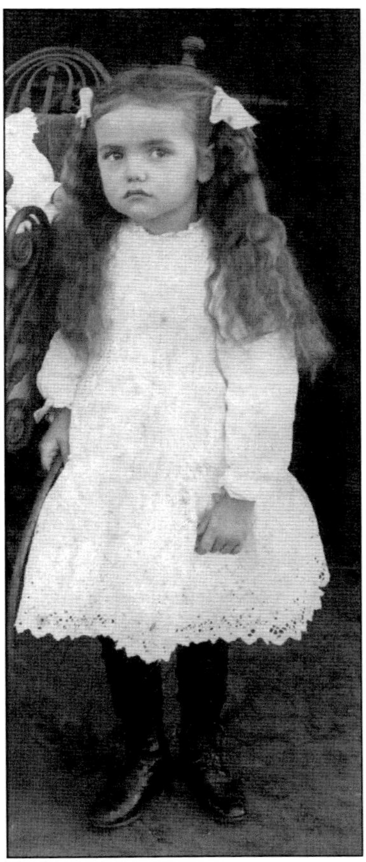

There are several stories handed down as to how the town of Jonesboro was named. One says that the men who built a mill in Macedonia did not like the current name, and it was tradition to name a town after the first-born girl in the community, which was Stella Blanche Jones. However, at the time, there was a woman who was in jail in Vernon named Stella who was creating unfavorable publicity, and Blanche was the name of another town. So, it is said that the town was named after the first known landowners, the Joneses. All of these people were from the same lineage, and it can be said that the town was named after the Jones family. (Courtesy of the *Jackson Independent*.)

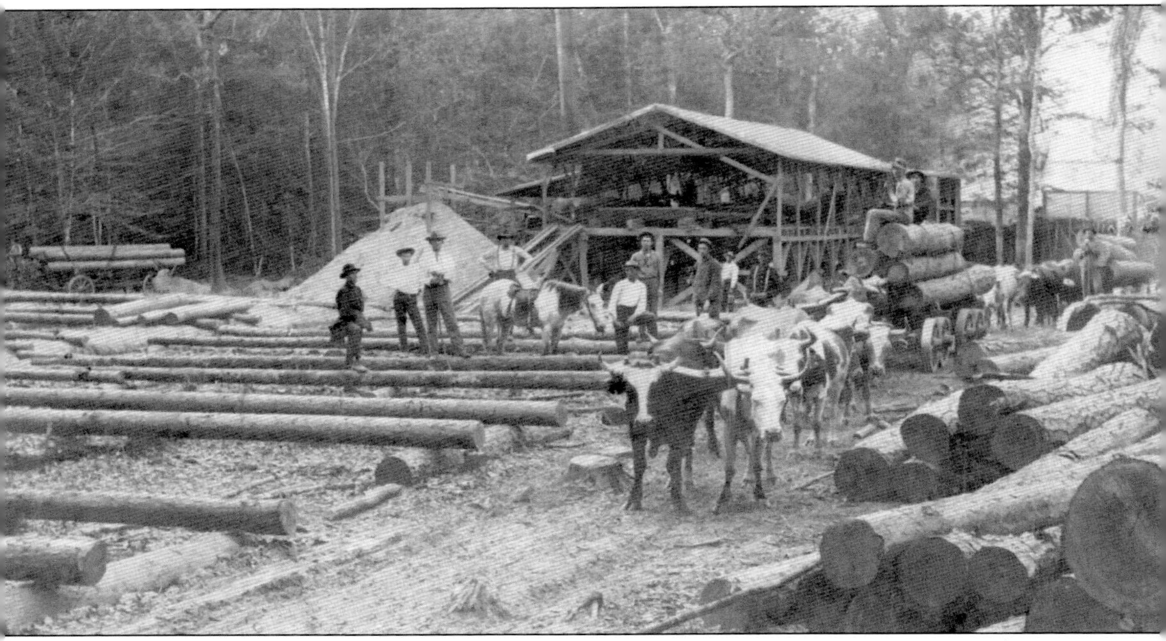

This is a sawmill in the Jonesboro community. The logs are drying in preparation for cutting. These trees were hand cut and then loaded on wagons pulled by oxen. At this time, oxen were used to pull logs into wagons. The logs were wrapped with chains and rolled up a ramp made of at least two logs that were leaned against the wagon. (Courtesy of the *Jackson Independent*.)

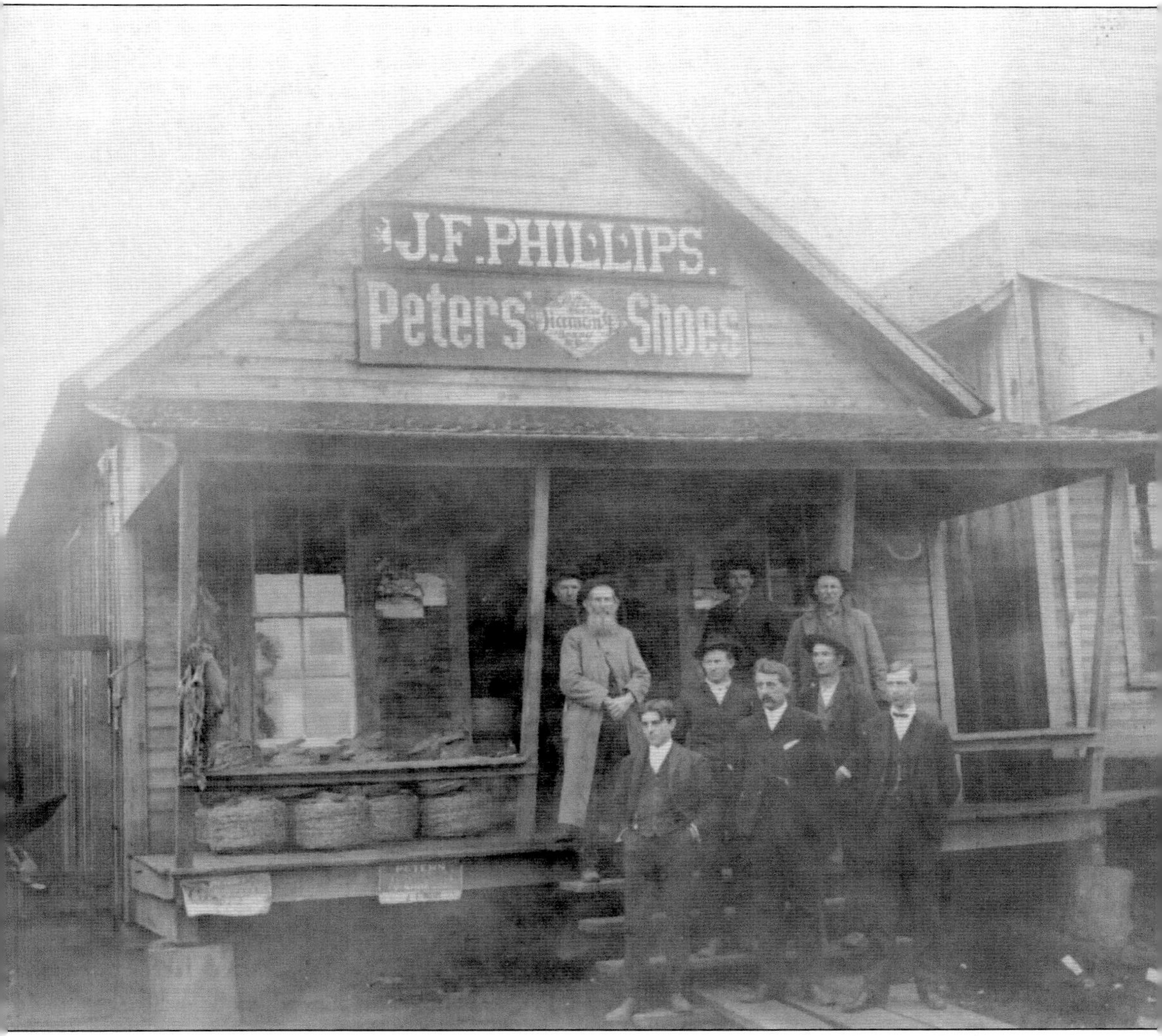


J.F. Phillips's store was one of the first businesses built on Main Street around 1901. The location of this store would later become the site of the first Jonesboro State Bank in early 1914. Men's shoes sold for $2.50, and women's shoes were $3. They also sold farming supplies, as evidenced by the barbed wire for fencing sitting out front. The store boasted a sign for Oxidine, which was used as a treatment for various maladies including "grippe" (flu), fever, chills, and malaria. (Courtesy of the *Jackson Independent*.)

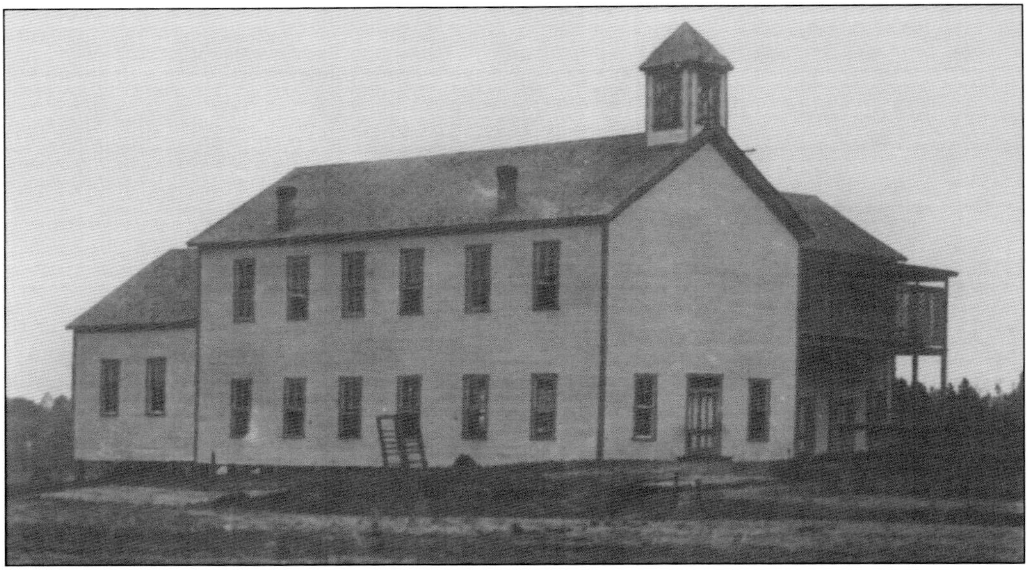

The first school in Jonesboro began in the Macedonia Baptist Church in 1901. By 1902, so many people moved into Jonesboro that a larger school was needed. In 1903, a two-story wooden building was erected, and in 1906, it became a high school. By then, additional rooms had been added to accommodate the increasing enrollment. This wooden building was located on Cooper Avenue. (Courtesy of Jackson Parish Museum.)

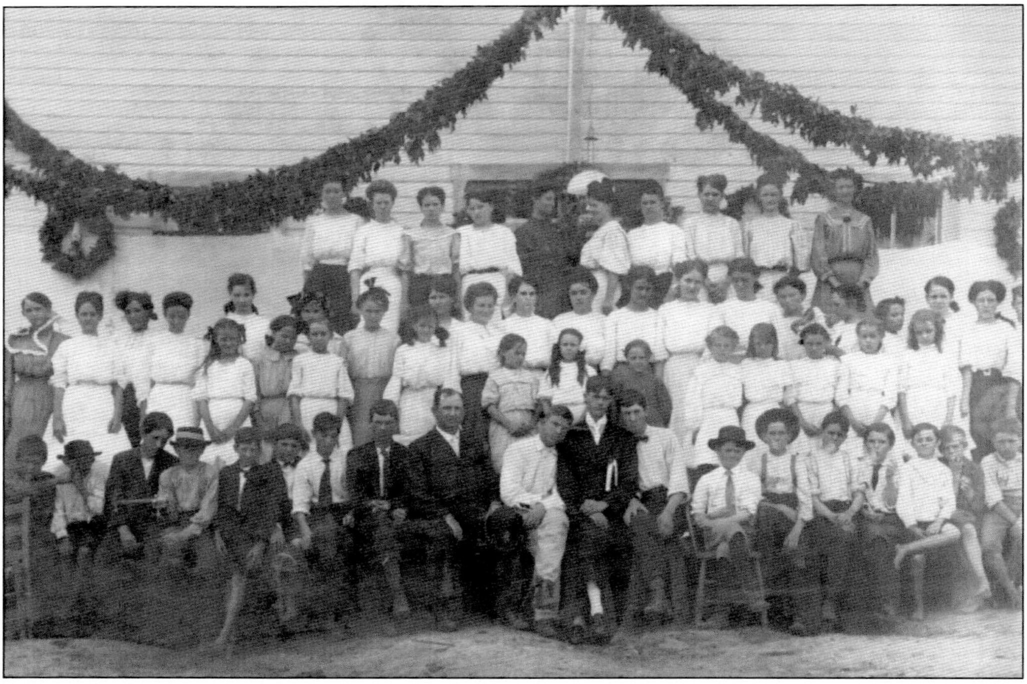

This early photograph of the students in the Jonesboro school shows the large student population. It was shortly after this that more rooms were added to the north side. The continual growth of the village of Jonesboro brought more students into the town. This wooden school would be replaced within the next 10 years. (Courtesy of the *Jackson Independent*.)

In 1903, the Jonesboro Methodist Episcopal Church was built on the corner of Fourth Street and Cooper Avenue. Earlier in the year, the Macedonia Baptist Church and school were moved from the area of the cemetery and separated. The church was constructed on First Street and Cooper Avenue. The Jonesboro school was built on Third Street and Cooper Avenue. This view down Cooper Avenue shows all three buildings. (Courtesy of the Jackson Parish Museum.)

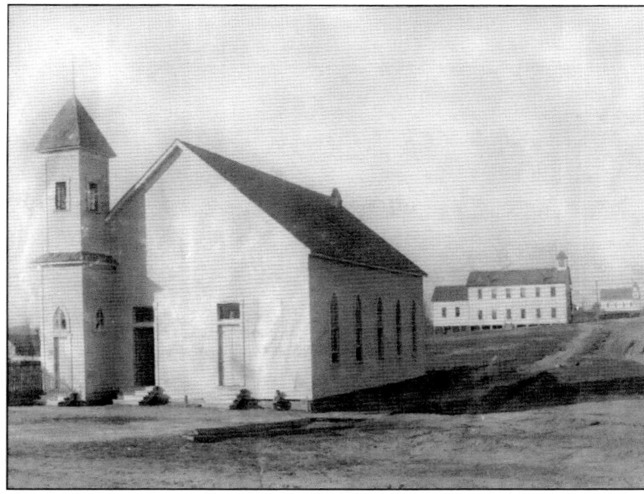

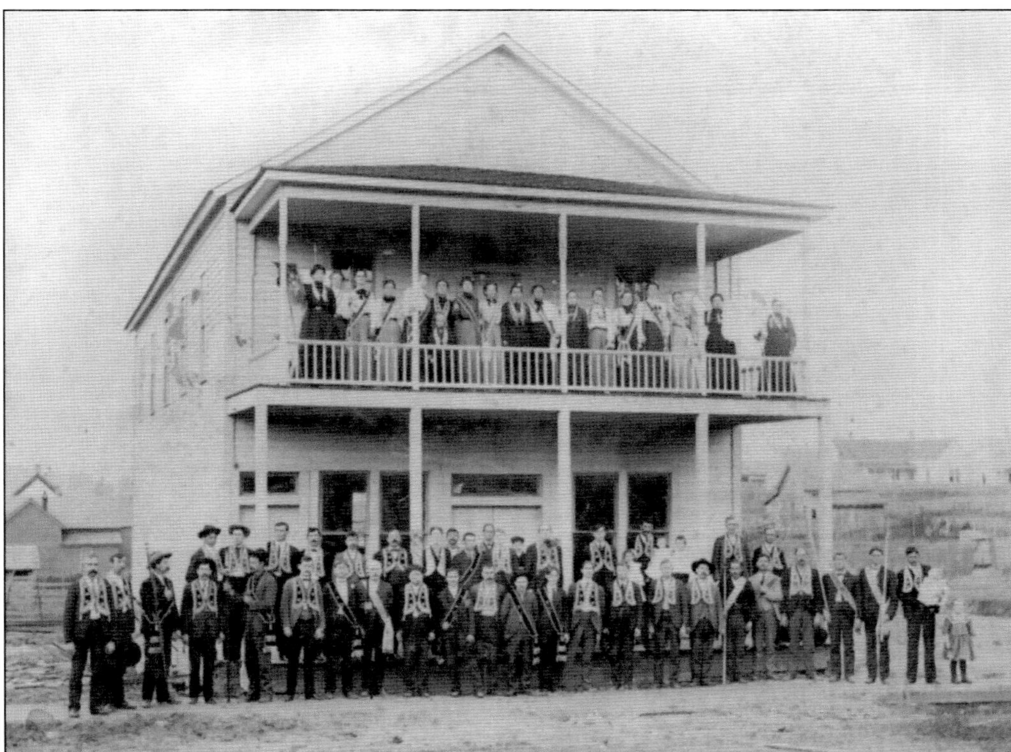

In England, it was odd to find people organized for the purpose of giving aid to those in need and pursuing projects for the benefit of all mankind. Those who belonged to such an organization were called "odd fellows." Odd Fellowship became the first fraternity in the United States to include both men and women in 1851. The Odd Fellows Lodge was built in Jonesboro in 1902 or 1903. (Courtesy of the *Jackson Independent*.)

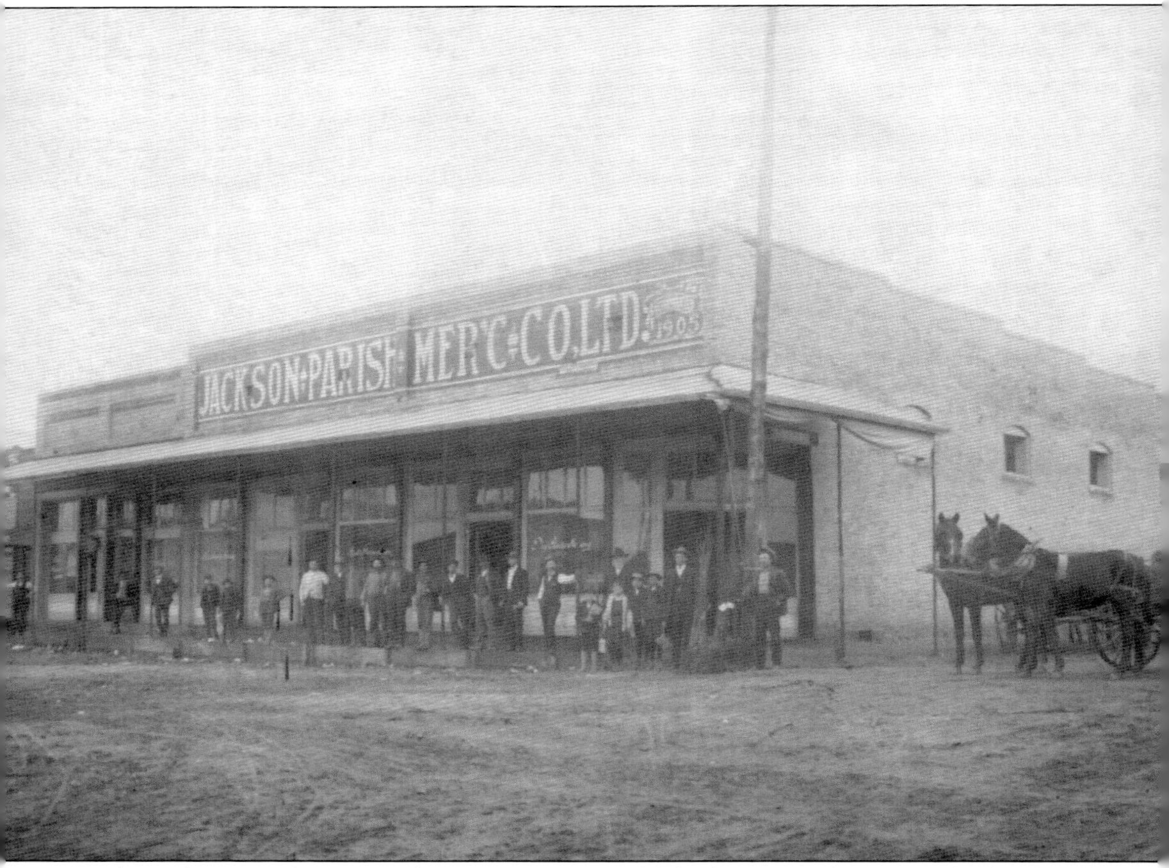


The Jackson Parish Mercantile Company was established in November 1905. The locals called this the "Mammoth store." There was a barbershop and post office next to this building on Main Street. This store has been sold and remodeled many times and has carried many different items over the years. This building still stands today on the corner of Polk Avenue and Main Street; until recently, it was Nash Pharmacy. (Courtesy of the Jackson Parish Museum.)

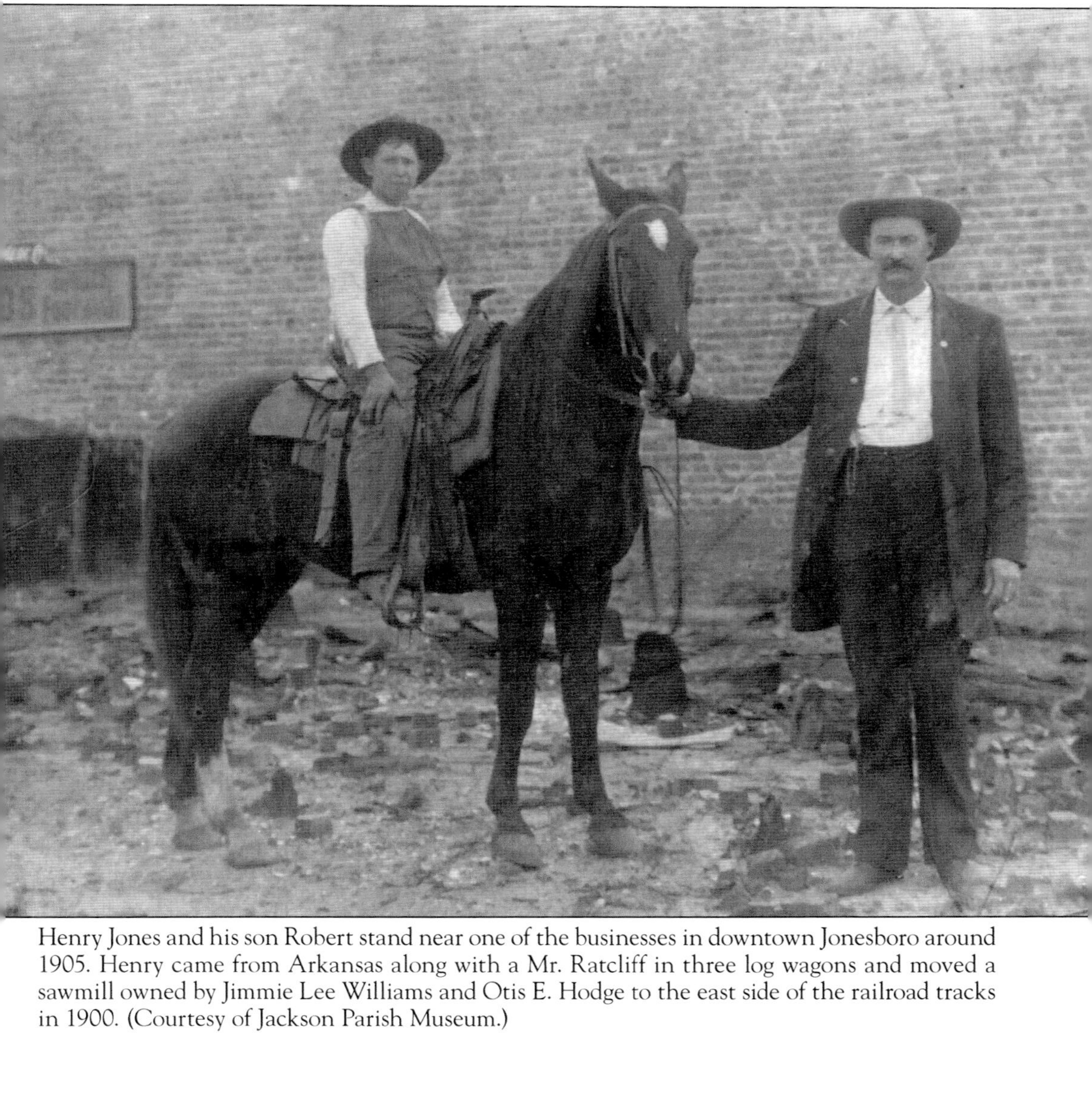

Henry Jones and his son Robert stand near one of the businesses in downtown Jonesboro around 1905. Henry came from Arkansas along with a Mr. Ratcliff in three log wagons and moved a sawmill owned by Jimmie Lee Williams and Otis E. Hodge to the east side of the railroad tracks in 1900. (Courtesy of Jackson Parish Museum.)

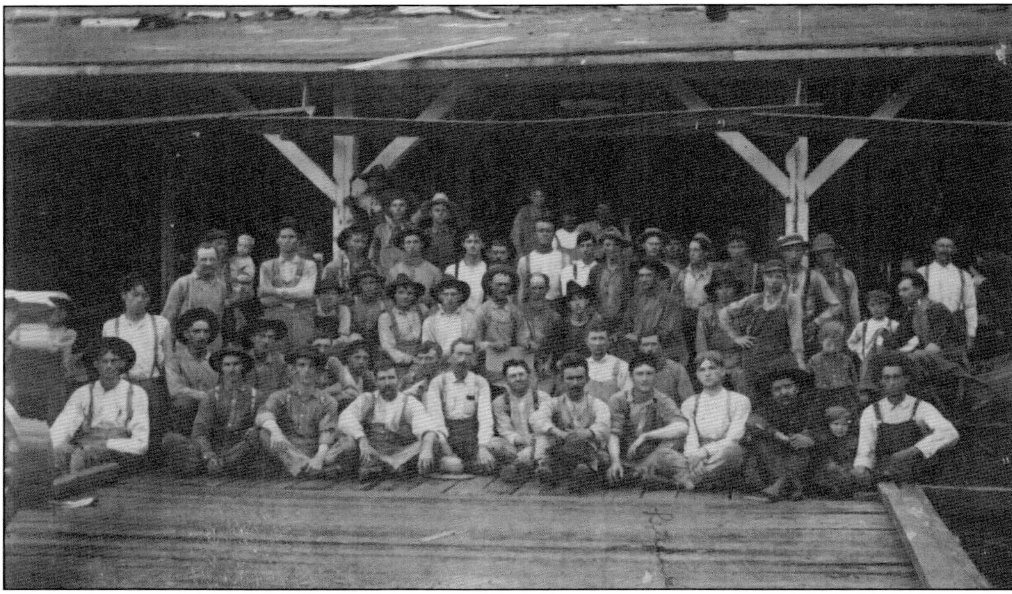

The Jonesboro sawmill was located on East Main Street, across the railroad from downtown, where Fred's Super Dollar sits today. The sawmill crew took time out for this picture in 1908. This mill later caught fire and was destroyed. It produced lumber that made up homes and another sawmill. (Courtesy of the Jackson Parish Museum.)

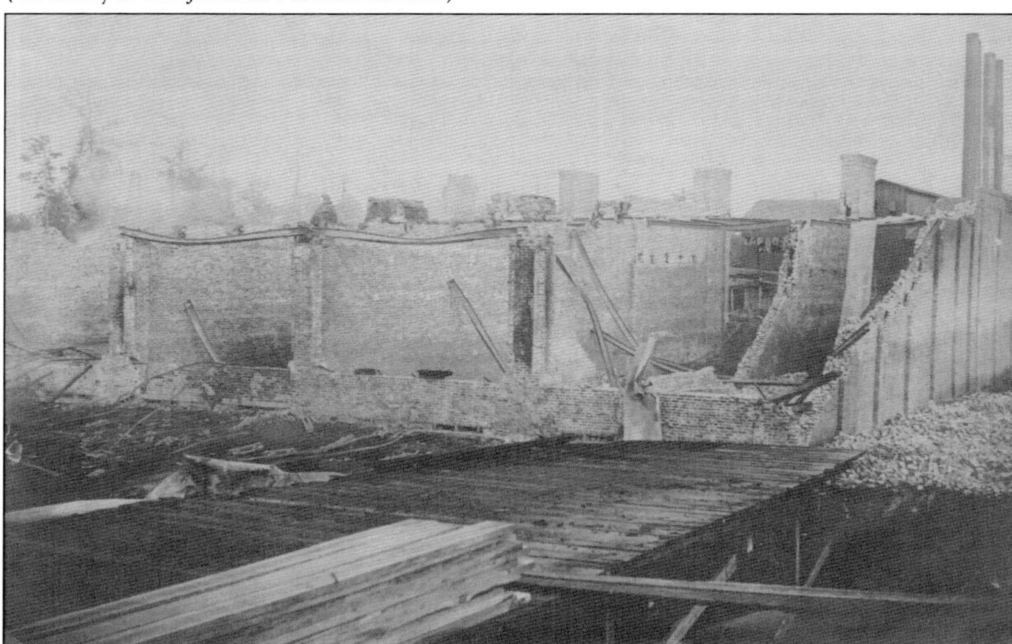

Green wood coming straight from a felled tree had far too much moisture to be used commercially because it would rot, warp, or split. So, a drying kiln was built, and heat was utilized to speed up the drying process. It took a very long time to air dry cut lumber. This image shows the burned-out remains of the Jonesboro sawmill in the early 1900s. The Jonesboro mill shut down in 1915. (Courtesy of the Jackson Parish Museum.)

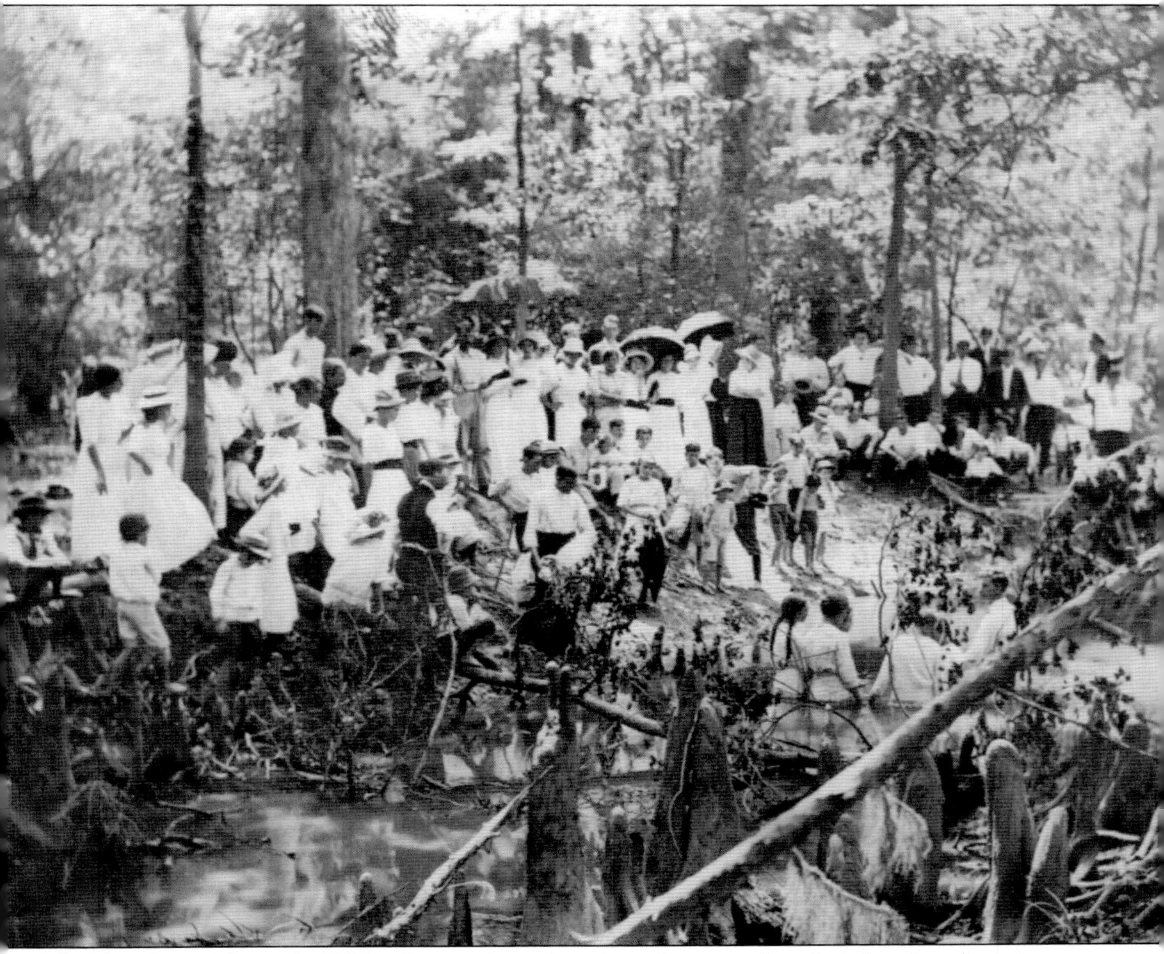

The churches of the early 1900s often used ponds and creeks to conduct their baptismal services. As seen here, one church uses the Dug de Mona creek. Baptisms were often made into postcards, such as this one, by worshippers documenting their personal faith and by tourists noting exotic practices and vanishing folk traditions. (Courtesy of the Jackson Parish Museum.)

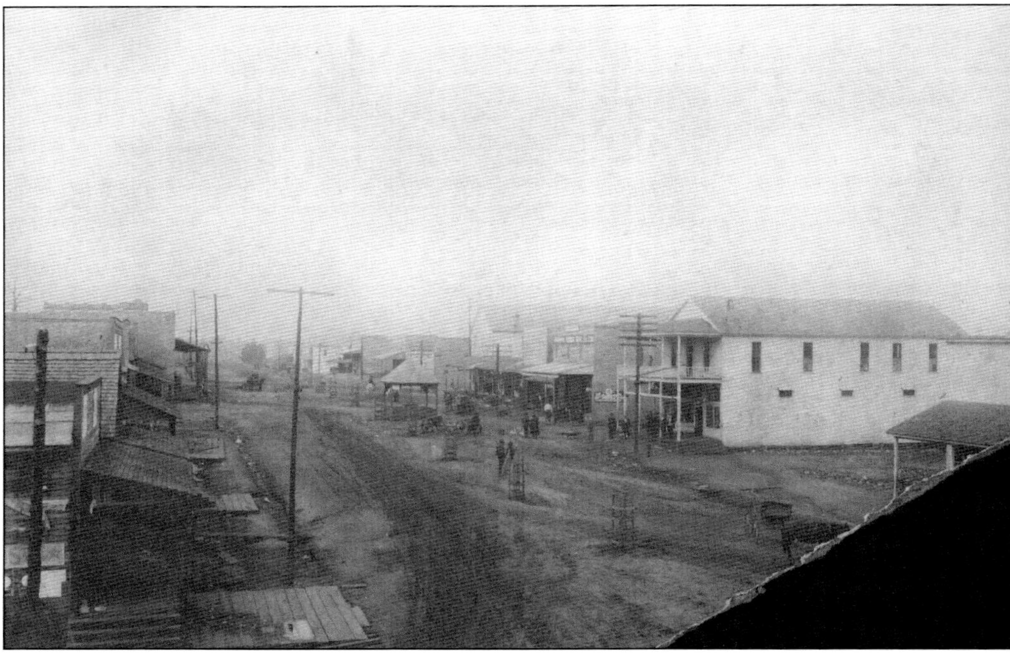

By December 1900, the blocks and streets had been surveyed, and the town was laid out. Lots were sold for homes and businesses. By 1912, the town of Jonesboro was continuing to grow and a main street was filled with businesses on either side of a boulevard. Trees were planted down the center, and a water well was built. The people were proud of their town. Sometime in 1905 or 1906, one block of downtown Jonesboro caught fire and burned down. It was immediately rebuilt and continued its growth. At lower right is part of a building that was the Tremont Lumber Company general merchandise store; beside this is the cross street Hudson Avenue. Tremont had built a small mill in Jonesboro by this time. (Both, courtesy of the Jackson Parish Museum.)

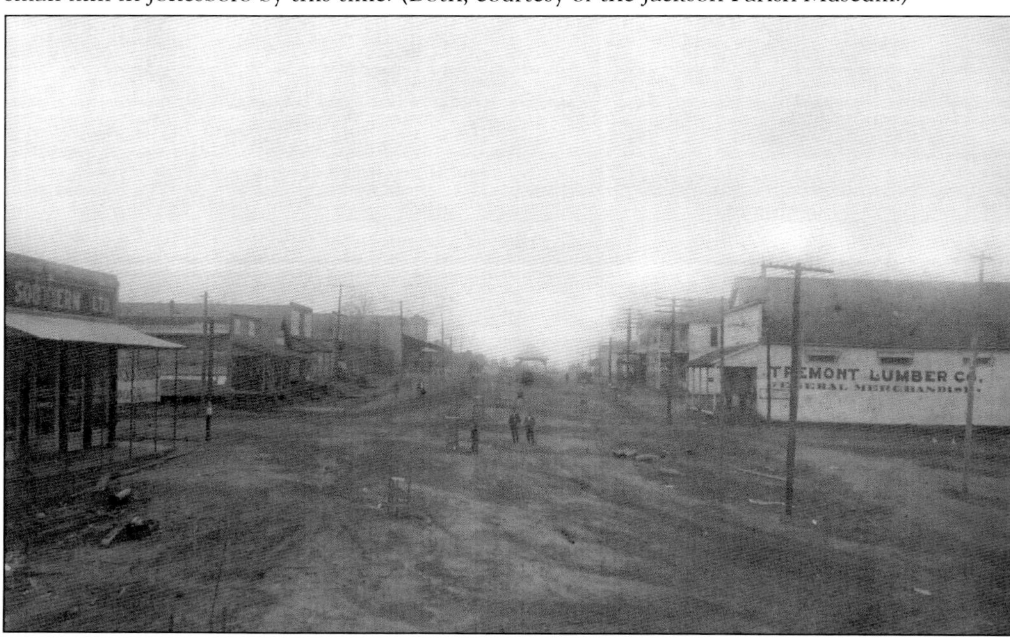

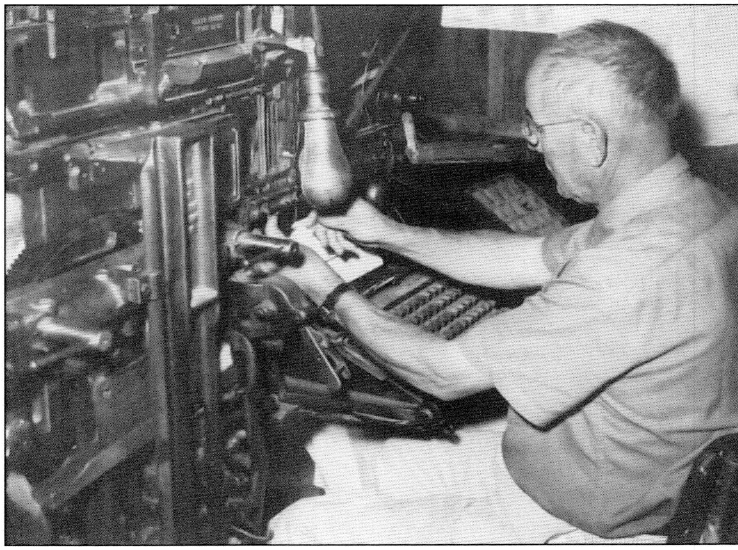

Ainsley H. Colvin Sr. bought the *Jackson Independent* on August 15, 1908, and moved it from Vernon to Jonesboro. It was first located behind the Colvin Jewelry store, owned by A.H.'s brother, on Main Street. It was published here for eight or nine years before moving to the rear of the old Jonesboro State Building until 1940, when it moved again. (Courtesy of the T.L. Colvin estate.)

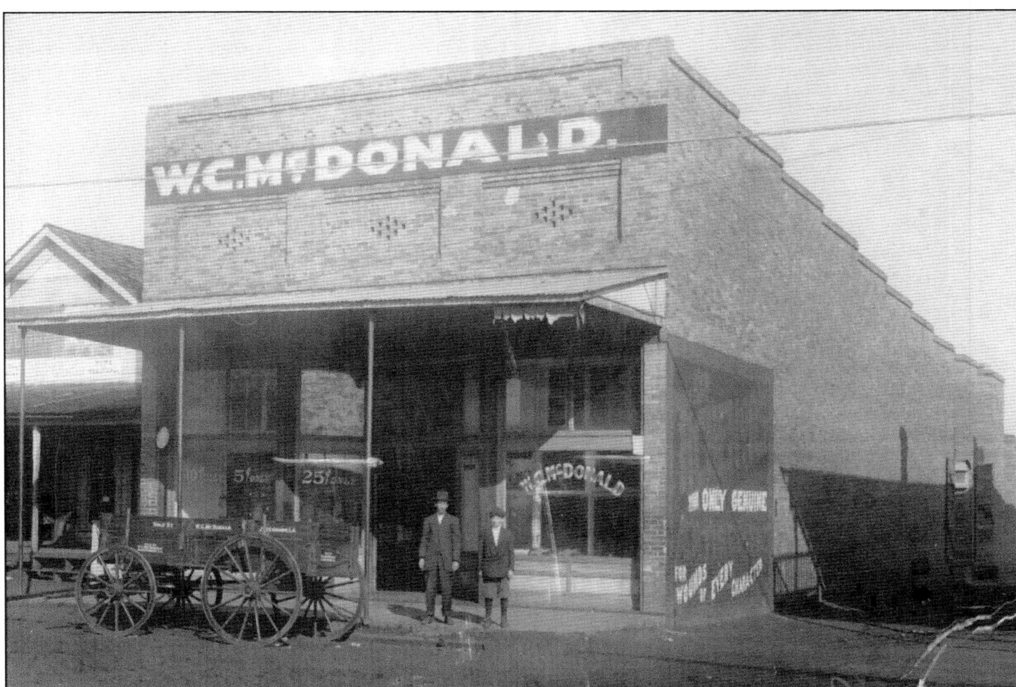


The store of W.C. McDonald was the first brick building in Jonesboro. This building, over the last hundred years, has been extensively remodeled and modernized. Its facade still stands today and serves the community. Mitchell's Pharmacy occupied the building for many years until it recently moved. (Courtesy of the Jackson Parish Bank.)

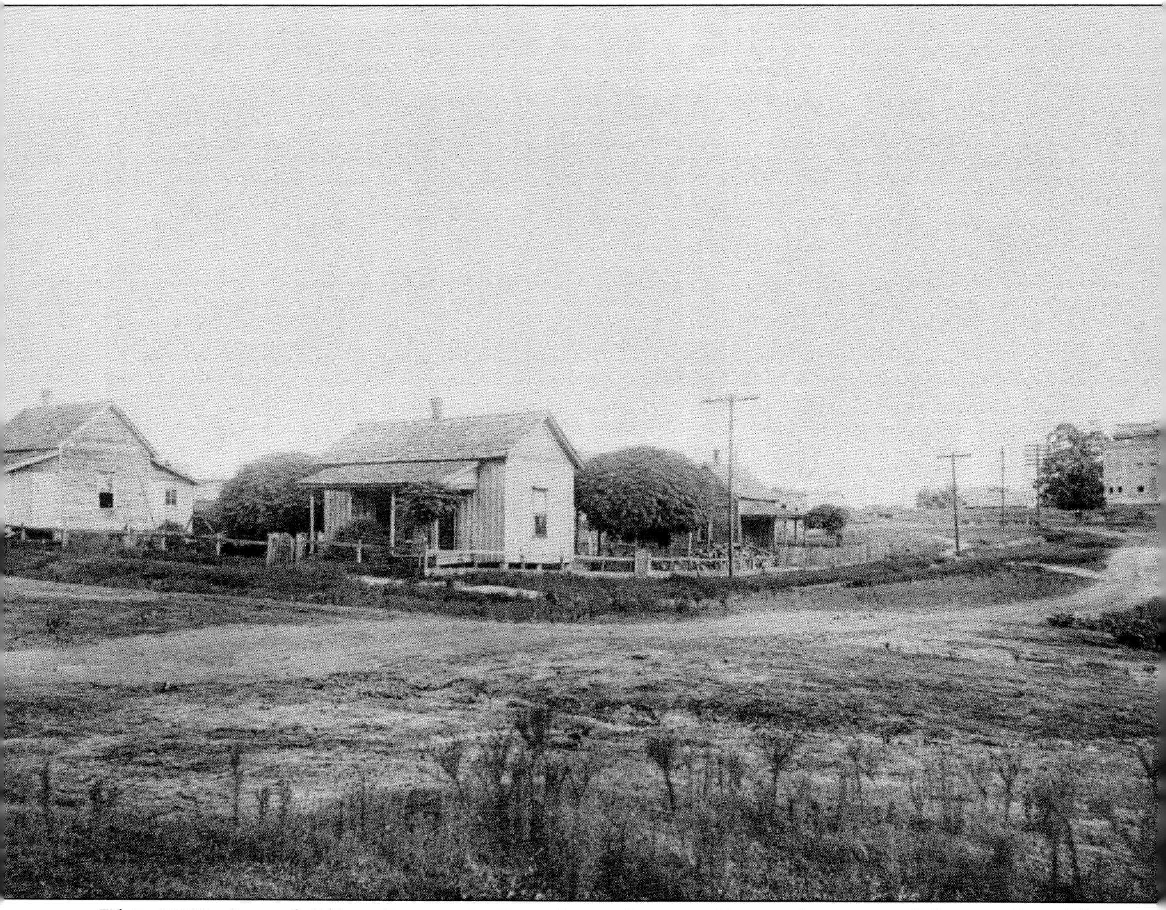

This 1912 view of Allen Avenue in Jonesboro shows a dirt road running left to right. Allen Avenue runs right up to courthouse knoll. The street was originally called Bullock Avenue but was renamed in 1902 in honor of W.H. Allen, the tax assessor. The building on the right is the newly built Jackson Parish Courthouse. (Courtesy of the Jackson Parish Museum.)

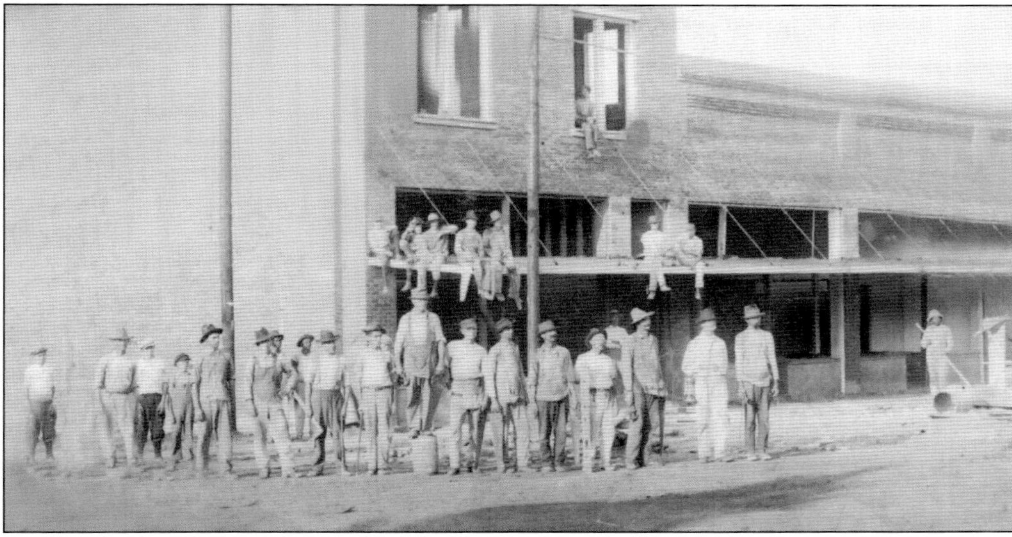

One of the first businesses in Jonesboro was a restaurant in a tent with a sawdust floor. There was a sawmill on the east side of the railroad tracks, and lumber was plentiful. Brick buildings started making an appearance in the town, and even though they took longer to erect and could be seriously damaged by fire, several of these buildings still stand in the town today. (Courtesy of the *Jackson Independent*.)

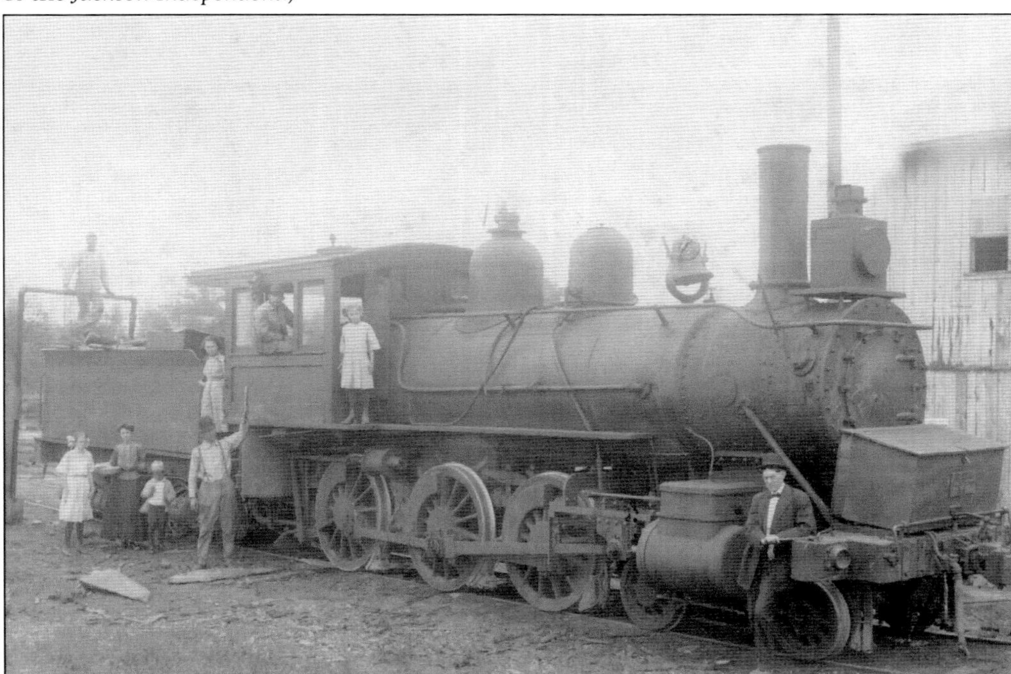

When the train stopped in Jonesboro, it was exciting. Spectators would be drawn to the depot to see what was being unloaded. Maybe it was visitors looking for jobs in the new town, distant family coming for long-awaited reunions, or even new merchandise for the town's businesses. This c. 1910 image shows children enjoying the chance to look inside a locomotive. (Courtesy of the *Jackson Independent*.)

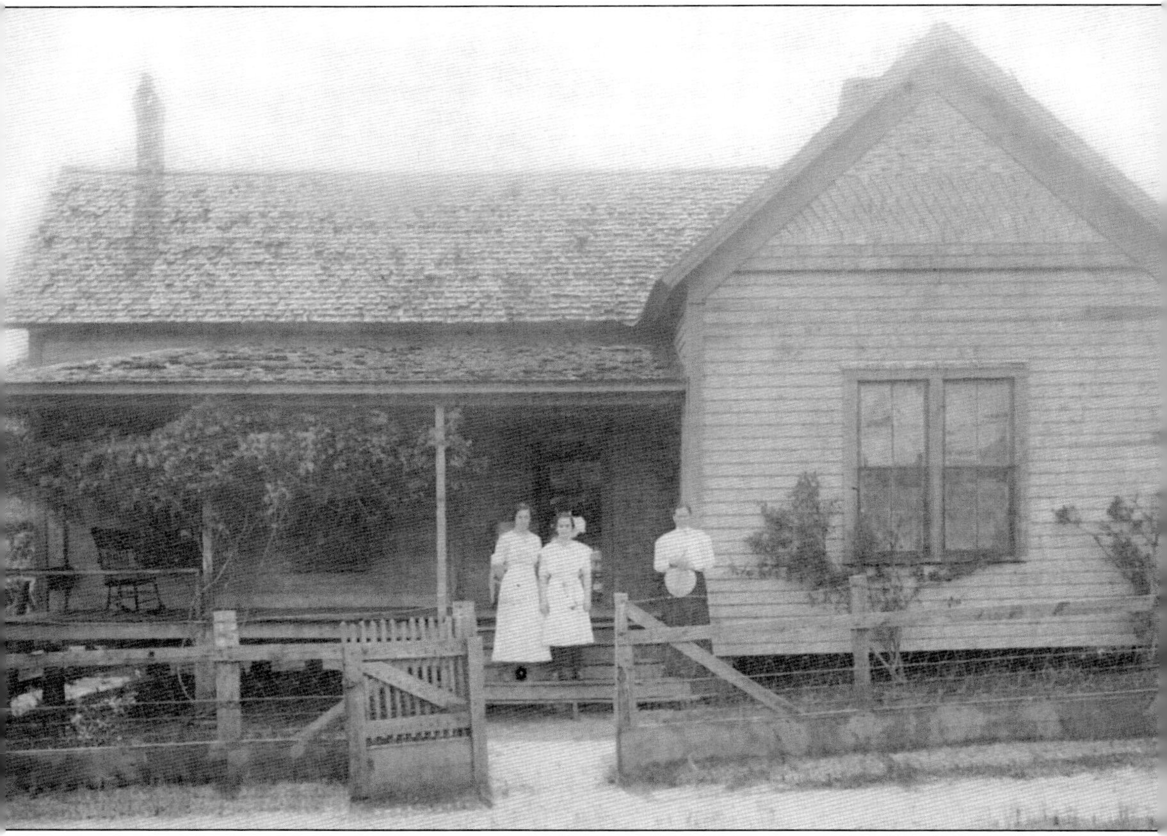

This is the home of Jackson Parish sheriff William J. McBride. It was one of the earliest homes built in Jonesboro. Sheriff McBride, who served from 1908 to 1916, moved back to Jonesboro when the parish seat was moved from Vernon in 1911. This home was built where the current Jackson Parish Library stands today. (Courtesy of the *Jackson Independent*.)

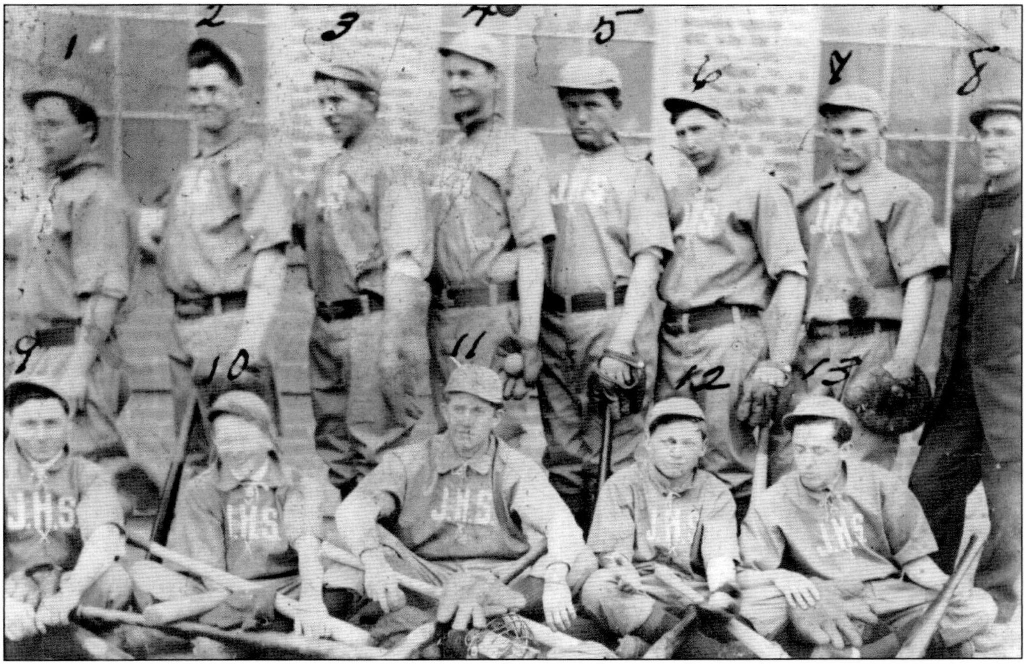

The first senior class of Jonesboro High School was set to graduate in May; however, money ran out in January 1910. Funds were then donated by the students' families, so it reopened as a subscription school. This baseball team stands beside the newly built school. (Courtesy of Jackson Parish Museum.)

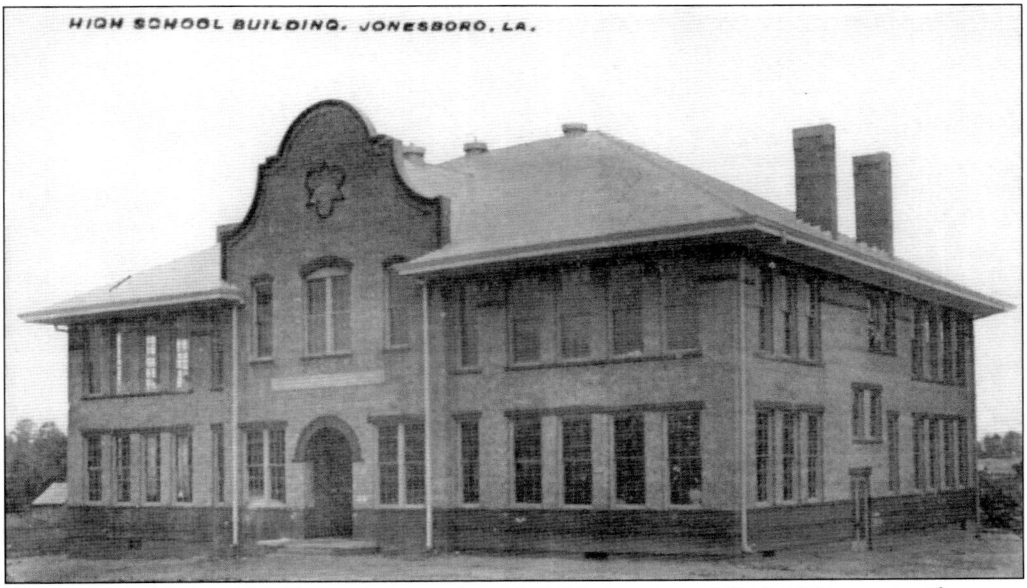


This new brick school building was erected in 1913. The session of 1916–1917 was significant to the now named Jonesboro-Hodge High School, as it was accredited as a secondary school. This meant the graduating class was issued diplomas with the seal from the Louisiana Department of Education. In 1920 "J-H," as it would be called, was accredited as a high school. This building was destroyed by fire in 1925. (Courtesy of Jackson Parish Museum.)

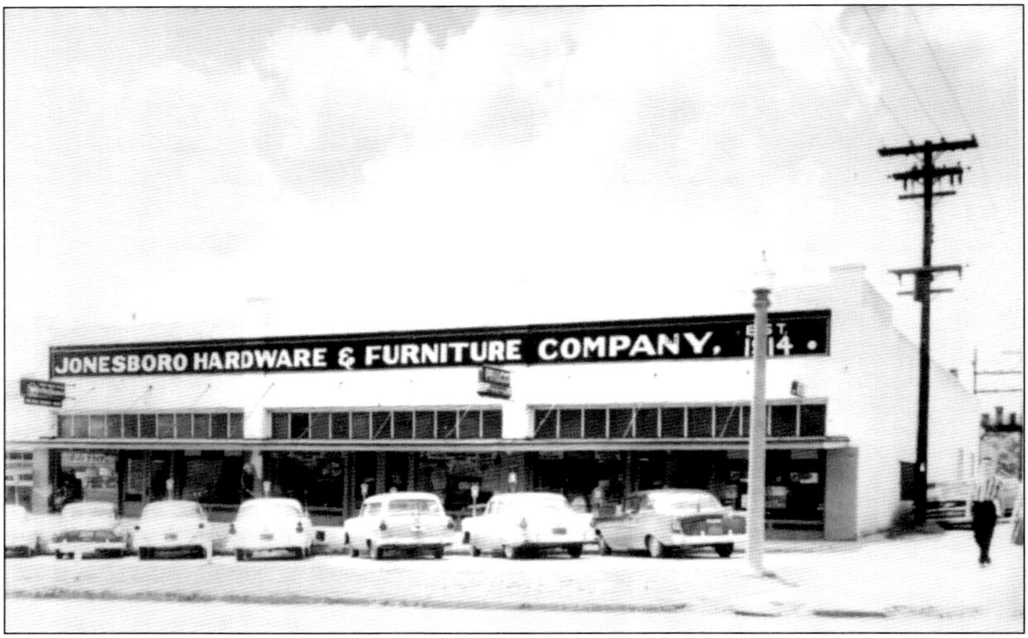


In 1911, C.J. Morton leased a two-story frame building on the corner of Main Street and Polk Avenue immediately following the announcement that Jonesboro would be the parish seat. In 1914, the Jonesboro Hardware and Furniture Company business was bought by J.E. Cox. (Courtesy of the Jackson Parish Museum.)

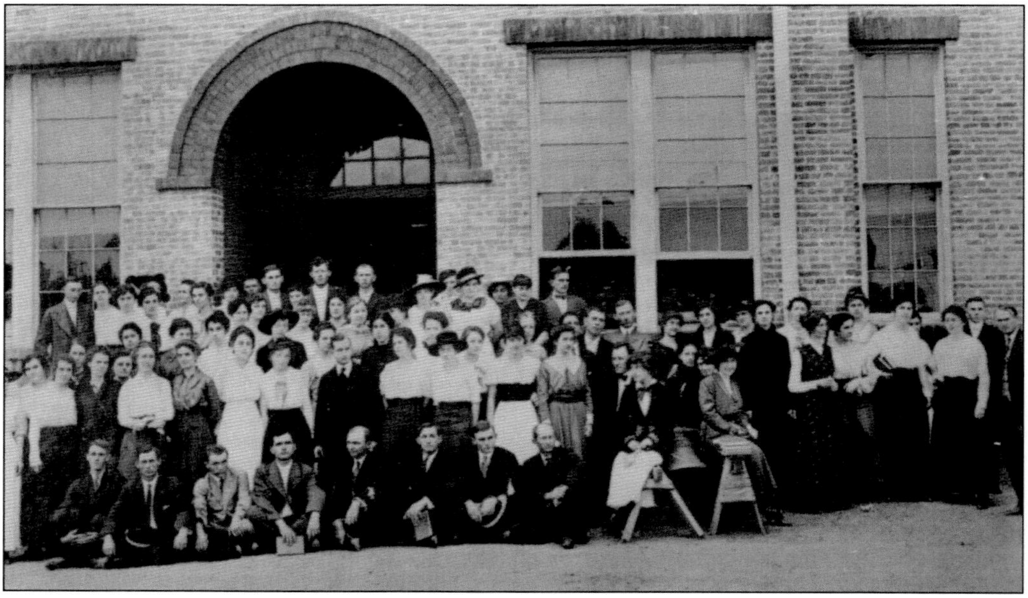

These future teachers pose outside of the Jonesboro-Hodge High School in 1915 during a break while taking the teachers workshop. After this workshop, the hopeful teachers with the highest scores were offered jobs for the next school year. (Courtesy of Sylvia Pagan.)

A political rally, most likely for a presidential election, was held on Main Street in 1916. The building on the right is the newly established Jonesboro State Bank. It opened for business in 1913. The first bank robbery was an inside job, and a suit was put forth against Rush Wimberly to pay back the money he had taken out of the bank without the knowledge of its directors. Wimberly was among the 19 men who bought stock to create the bank. (Courtesy of the Jackson Parish Museum.)

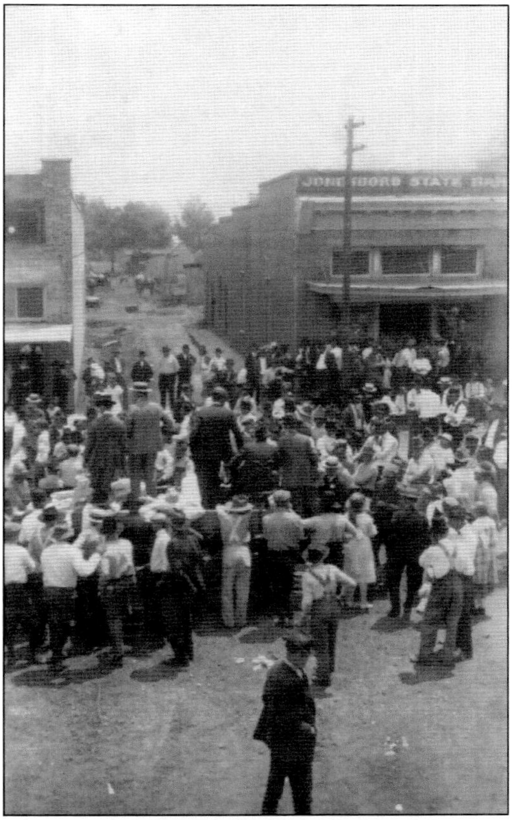


The Jonesboro Town Band is pictured here in the early 1920s. The band was directed by Mike Kelley of Hodge; he also conducted the Southern Advance Band in Hodge. This band was known to play concerts during the spring and summer. It was also available to play during town parades and picnics. (Courtesy of the *Jackson Independent.*)

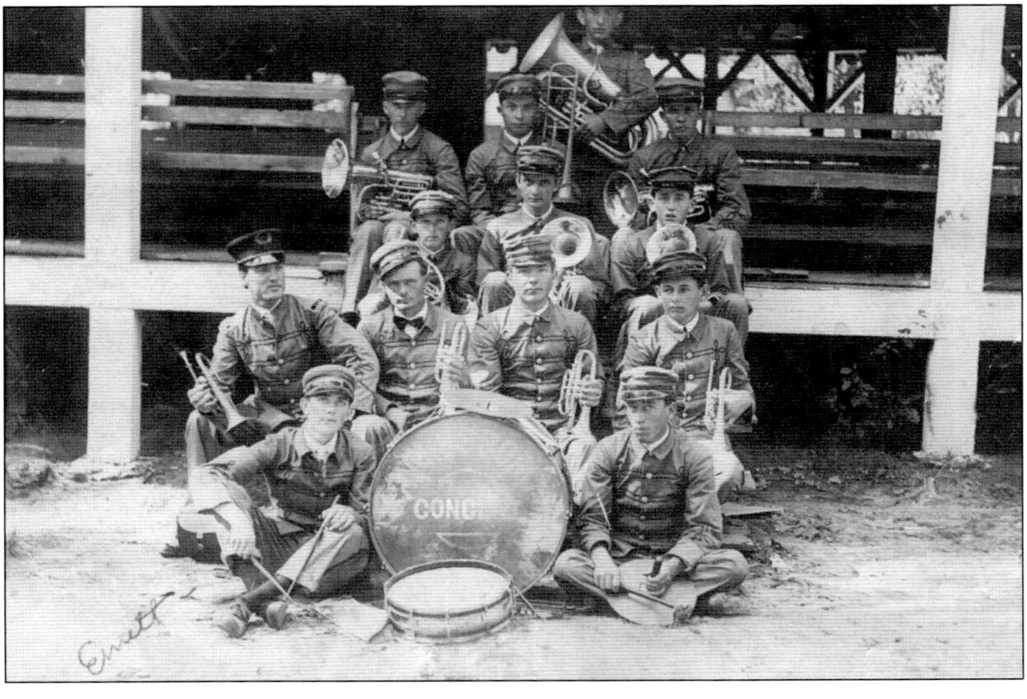

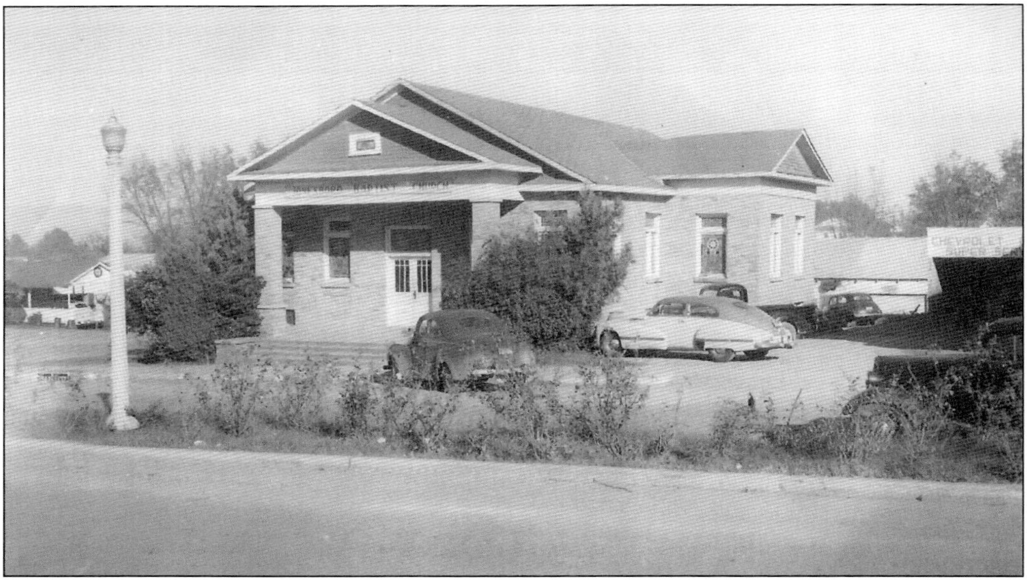

In 1920, Rev. A.N. Murray became pastor and soon after organized the construction of a two-story brick house of worship with ample space on the corner of Allen Avenue and Main Street. This was the first brick church built in the parish. By 1921, church membership had risen to 200. Church services were on the second and fourth Sunday of the month. (Courtesy of First Baptist Church.)

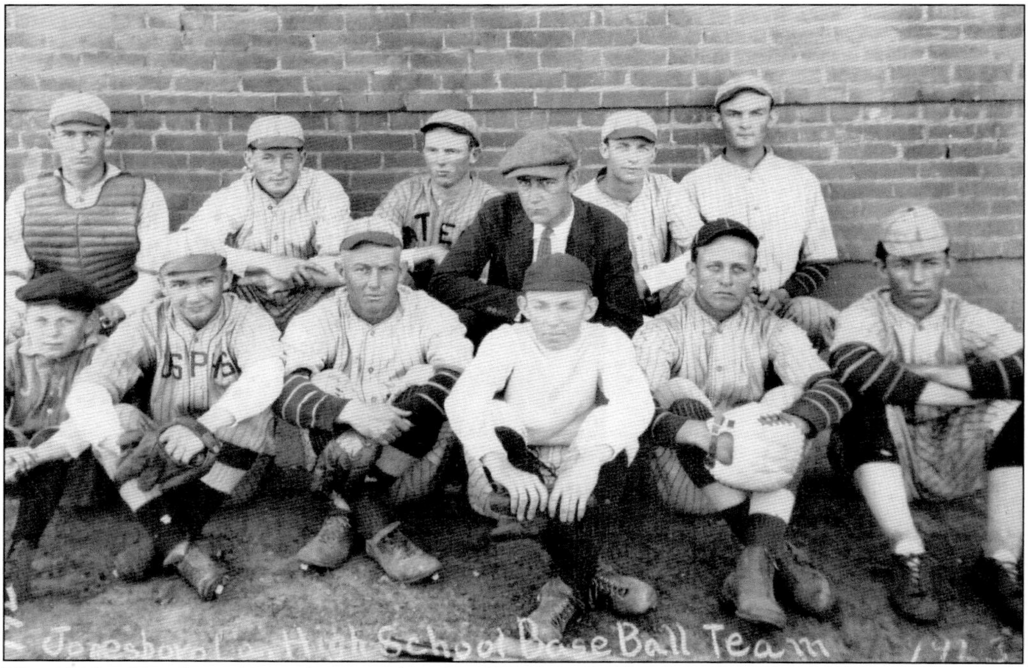


The 1923–1924 class of Jonesboro High School had 23 graduates. Jonesboro was seeing an increase in population, and the number of students was increasing as well. After the 1913 school building burned in 1925, construction of a larger brick building on Fourth Street and Cooper Avenue began and was completed in 1927. This new school building only lasted a few years before it too burned. (Courtesy of Jackson Parish Museum.)

Sheriff Eli Rentz (pictured) and Deputy Luther Barnes arrested three men making moonshine in the community of Ansley. After handcuffing each one, Rentz ordered Barnes to get the car and he would meet him with the prisoners. Barnes had only gone a short distance when he heard gunfire and returned to find that the sheriff had been killed. This began one of the largest manhunts in the parish. The men were captured separately and sentenced to hang. (Courtesy of the Jackson Parish Sheriff's Department.)

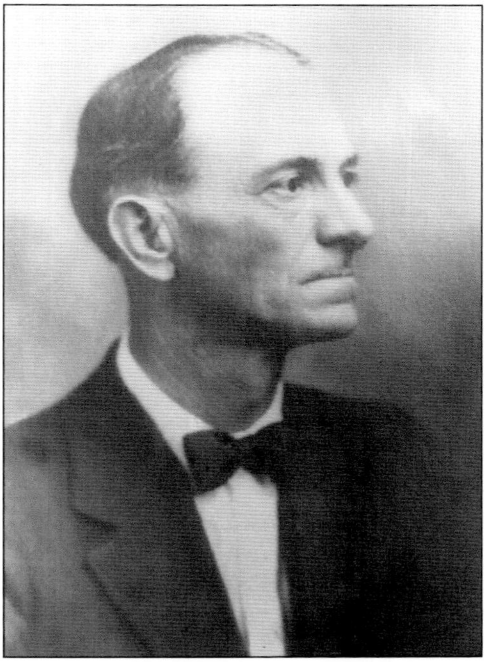

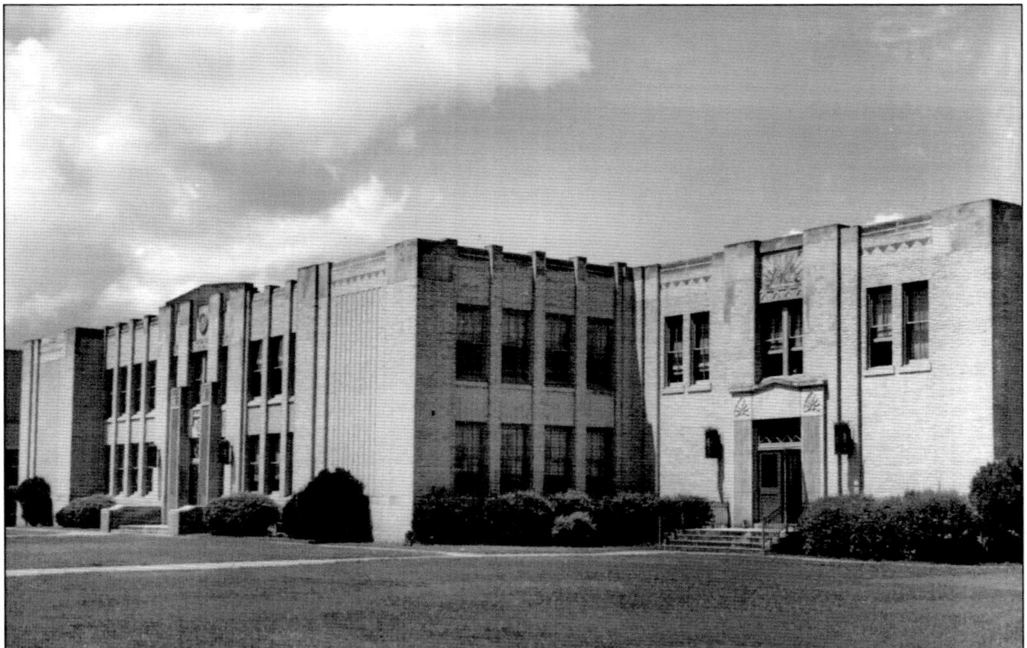

A new, larger school was built in 1932 on Pershing Highway. This became its permanent setting, and the cafeteria and band hall were constructed in 1954. A new stadium for football games, a gymnasium, and a home economics building were constructed in 1959–1960. Several years later, an auditorium was built. The architecture of the building came to symbolize Jonesboro-Hodge High School. In June 2000, the senior high school was set on fire by arson, and another building was constructed during the 2002–2003 school year. (Courtesy of the T.L. Colvin estate.)

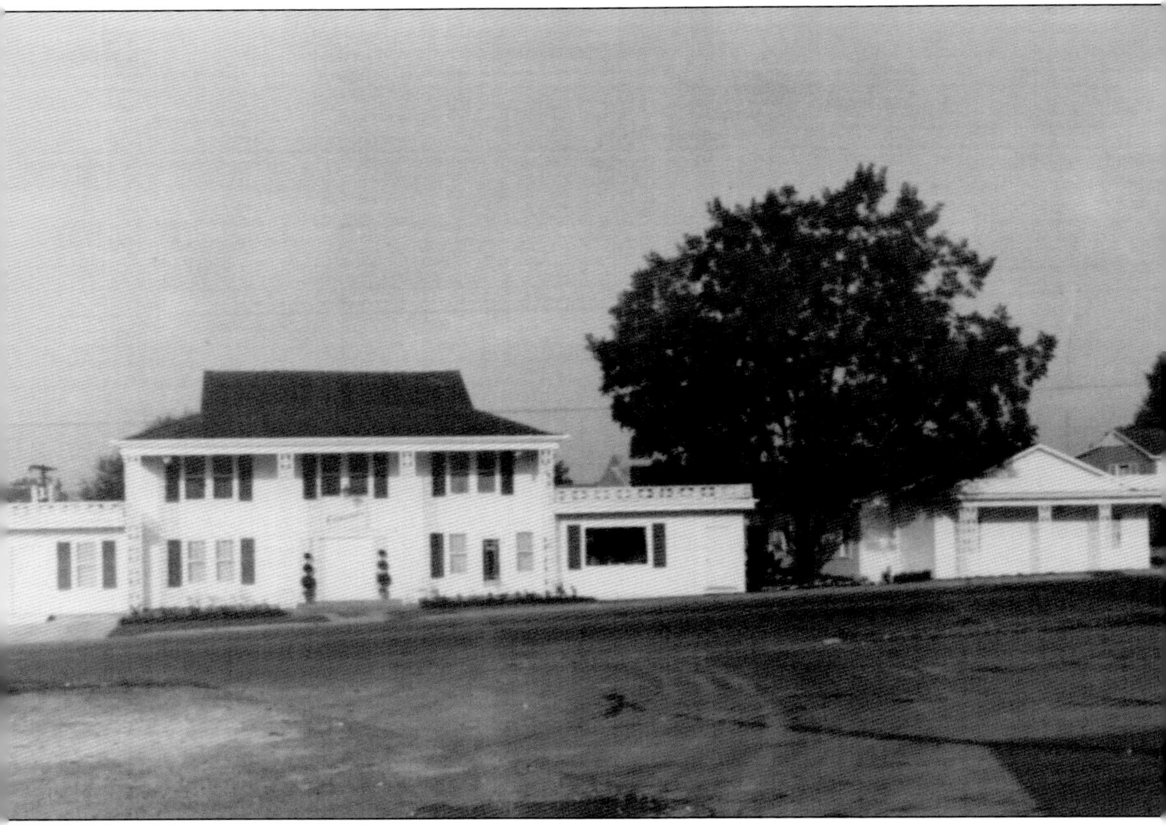

In 1937, Mr. and Mrs. E.L. Edmond came to Jonesboro and established a funeral home. It took a lot of courage to come to a small town and start a business during the Depression. The Edmonds built their funeral home on the corner of Allen Avenue and Third Street, opposite the Talbot house. A new, larger building was erected in 1961. Edmonds Funeral Home still serves the community today. (Courtesy of the T.L. Colvin estate.)

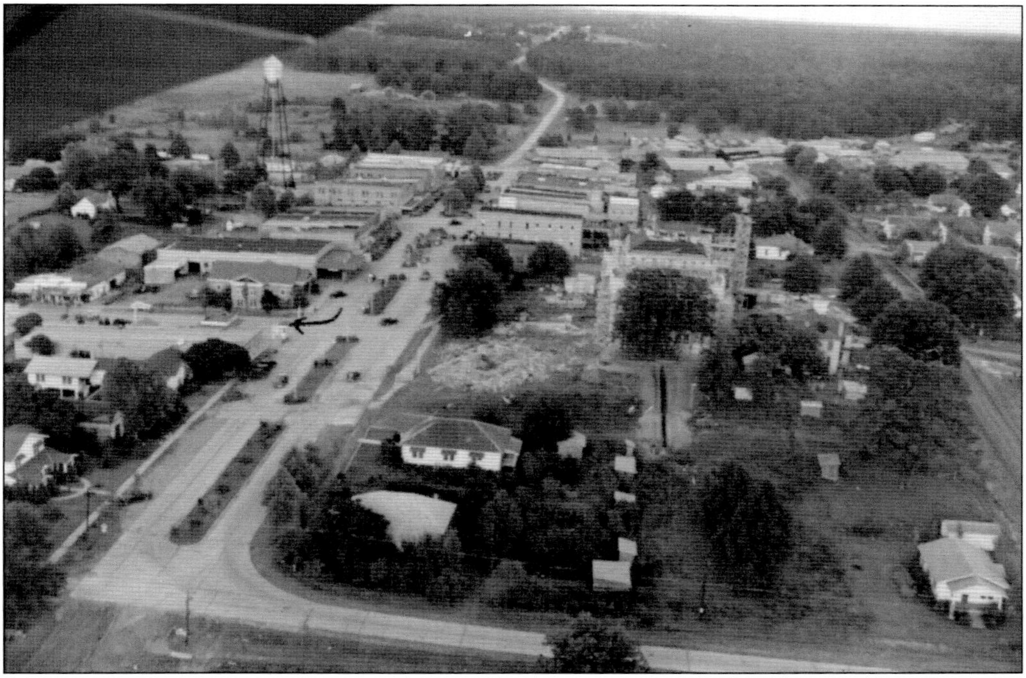

This aerial view of downtown Jonesboro in 1937 shows the layout of the town. The scaffolds on the new courthouse, still under construction, are visible. The black arrow at left center points down Allen Avenue. T.L. Colvin Sr. was an avid aviator took pictures from his airplane, offering unique views of the towns he flew over. (Courtesy of the T.L. Colvin estate.)

I.J. Allen bought full ownership of the Jackson Gin and Ice Company around 1934. In 1938, the company was completely destroyed by fire. During the fire, an ammonia tank and air tank exploded, damaging several nearby buildings. The ice building was minimally damaged, but Allen did not rebuild the gin building. (Courtesy of the T.L. Colvin estate.)

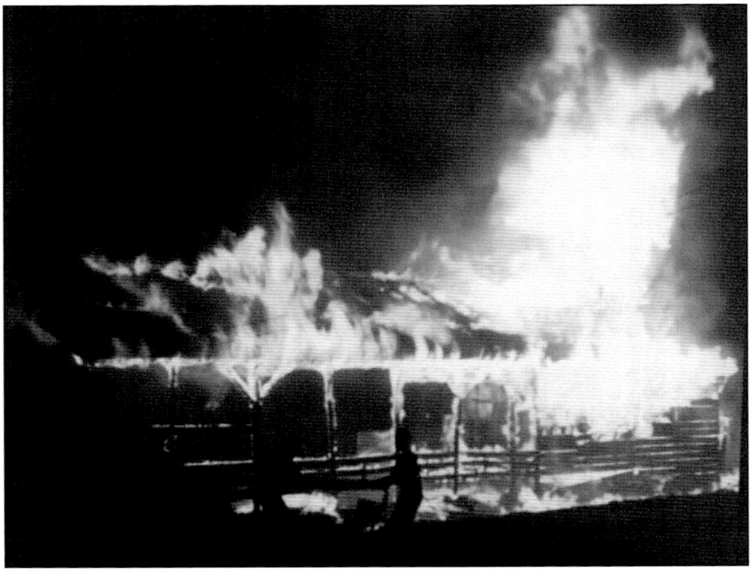

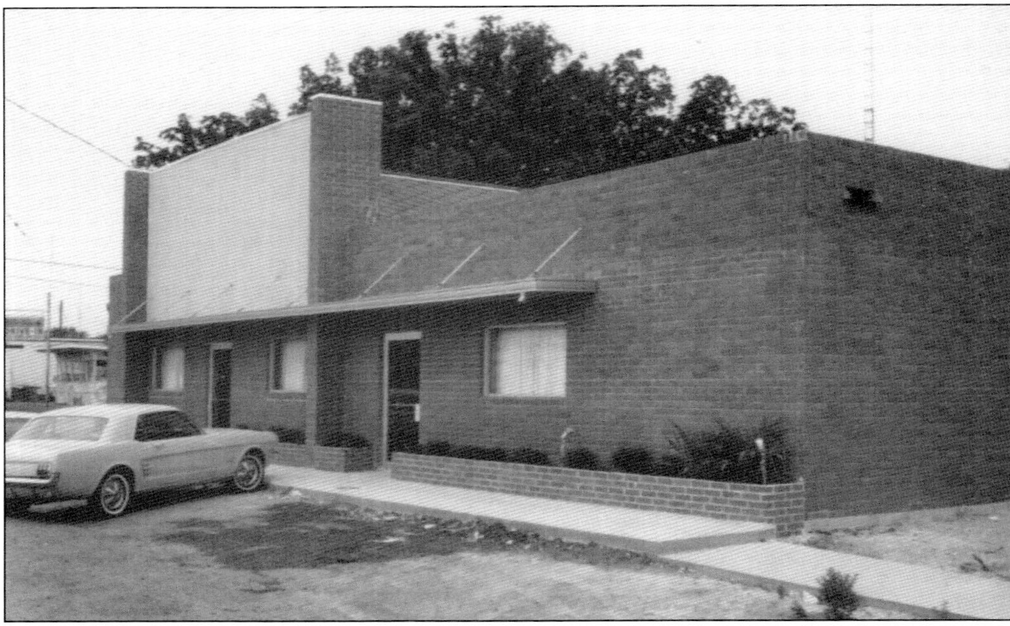

The *Jackson Independent* office was moved to its present location on Hudson Avenue around 1940 when it needed more space. A.H. Colvin Sr. retired in October 1956 and sold his interest to his children Ansley and T.L. Colvin Sr. The *Jackson Independent* upgraded its machines and continued to publish the weekly news. This building is still in use today. (Courtesy of the T.L. Colvin estate.)

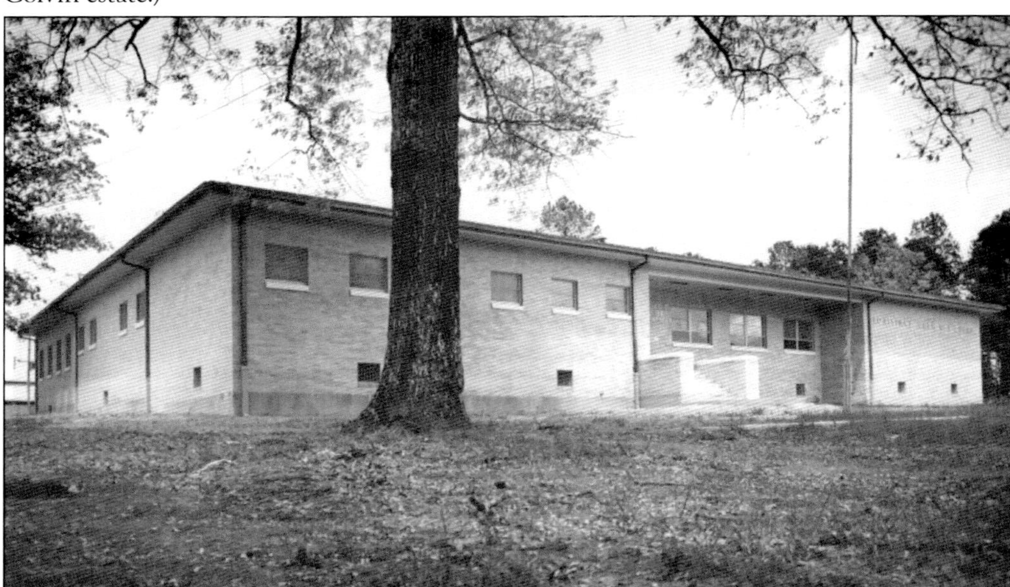

Company C, 199th Infantry Regiment of Jonesboro, Louisiana, was activated on March 31, 1947, with two officers and 25 enlisted men. Federal recognition was accorded to the unit on April 10, 1947. From the time of activation, the unit has grown constantly, reaching full strength in early 1949. It was moved from the old jail building to its current location on the fairgrounds hill just east of Jonesboro. (Courtesy of the T.L. Colvin estate.)

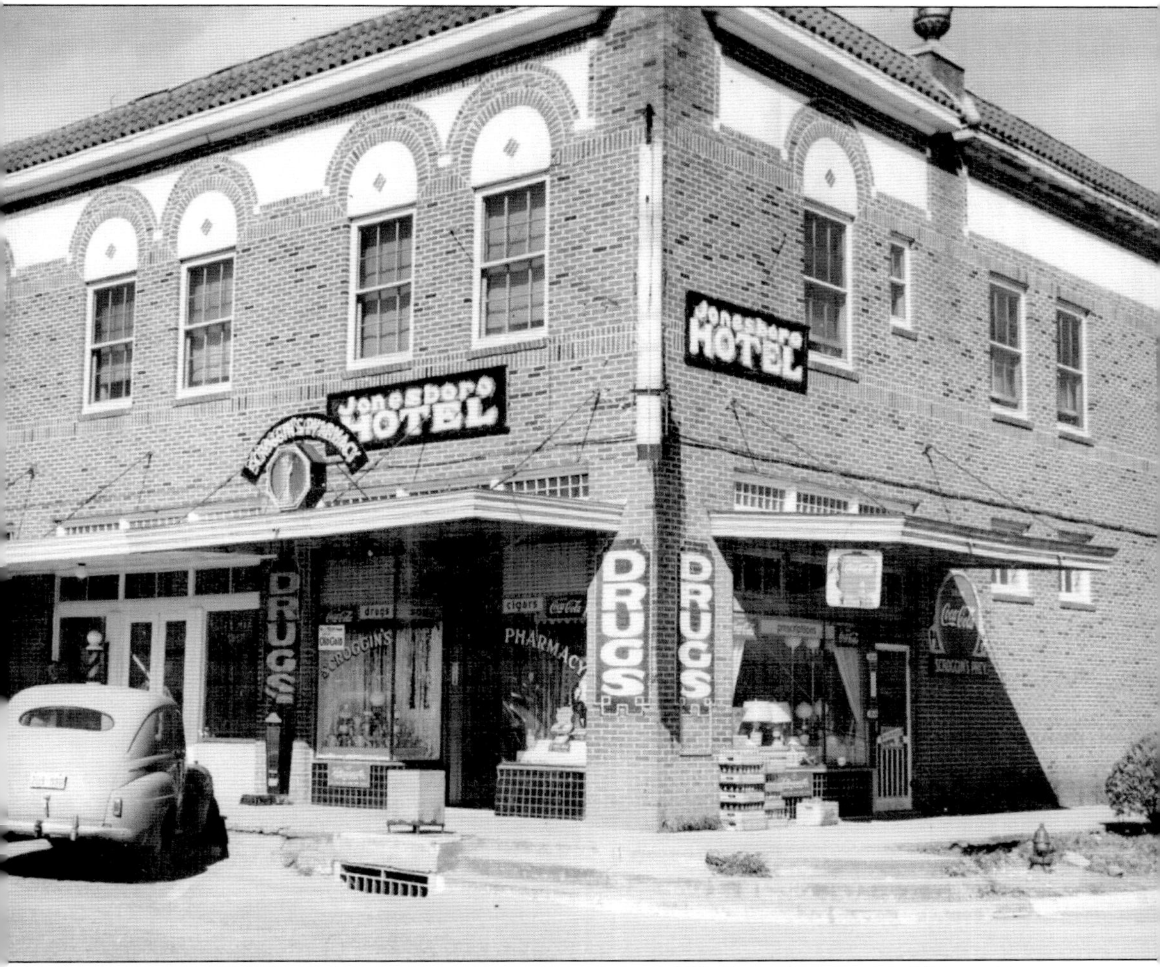


The Jonesboro Hotel was built in 1926 on the corner of Hudson Avenue and Main Street and was owned and operated by the George Nomey family. Inside the hotel was a coffee shop, Ayres record and book shop, Ed May's barbershop, and May's beauty parlor. In 1961, smoke was discovered coming out of the kitchen, and an alarm was sent out. However, within minutes, the building was engulfed in flames. The entire structure was destroyed. (Courtesy of the Jackson Parish Museum.)

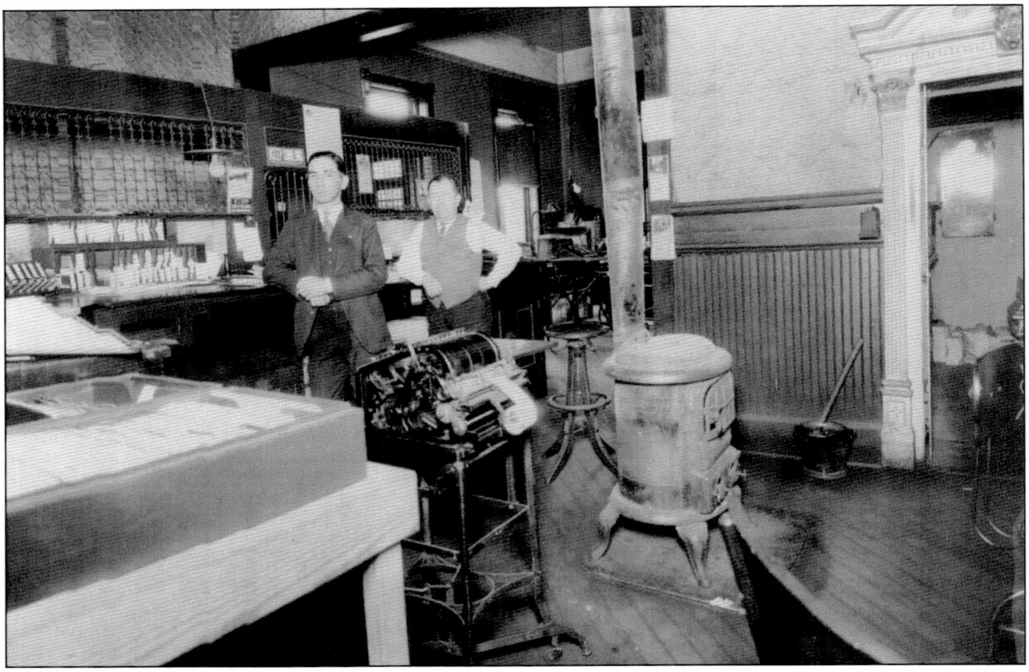

In 1904, land on the corner of Polk Avenue and Main Street was purchased from Warren E. Bush and William "Bill" McBride, and construction began on Jackson Parish Bank; it opened in June that year. These images show the early days of the bank around 1925, with Wilbur McDonald (above left), a cashier, and Waylon McDonald (above right), assistant cashier. The growing bank became cramped with its volume of business, so the old building was torn down and a new one was erected in its place. Pictured below from left to right are Wilbur McDonald, Stanley Lewis, Guy Cox, and Waylon McDonald. (Both, courtesy of the Jackson Parish Bank.)

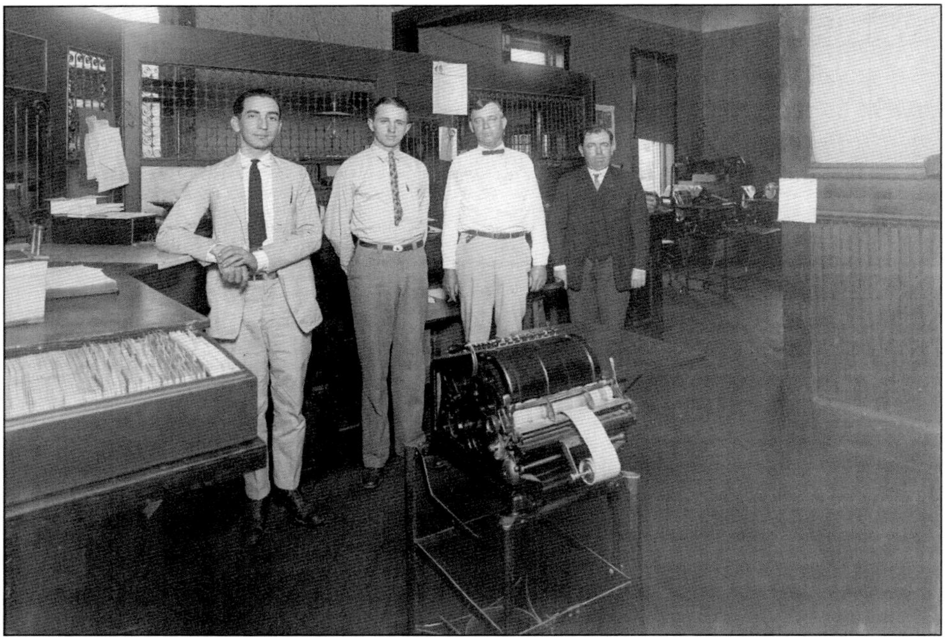

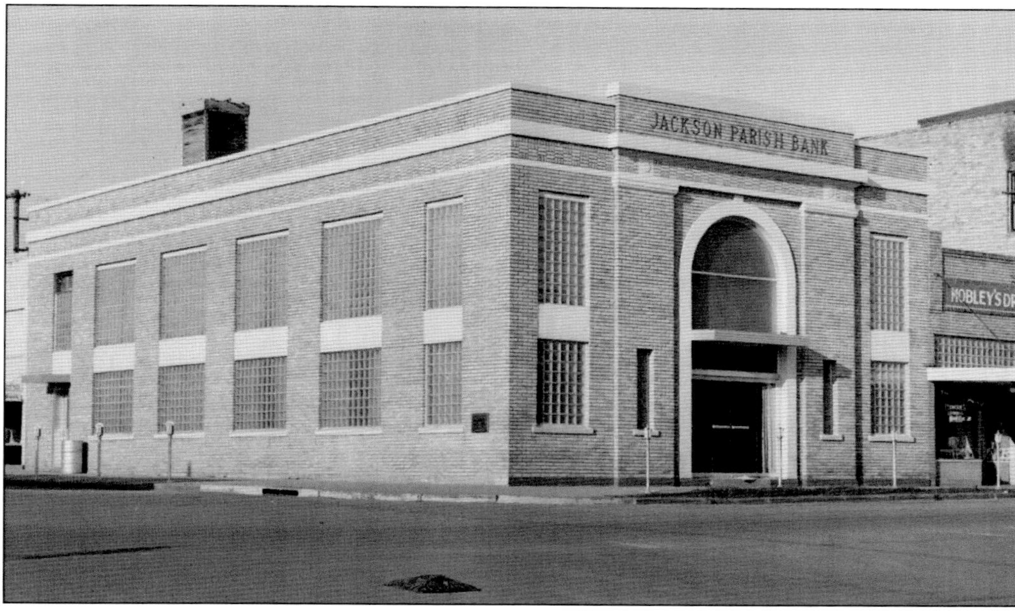


After tearing down the old building, the bank reopened in November 1927. Then, the 21-year-old bank was remodeled in 1948. In general, the main structure stayed the same, but the inside was completely remodeled. In 1969, the directors decided it was time to rebuild and grow in size. The 1927 building was demolished, and on April 13, 1970, a new structure (pictured below) opened that still serves the community to this day. (Above, courtesy of the T.L. Colvin estate; below, courtesy of Mary Smith.)

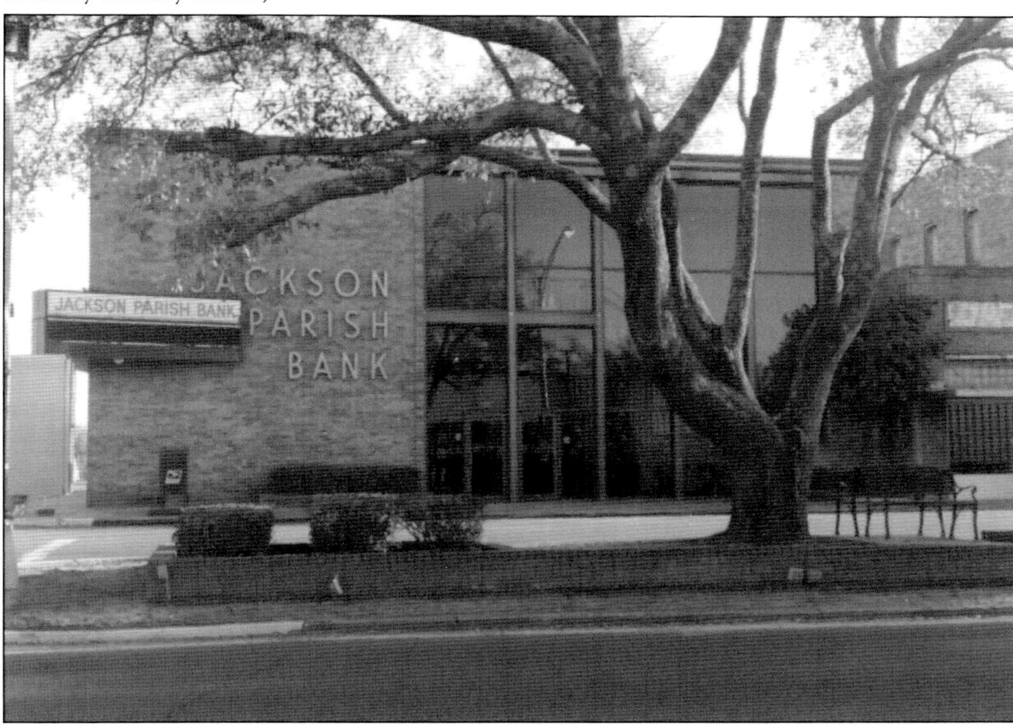

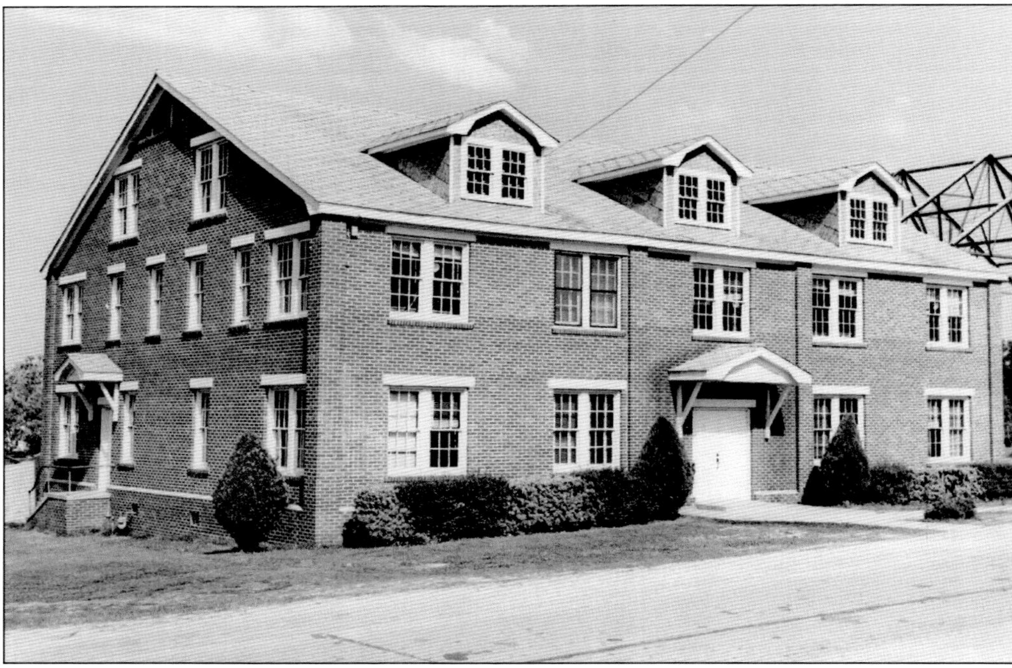

By 1934, the training union at Jonesboro Baptist Church had an enrollment of 119. An educational building erected at the west end of Main Street was dedicated in 1944. At this time, church enrollment was over 900. A new auditorium was built in 1948 next to the educational building. The church built a large auditorium with a seating capacity of 750. The name was changed to First Baptist Church of Jonesboro in the early 1950s. The church has continued to grow and be renovated. A new educational building was constructed, and the old one torn down. A new Family Life Center was built in 2006. (Both, courtesy of First Baptist Church.)

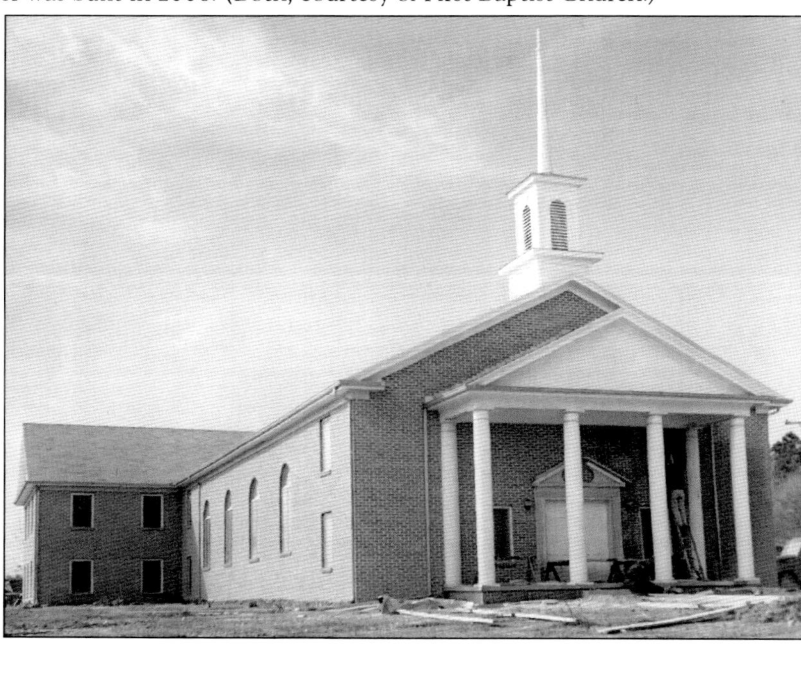

In the days before pine tree farming, cotton was the major crop in Jackson Parish, and for a short time, tomatoes were a cash crop for local farmers. The profitability of these crops began to decline, and the parish realized the sustainability of the trees. Henry Hardtner became known as the local father of forestry when he began pushing the reforestation program. He realized that cut-over land could be planted, left alone to grow, and then cut again. This is what currently sustains the parish, as lumber is the only local industry. (Courtesy of the *Jackson Independent*.)

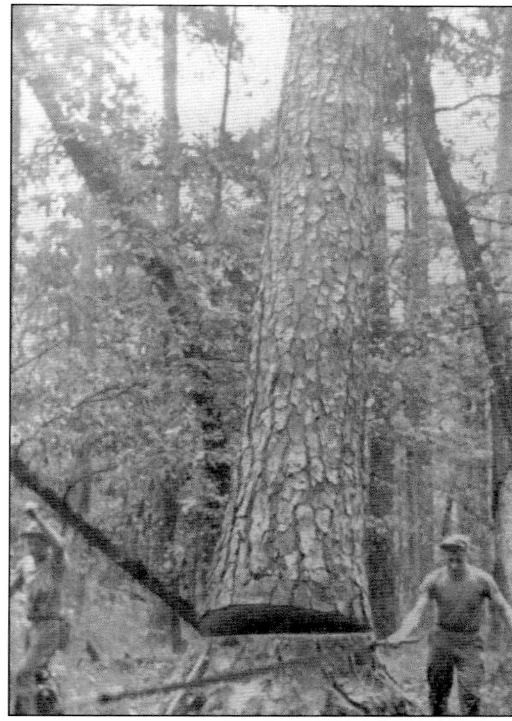

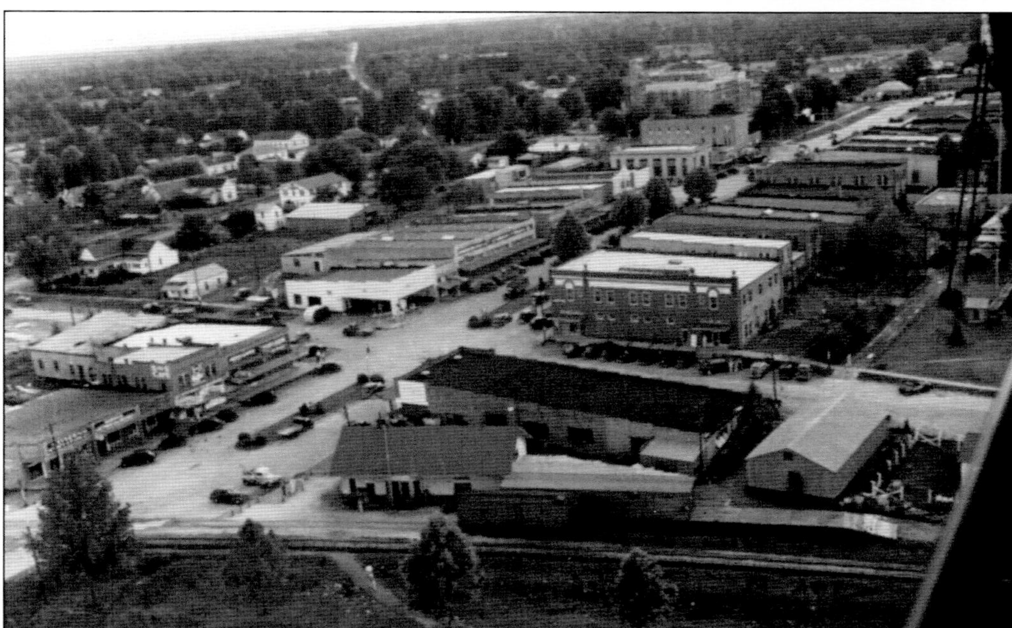

This is an aerial view west of downtown Jonesboro in the late 1937. The buildings on the left side of Main Street, up to the old State Bank, have all been torn down and replaced. The first building immediately past the train tracks on the right, and the Jonesboro Hotel building, have been replaced. Downtown Jonesboro, west of the train tracks, has seen minimal change over the years; the past is clearly visible while driving down Jimmie Davis Boulevard. (Courtesy of the T.L. Colvin estate.)

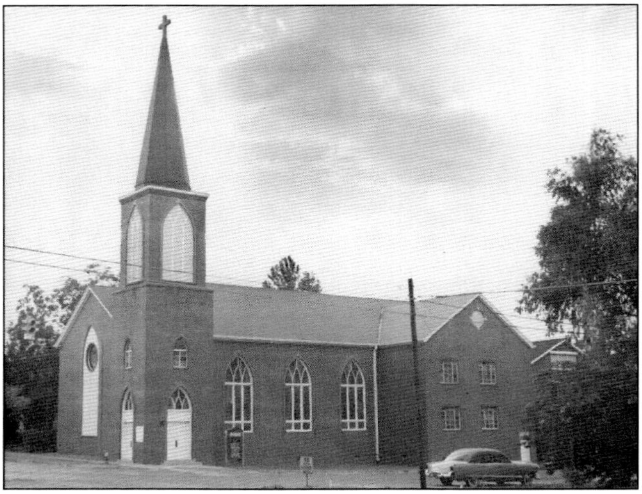

The Jonesboro Methodist Church South and the Jonesboro Methodist Protestant Church merged in 1939 and became Jonesboro Methodist Church. A new building was constructed on Cooper Avenue, and the first service was held in 1941. A new parsonage was built in 1959, and the old one was moved and used as a kindergarten and church school until 1968. A new educational building was erected in 1968. The church building caught fire in 2005 but has since been rebuilt. (Courtesy of the T.L. Colvin.)

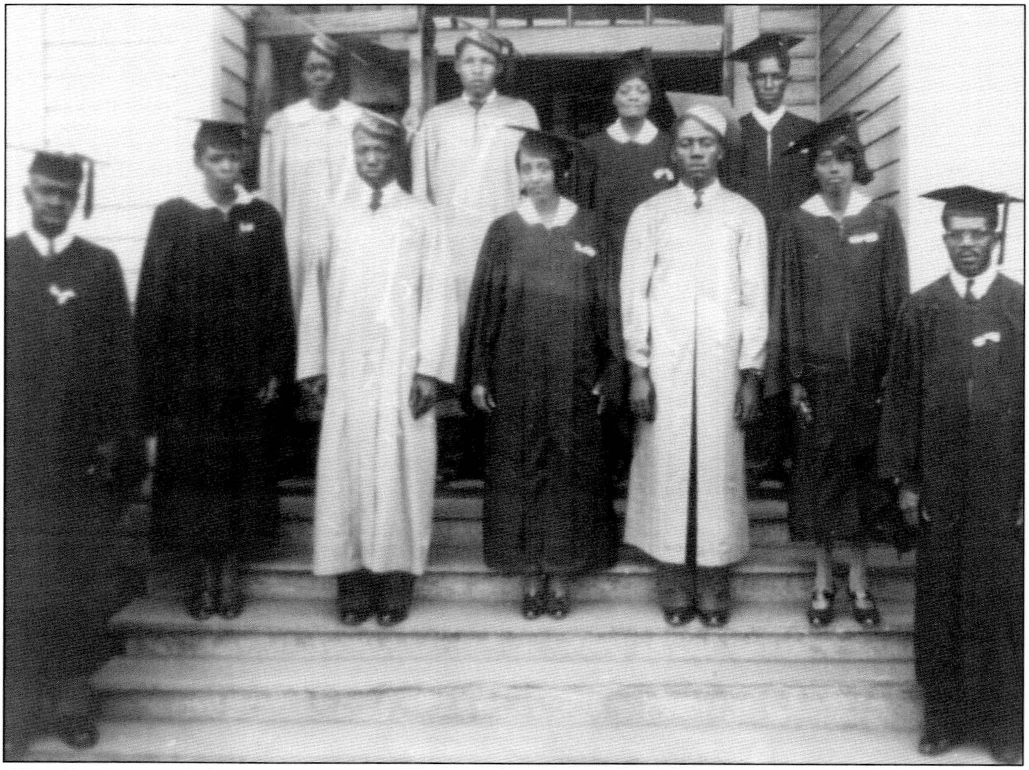

G.L. Hawk, at far left, was asked to establish a school, and Jonesboro Colored High School opened. Later, the name was changed to Jackson High School, and a second building was constructed after World War II using salvaged lumber. This building, located on the corner of Cedar Street and Beech Springs Road, was demolished after 1970. Pictured is the first graduating class in 1937. (Courtesy of the *Jackson Independent*.)

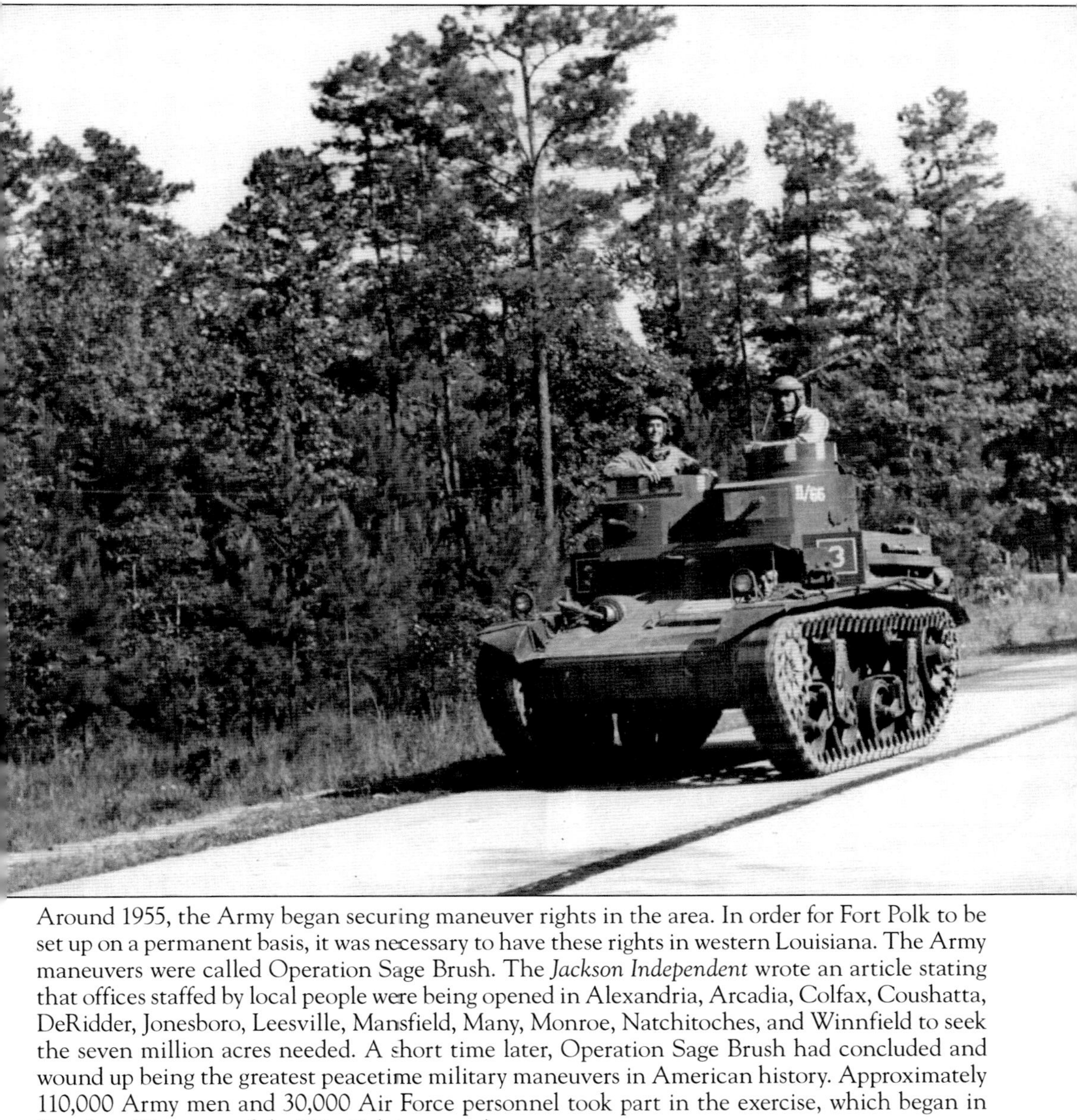


Around 1955, the Army began securing maneuver rights in the area. In order for Fort Polk to be set up on a permanent basis, it was necessary to have these rights in western Louisiana. The Army maneuvers were called Operation Sage Brush. The *Jackson Independent* wrote an article stating that offices staffed by local people were being opened in Alexandria, Arcadia, Colfax, Coushatta, DeRidder, Jonesboro, Leesville, Mansfield, Many, Monroe, Natchitoches, and Winnfield to seek the seven million acres needed. A short time later, Operation Sage Brush had concluded and wound up being the greatest peacetime military maneuvers in American history. Approximately 110,000 Army men and 30,000 Air Force personnel took part in the exercise, which began in October. (Courtesy of the T.L. Colvin estate.)

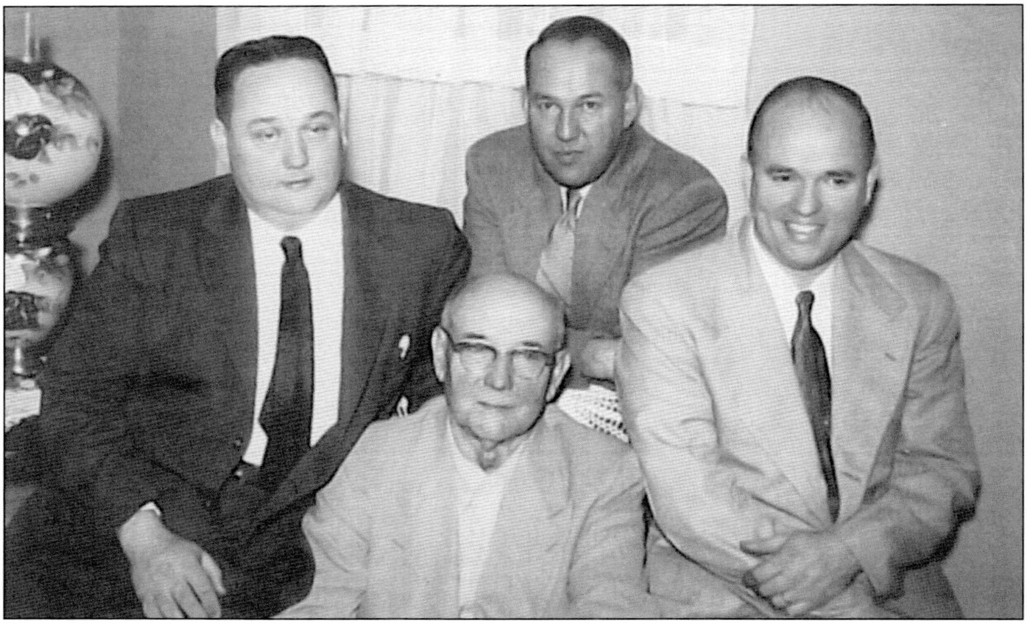

Ansley Colvin Jr. retired from the newspaper business in 1976, and T.L. Colvin Sr. and son Ted acquired his interest. T.L. served as publisher and Ted as editor until T.L. retired and sold his interest to his son Ted and grandson Tre. Lester G. Colvin was a pressman and darkroom technician, and after he retired, was involved in distribution. After almost 93 years, the Colvins sold the newspaper. (Courtesy of the T.L. Colvin estate.)

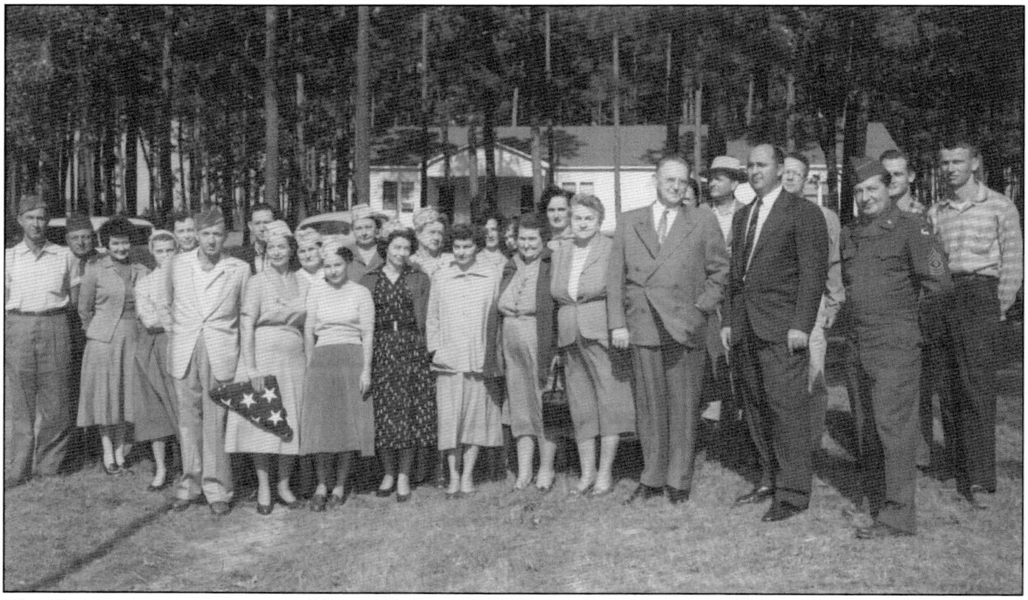

The flag-raising ceremony on Veteran's Day 1955 shows the Veterans of Foreign Wars Edwin Brown Post No. 4317 in the background. This post, located on east Main Street, was named after Edwin Brown, who died as a prisoner of war at a Japanese prison camp on Luzon in the Philippines. He was forced along the Bataan Death March and never reached his destination; he had been a prisoner for five months. (Courtesy of the T.L. Colvin estate.)

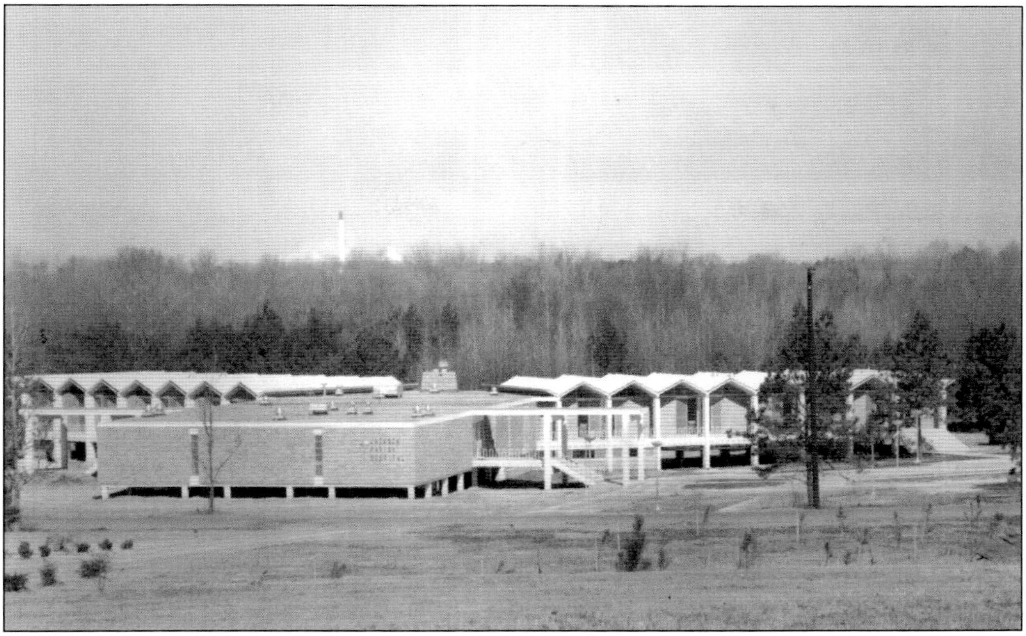

Efforts to establish a hospital began in 1959. On February 5, the Jackson Parish Jaycees announced the completion of a survey to determine local interest in securing a hospital. The Jackson Parish Junior Chamber of Commerce, along with the Jackson Parish Police Jury, was instrumental in creating interest in a parish hospital. The ultra-modern 38-room hospital was built and dedicated in 1962. The hospital is located in the Jonesboro city limits on a seven-and-a-half-acre tract on Beech Springs Road and Alexander Street, just off highway 167. (Both, courtesy of the T.L. Colvin estate.)

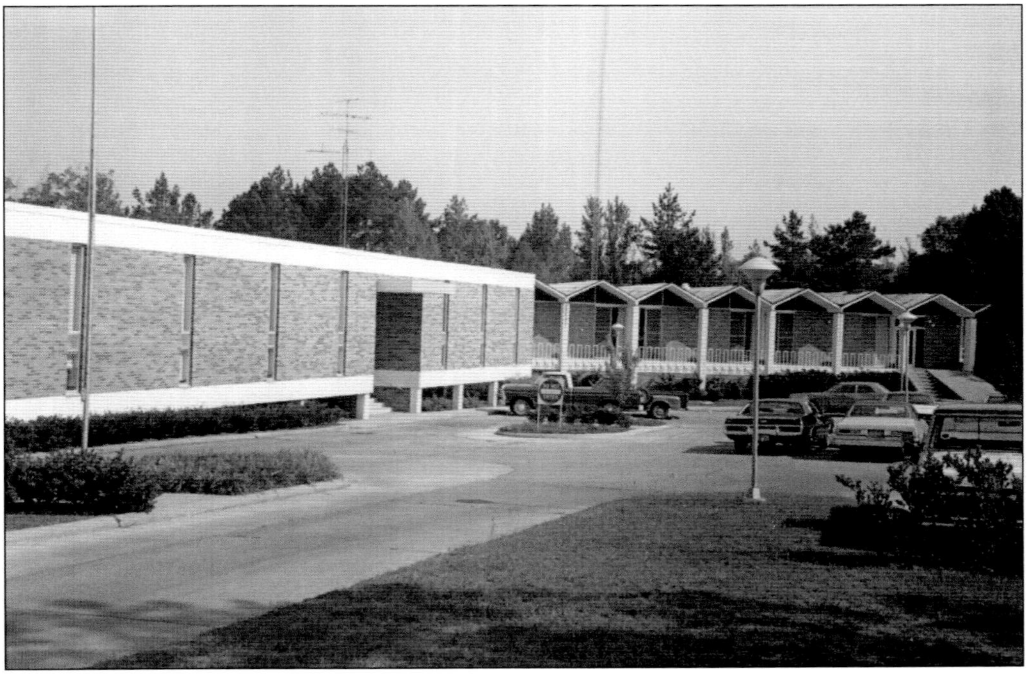

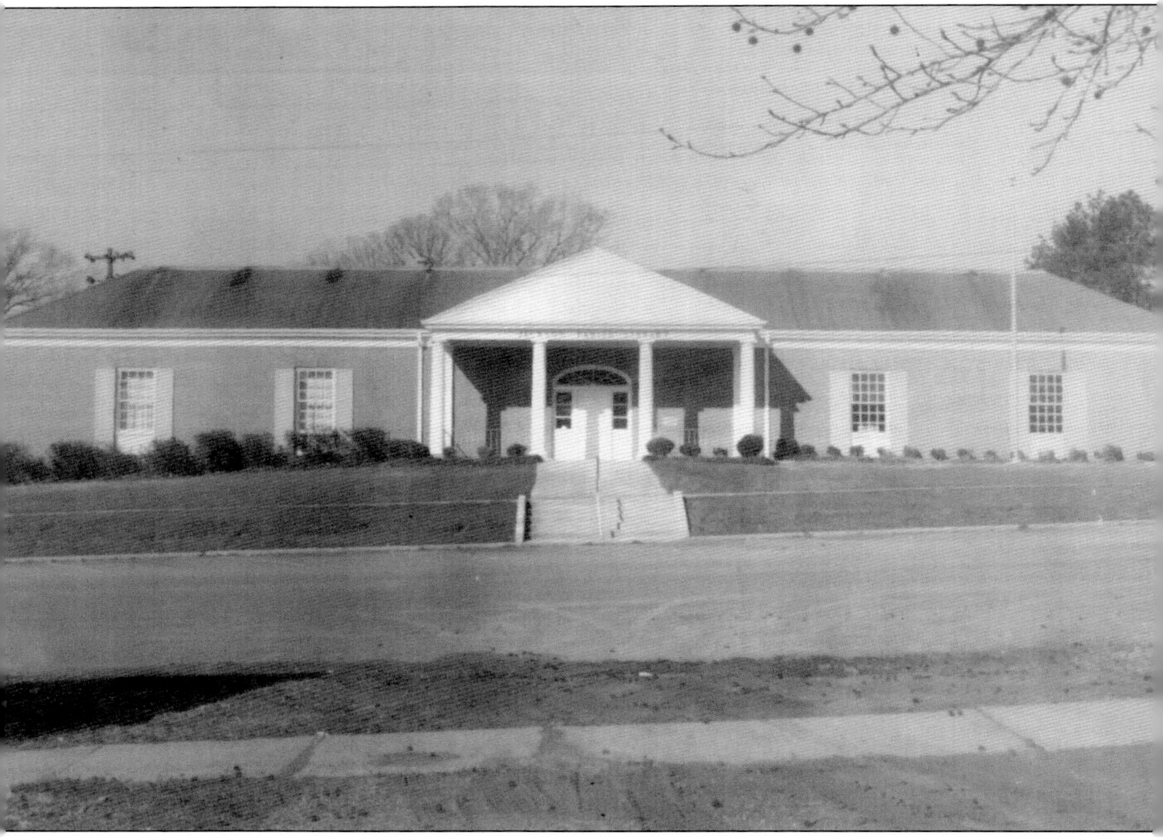

After six months of planning, in 1960, the Jackson Parish Library became a reality. The former post office building, the Holliday building on the corner of Polk Avenue and Sixth Street, was rented and housed 9,000 books. A bookmobile was ordered to serve the entire parish. In 1971, the Jackson Parish Police Jury voted to purchase the William J. McBride property, and construction began on a 9,000-square-foot building. It was opened to the public in September 1972. In 1999, it was remodeled, and the building was doubled in size. The library just recently added a second branch in Chatham. (Courtesy of the T.L. Colvin estate.)

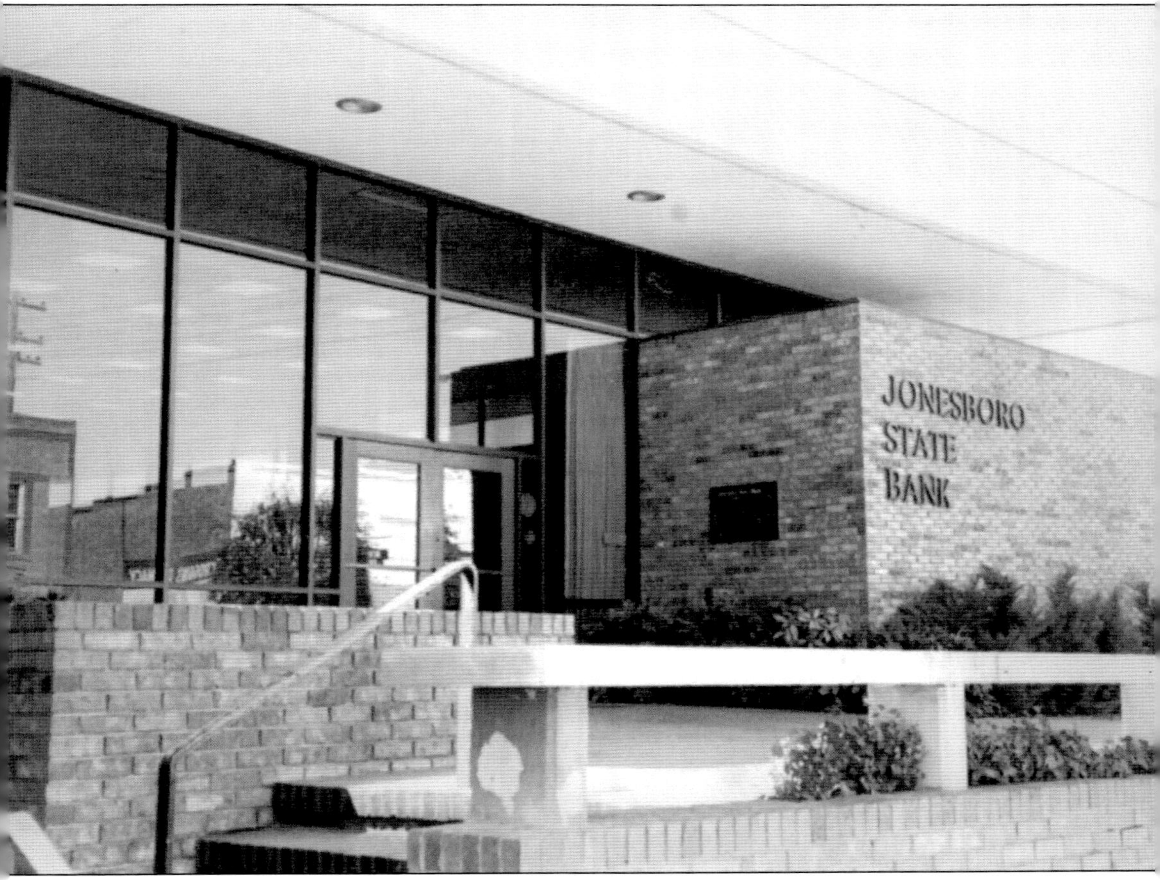


The old Jonesboro State Bank was remodeled in 1958. In 1975, I.J. Allen, who became president in 1939, signed a contract to build a new bank on the corner of Hudson Avenue and Main Street beside the old structure. In 1975, the Jonesboro Hardware and Furniture store was torn down, and the current Jonesboro State Bank was built; its doors opened in December 1976. (Courtesy of the T.L. Colvin estate.)

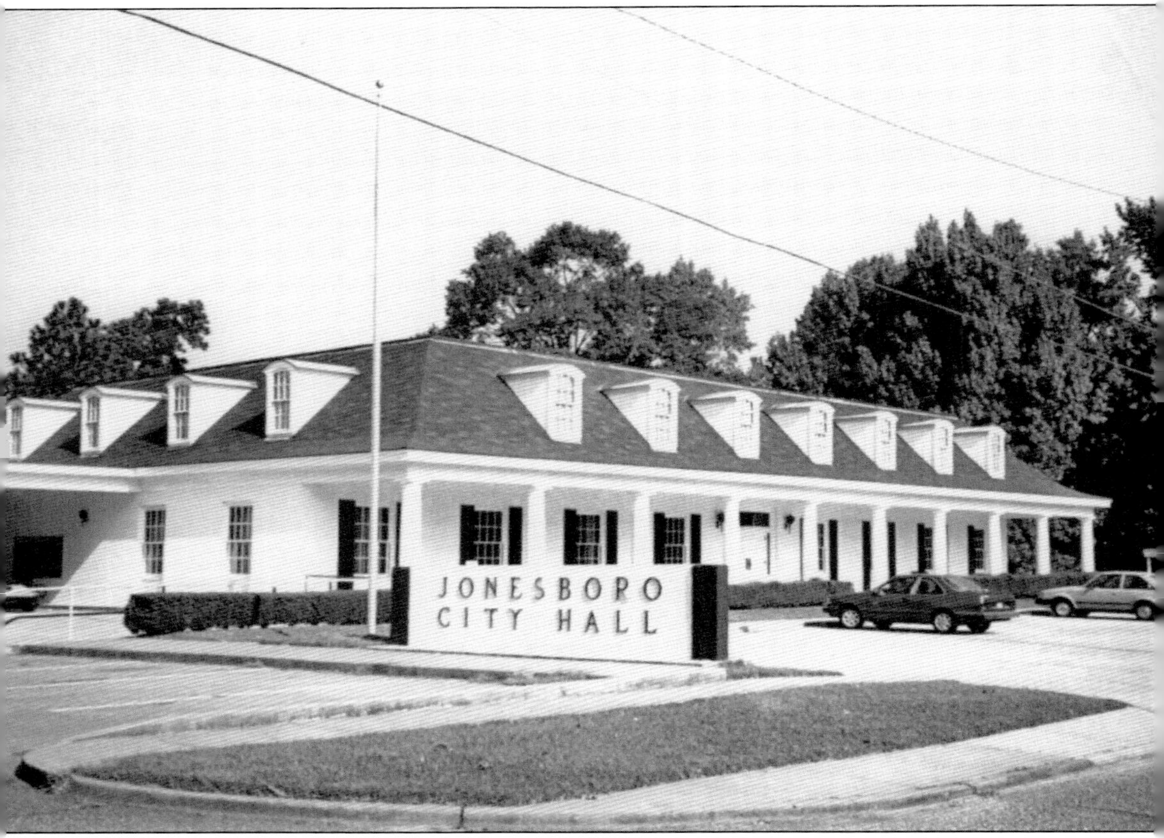


The Town of Jonesboro purchased the old Federal Savings and Loan building and began using it as a town hall with the mayor's office in 1992. This building, located on Allen Avenue, is still in use today. (Courtesy of the T.L. Colvin estate.)

# *Five*

# Hodge

In 1899, Robert Huie and Otis E. Hodge operated a temporary mill in Macedonia until they constructed a permanent mill in Hodge. In 1906, O.E. Hodge and John S. Hunt bought out Robert Huie and formed the Hodge-Hunt Lumber Company. Hodge-Hunt started a joint venture in 1926 with the Southern Advance Bag and Paper Company, and the first paper machine began production in 1928. By 1940, production increased; however, World War II was hard on the paper industry, which was called upon to produce large amounts of pulp and special paper necessary to the war effort. The 10 years following the war were spent in rebuilding and increasing capacity.

Steve Michaud from Maine came to work for the mill in 1928, when it was at full-time paper production and the little village of Hodge was developing into a full-scale company town. The company, through Steve Michaud, got fully involved with the town and laid out the streets, installed the water and sewer lines, and built wood frame houses for its employees. People remember that the row of company houses were painted red, as it was the cheapest paint available. The company donated land to the churches and built a small medical clinic for the employees and their families. A town swimming pool was built, as was a nine-hole golf course, a recreation center, a community dance hall, a meeting center, and a baseball park complete with a baseball team dressed in company uniforms. Each labor day, the employees were treated to a big celebration with a parade and floats.

In 1955, the Robert Gair Company acquired the mill and merged with Continental Can Company, making the Hodge plant a part of the largest manufacturer of packing materials in the world. The mill ceased to own the town. The houses were sold to the people who lived in them. Life in the town slowed, and businesses began closing. The mill was sold to Stone Container in 1984 and later to Rock Ten. The little village of Hodge has seen the mill change hands many times, but the owners of Southern Advance are remembered with fondness.

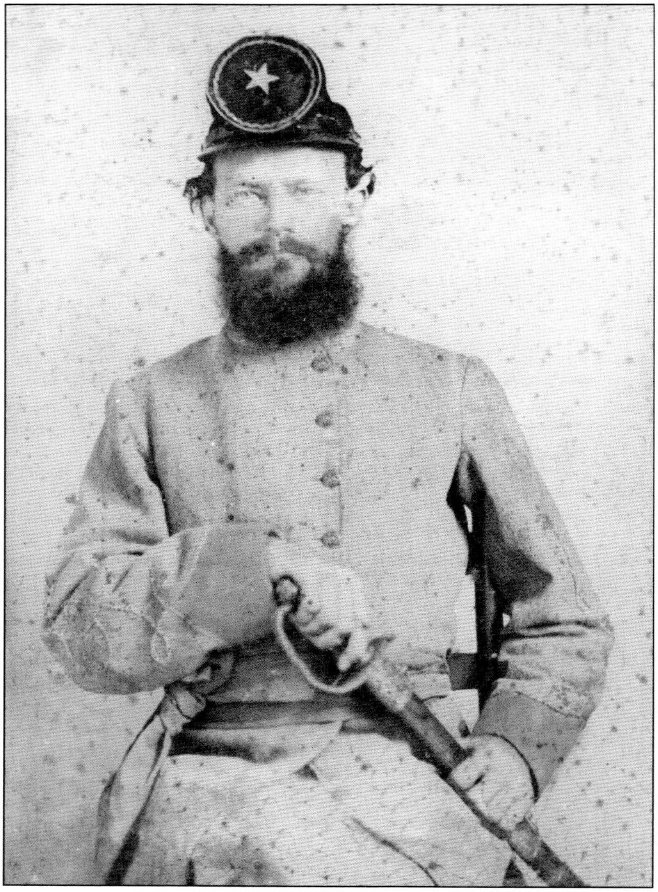

Willis Marion Jeffress, shown here in his Civil War uniform, joined the Jackson Sharpshooters, which became a member of the 12th Louisiana Infantry. He saw action during the campaign of 1862 and died in Tennessee on April 28. The Civil War brought casualties to many families in the parish, leaving them very poor when their husbands and fathers were killed or disabled. (Courtesy of Holbrook McLean.)

Southern Advance Bag and Paper Company started production in 1928. The company was truly the beginning of the village of Hodge. Southern employed almost 500 people when they bought the lumber company and brought life to this little town. Southern produced paper and ran its productions until they sold their holdings to the Robert Gair Company in 1955. (Courtesy of Jud Rogers.)

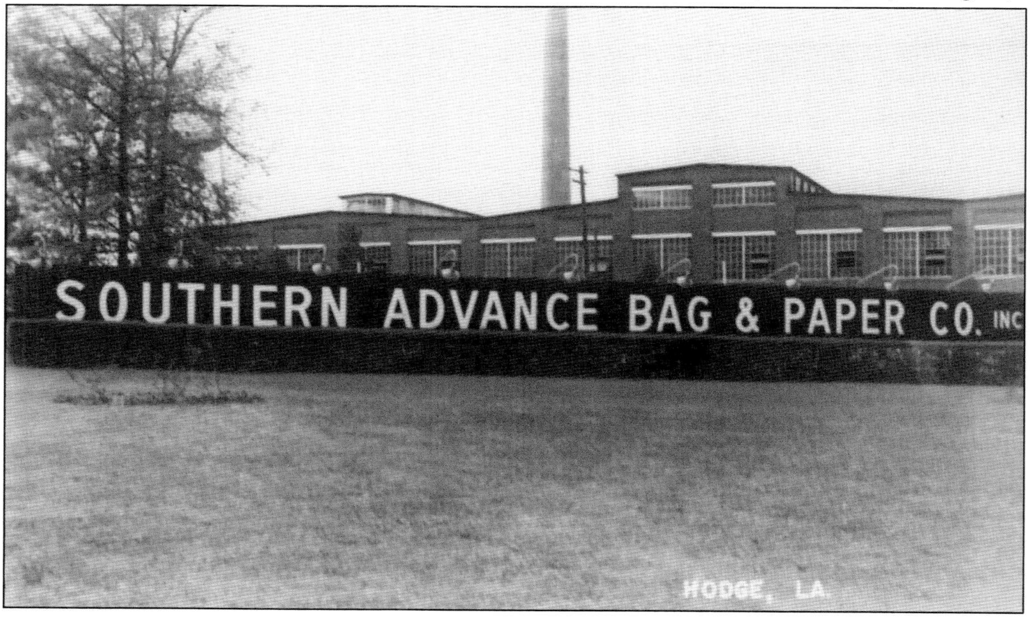

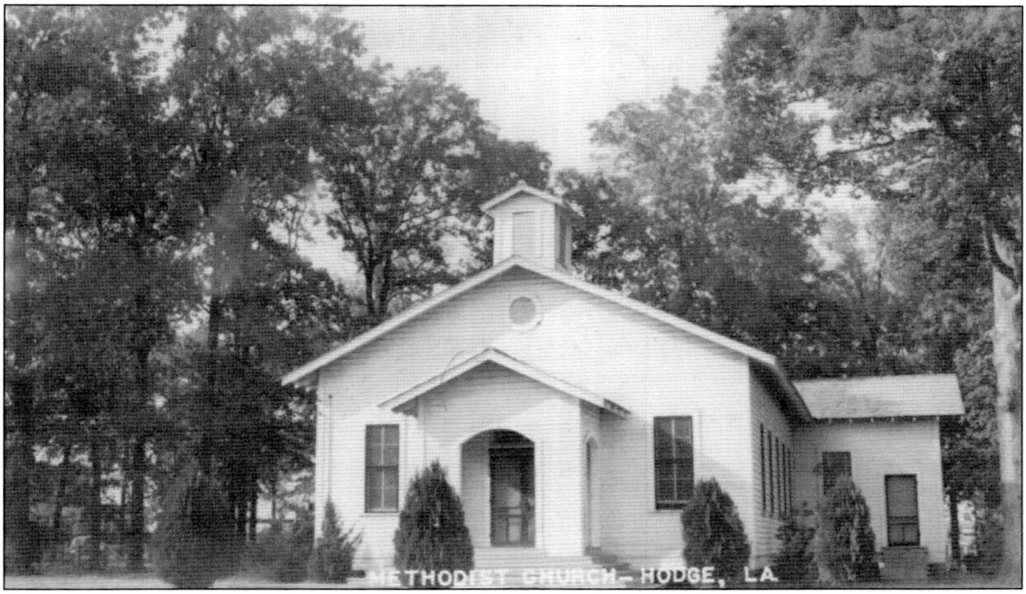


The first church in Hodge was built by the Huie-Hodge Lumber Company in 1903 and used by the Baptists, Methodists, and the Presbyterians. In 1926 the building was condemned, and the second Union Church was built by the Hodge-Hunt Company. In October 1932, the Southern Advance Bag and Paper Company, which by then owned the building, gave sole authority to the Methodist Church. It became the Hodge Methodist Church in May 1939. In 1959, the church building and the parsonage were deeded to the church by the Continental Can Company, which then owned the paper mill. In 1970, a new structure was erected, and the old church building was sold and moved. During construction of the new church, Saint Lucy's Catholic Church offered the use of their old building as a place of worship until the church was completed. (Both, courtesy of Hodge Methodist Church.)

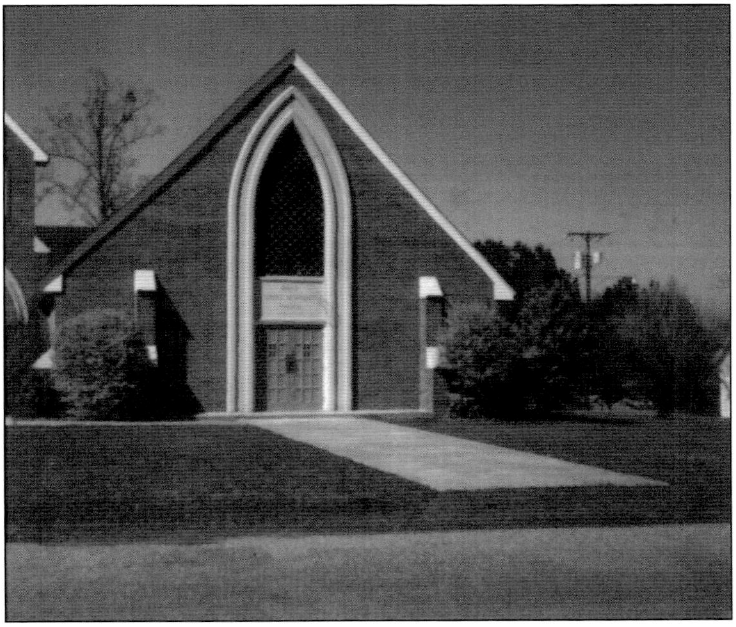

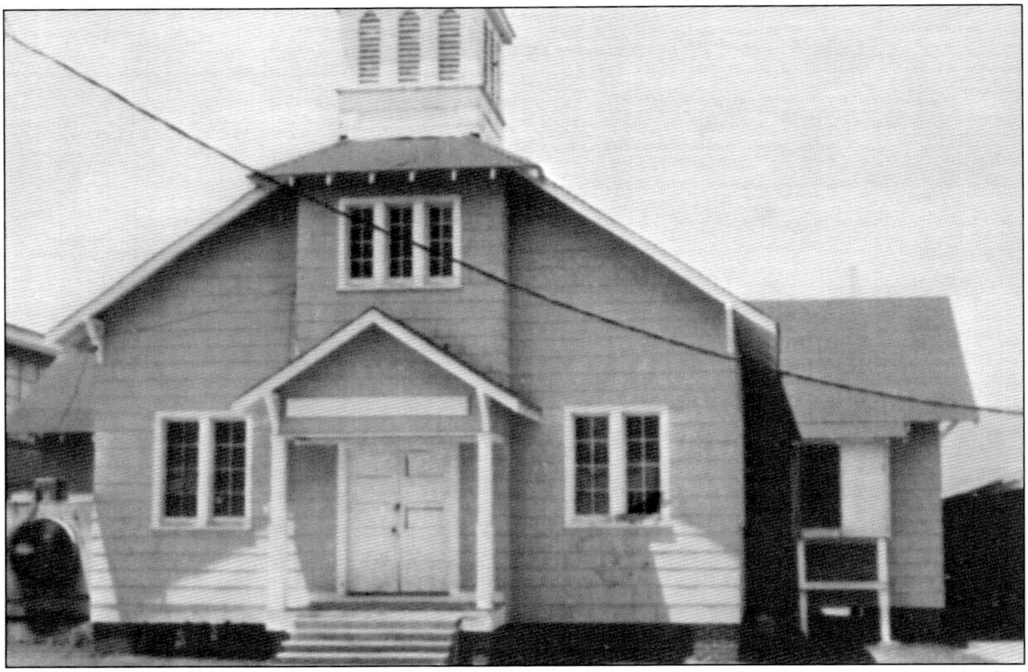

After Southern Advance Bag and Paper Company gave the Union Church to the Methodist fellowship, the company decided to build Hodge Baptist Church an auditorium with two small classrooms at the front, omitting rooms at the side and back as originally planned. The company told the church committee if they wanted the original space, they would build it for cost. During the church's ministry, the building was greatly enlarged, and other buildings were added. (Both, courtesy of the T.L. Colvin estate.)

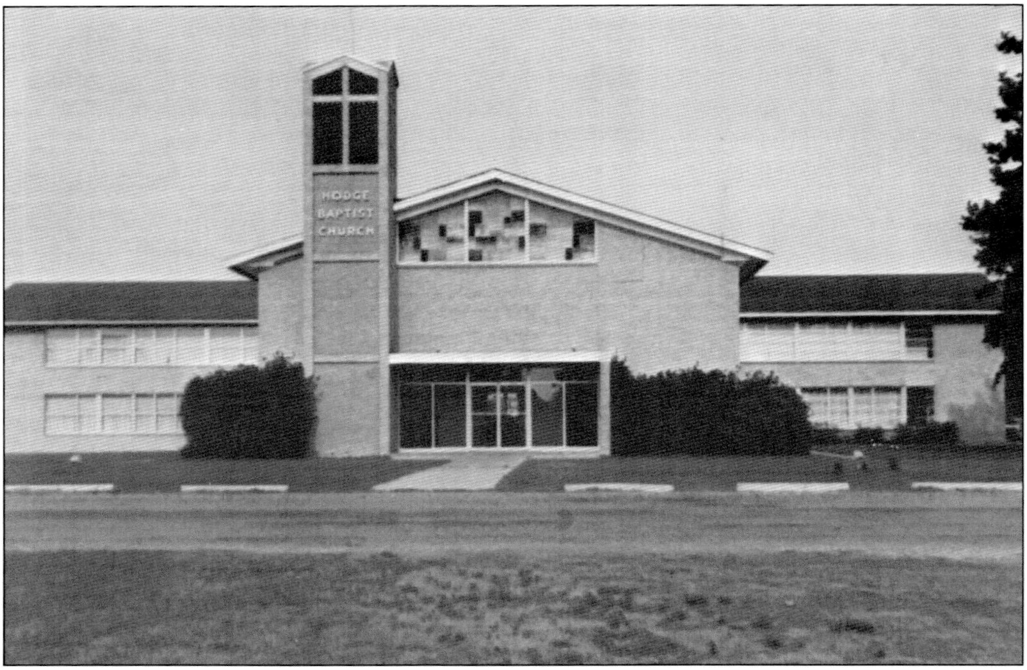

The few Catholics of Hodge who met for mass in the home of S.E. Michaud at least once a month decided that a church should be built. A site for the building was provided by the Southern Advance Company, and construction began immediately. Saint Henry Catholic Church was blessed by Bishop Van deVen in February 1929. A new church was built in 1961, and the name was changed to Saint Lucy Catholic Church in 1962. (Both, courtesy of Saint Lucy Catholic Church.)

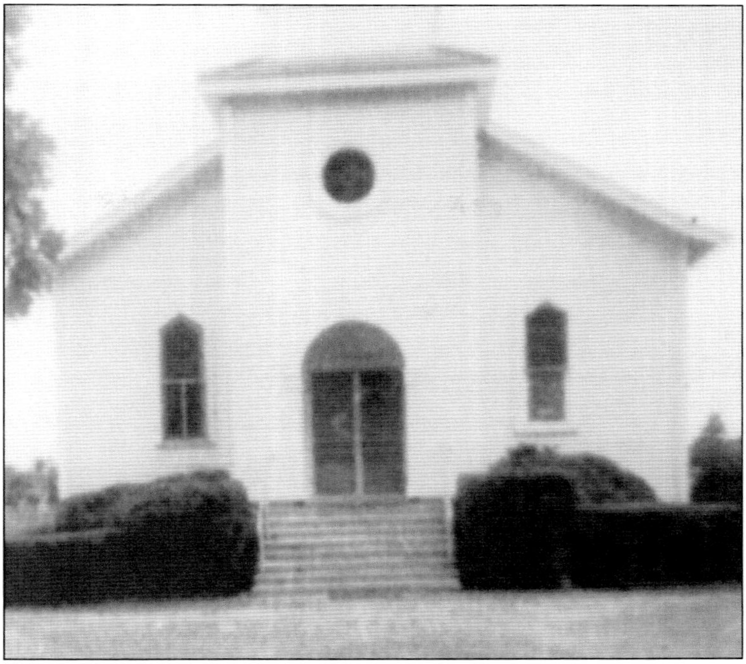

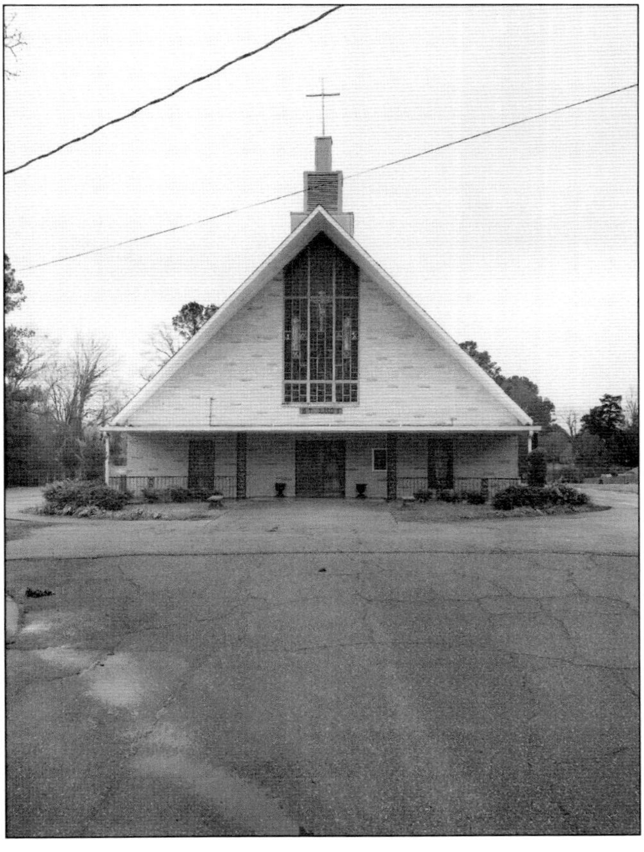

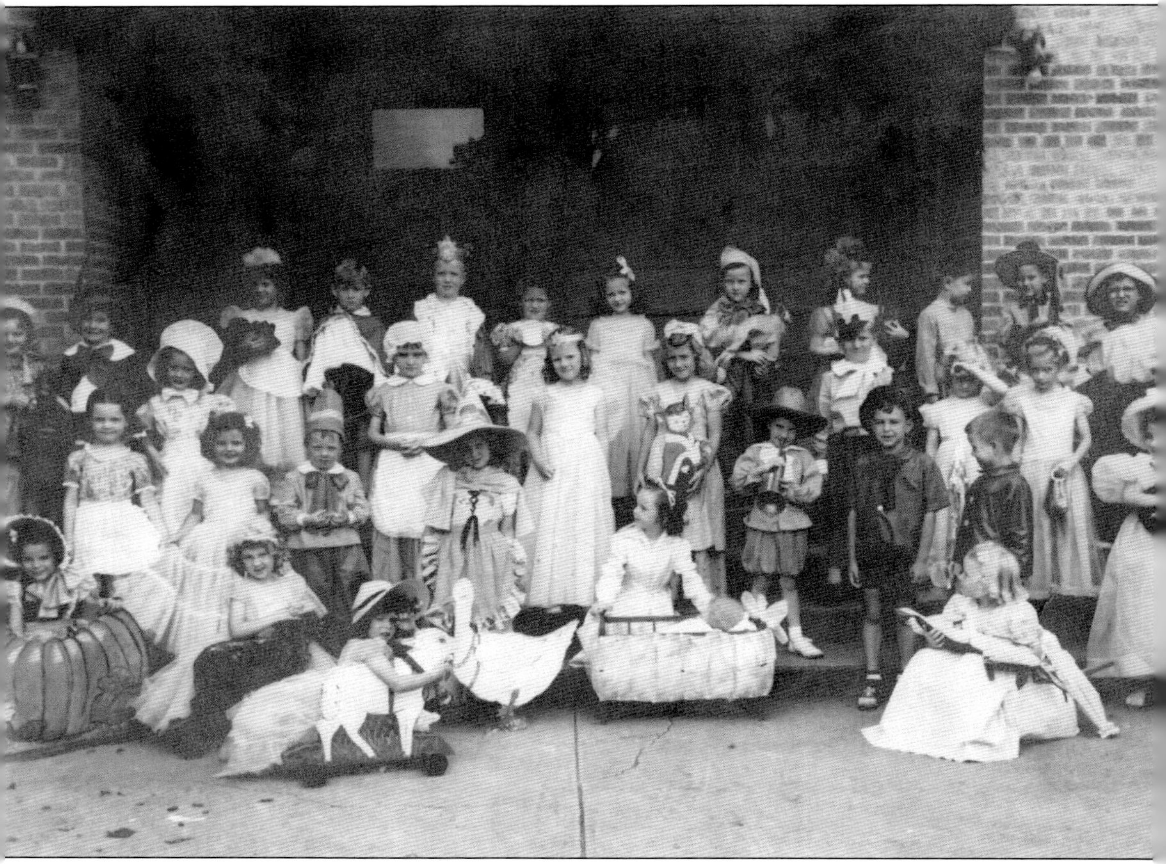

Saint Henry Catholic Church began a kindergarten and school of music in September 1941. The kindergarten was a 28-foot-by-28-foot room with double doors opening to a playground. Children from ages 3 to 6 came to learn before moving on to Hodge Elementary School. The first commencement was held May 31, 1942, in conjunction with a musical presented at the community hall by piano pupils. The school remained open for 10 years. The children of Saint Henry's are pictured in front of Hodge Elementary School, where they put on a play depicting Mother Goose characters. (Courtesy of Holbrook McLean.)

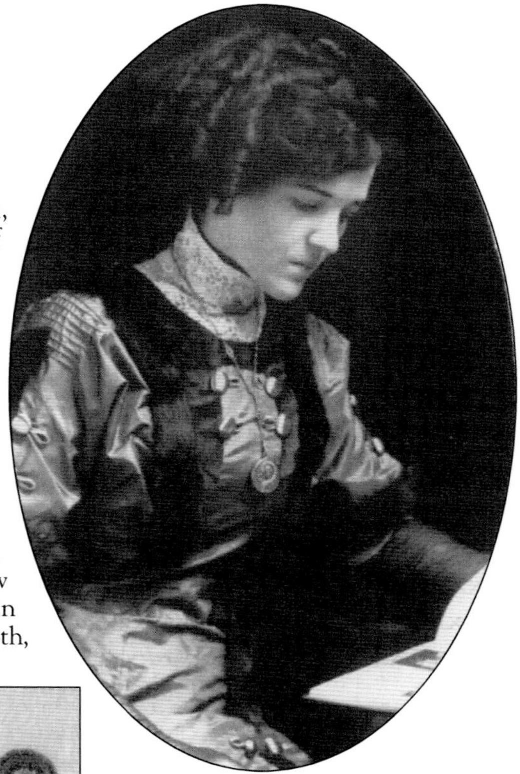

Callie Elizabeth Jeffress Fanning Smith, granddaughter of W.M. Jeffress and daughter of John Jackson Jeffress, attended the Academy of Fine Arts in St. Louis, as well as Eastman College and Conservatory of Music and Art in Sulphur Springs, Texas. On March 28, 1940, Smith wrote a letter to Eleanor Roosevelt, telling her how much she admired her. The letter was accompanied by a quilt that was divided into 12 frames portraying Roosevelt at different stages of her life. The illustrations of her life were made of appliqué and hand-painted figures. The design features 20 rosettes at the corner of each frame, and within each rosette is a hand-painted yellow rose. This quilt currently hangs in the Franklin Roosevelt Library and Museum in Hyde Park. (Both, courtesy of Holbrook McLean.)

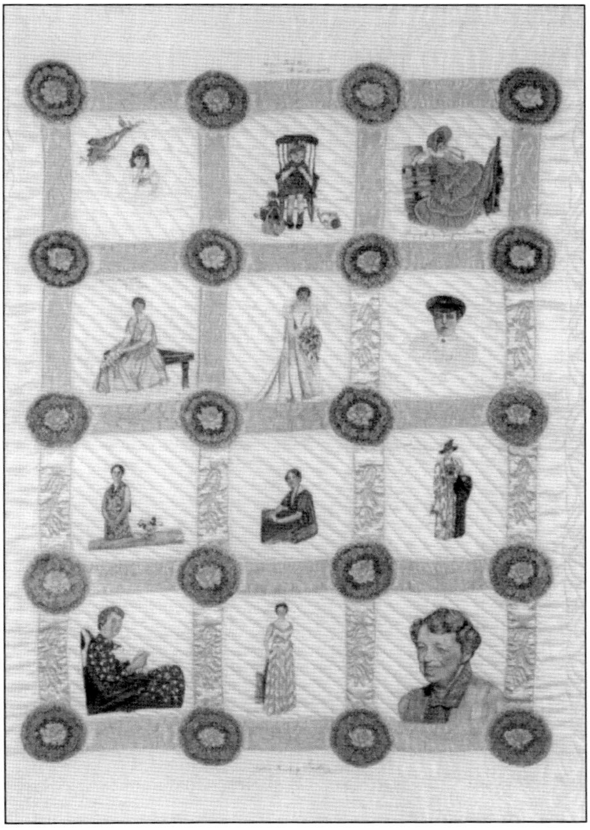

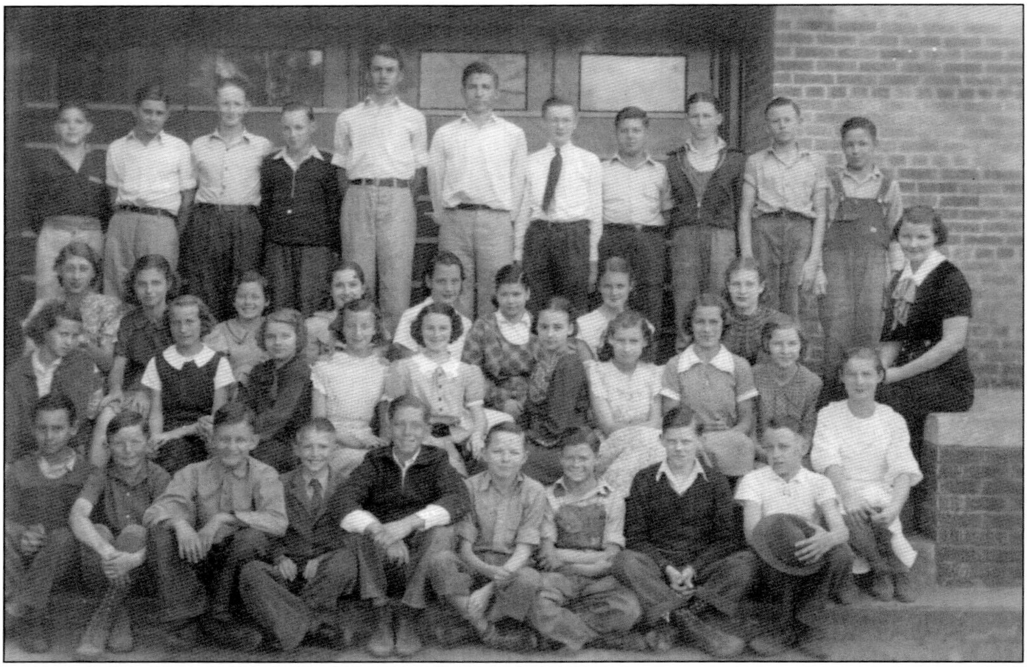

Hodge Elementary's first school was on the bottom floor of the Masonic building until a wooden structure was erected near the site where Hodge Elementary currently sits. When the new brick building was constructed, the old school was converted into the Crystal Ballroom. A large crystal ball hung from the ceiling and revolved during dances. During maneuvers prior to World War II, the ballroom was used to provide entertainment for the soldiers. The elementary school sits on its lot, completely abandoned since it was consolidated with Jonesboro. (Above, courtesy of T.L. Colvin; below, courtesy of Hodge Town Hall.)

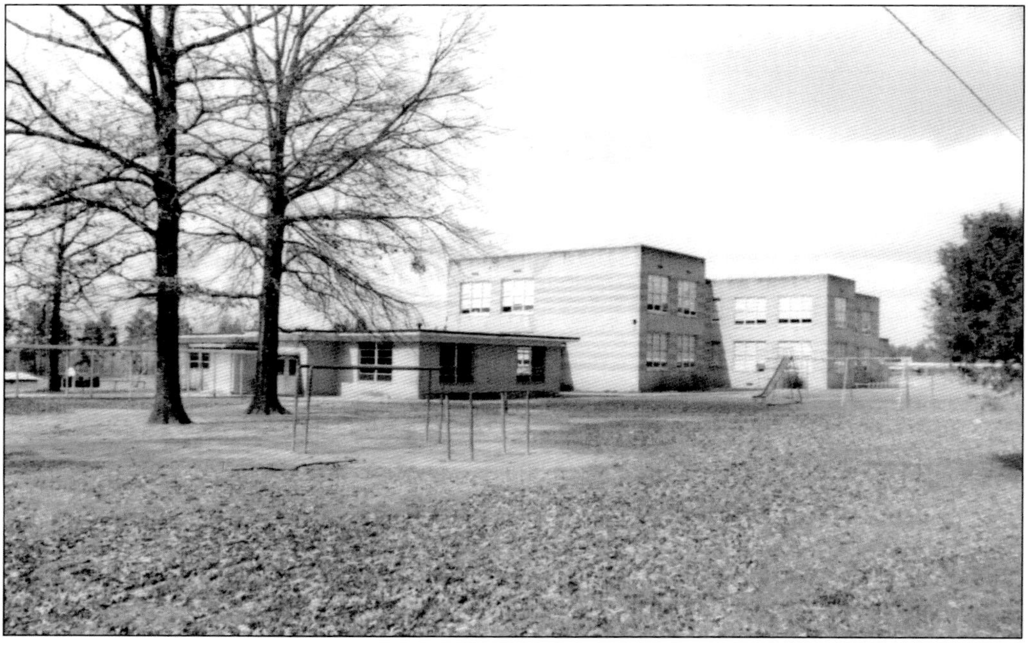

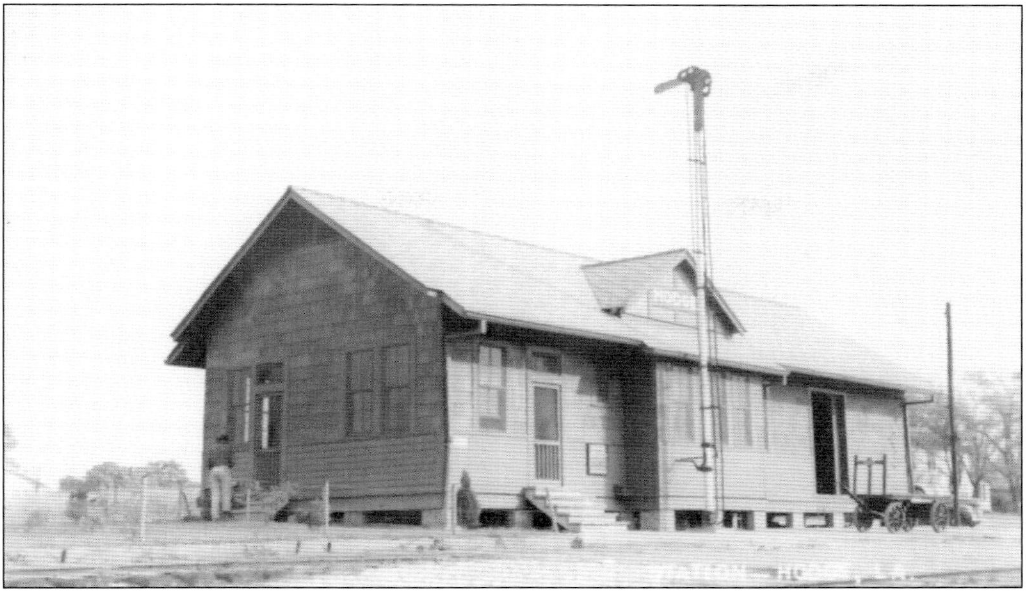

The Hodge train depot has seen lots of activity throughout the years. On Sundays, most of the town would come to watch the train arrive and meet the arrivals. It was the main stop in Hodge for employees of the mill and sat next to the railroad and across the street from the Hodge Hotel. It was on one such day that F.A DeJean, a timber inspector from Opelousas, met his future wife, Olive Jenkins, who had come to see the train. The train depot was remodeled, and the outside was bricked. It is still in use today. (Above, courtesy of Jud Rogers; below, courtesy of Hodge Town Hall.)

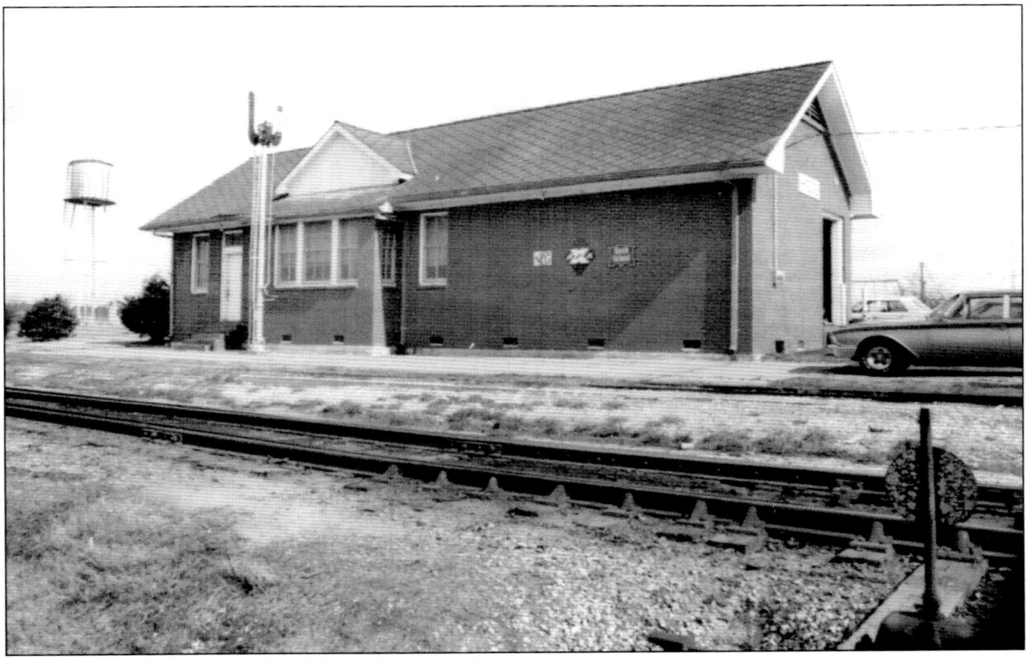

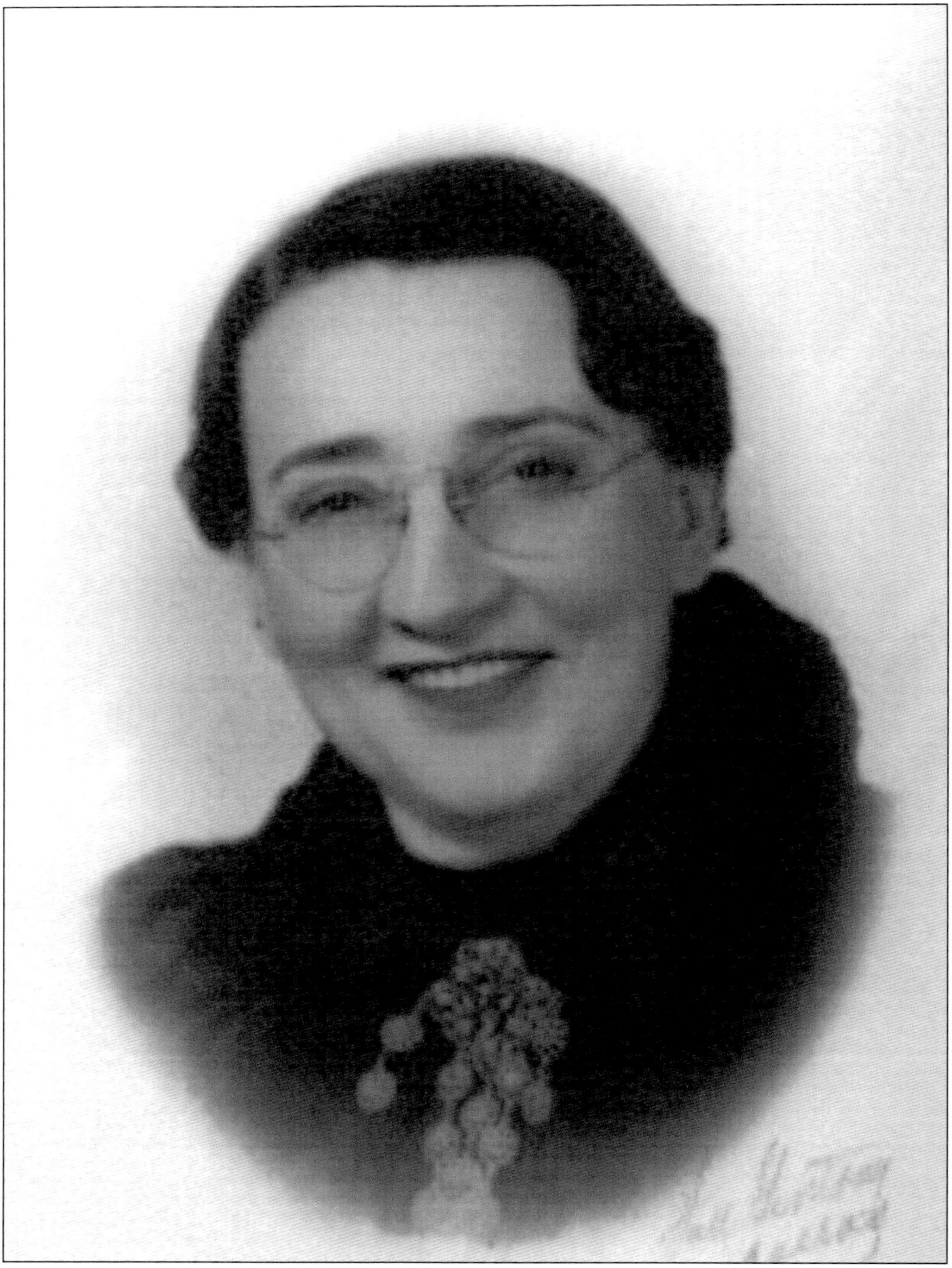

Ella A. McDowell was appointed Hodge postmistress on August 22, 1940. She served faithfully until her retirement in 1958. Her sister Olive DeJean was appointed postmistress after her. She was a native of Winnfield when she moved to Hodge and was a resident for approximately 50 years. (Courtesy of Jud Rogers.)

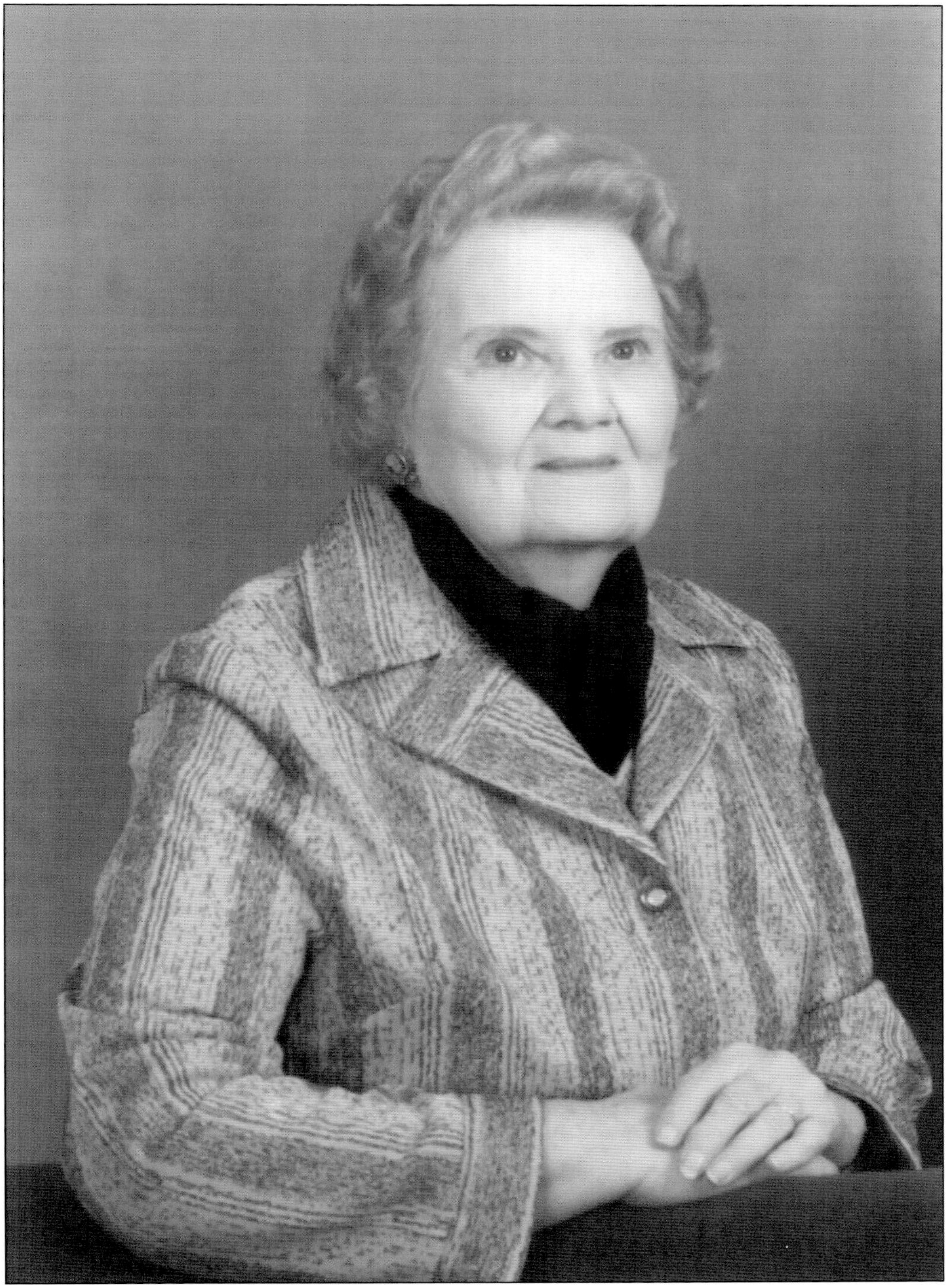

Olive DeJean, along with her sister Ella A. McDowell, was the first postmistresses of the Hodge Post Office. DeJean was acting postmaster on June 30, 1957, and was appointed postmaster on March 19, 1958. After McDowell retired, DeJean served the post office faithfully for 38 years. She retired in 1972. (Courtesy of Jud Rogers.)

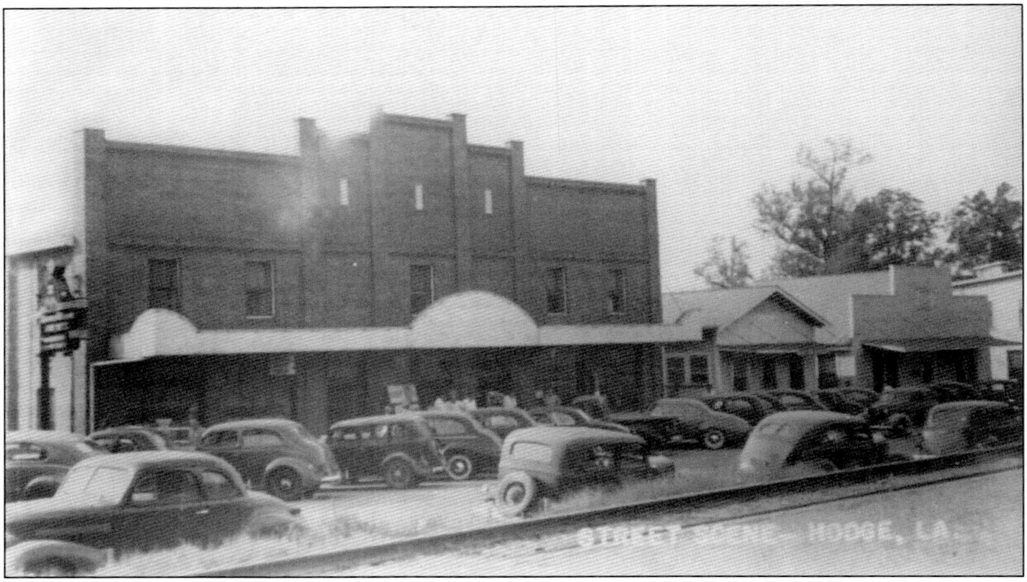


The shopping complex at Hodge featured a hardware store, a furniture department, a shoe department, and many other necessities. It is possible that it was one of the first shopping malls to be built. The stores were connected in such a way that one could cross from one store to another without having to go outside. The recreation building also had a movie theater, a pool hall, bowling alley, basketball court, and a pool hall. (Both, courtesy of Holbrook McLean.)

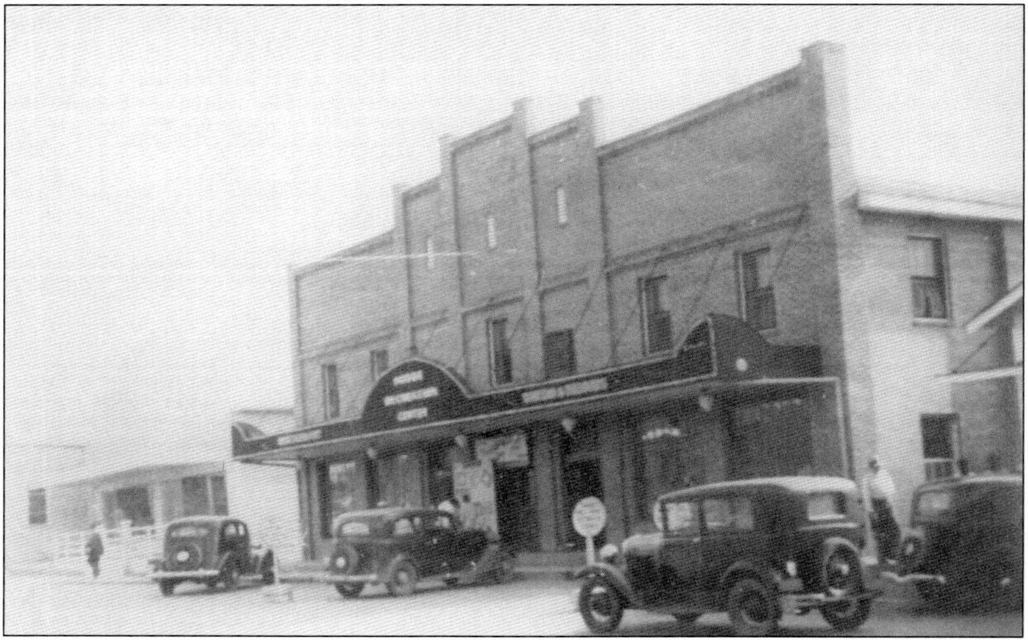

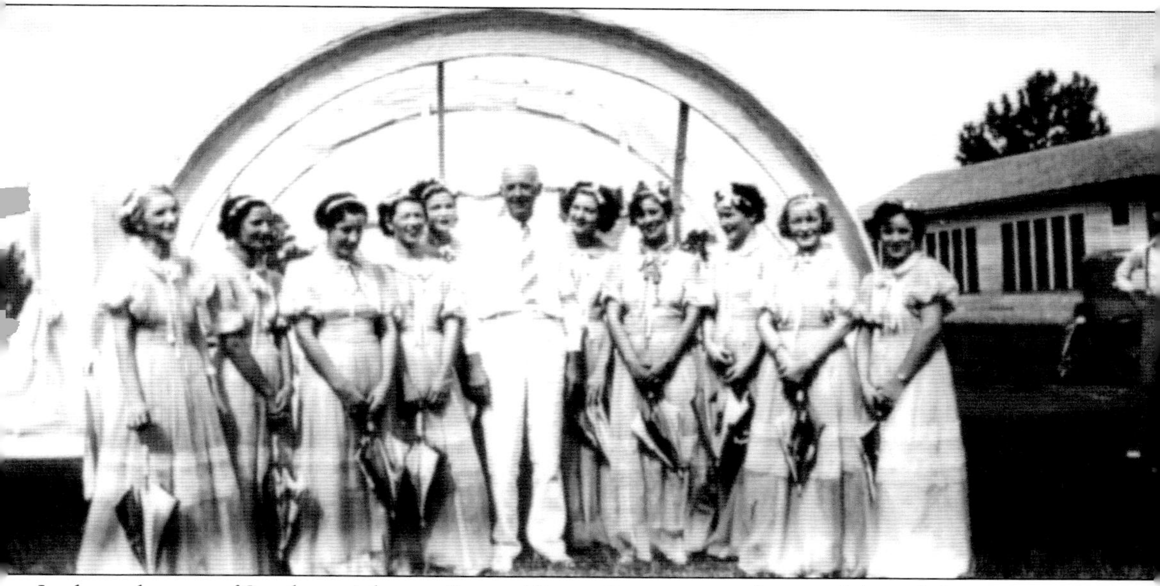

In the early years of Southern Advance Bag and Paper Company, employees celebrated the opening of the plant on Labor Day with a day of food, games, and a parade that featured floats representing the various departments at the plant. These ladies dressed in rainbow colors are on the Bag Mill No. 2 float. They were machine operators, and a sign on the float declared, "If it's a bag, it's made in the Bag Mill No. 2. If it's pretty girls they come from Bag Mill No. 2." William McLean served as superintendent of Bag Mill No. 2 until 1944. (Courtesy of Holbrook McLean.)

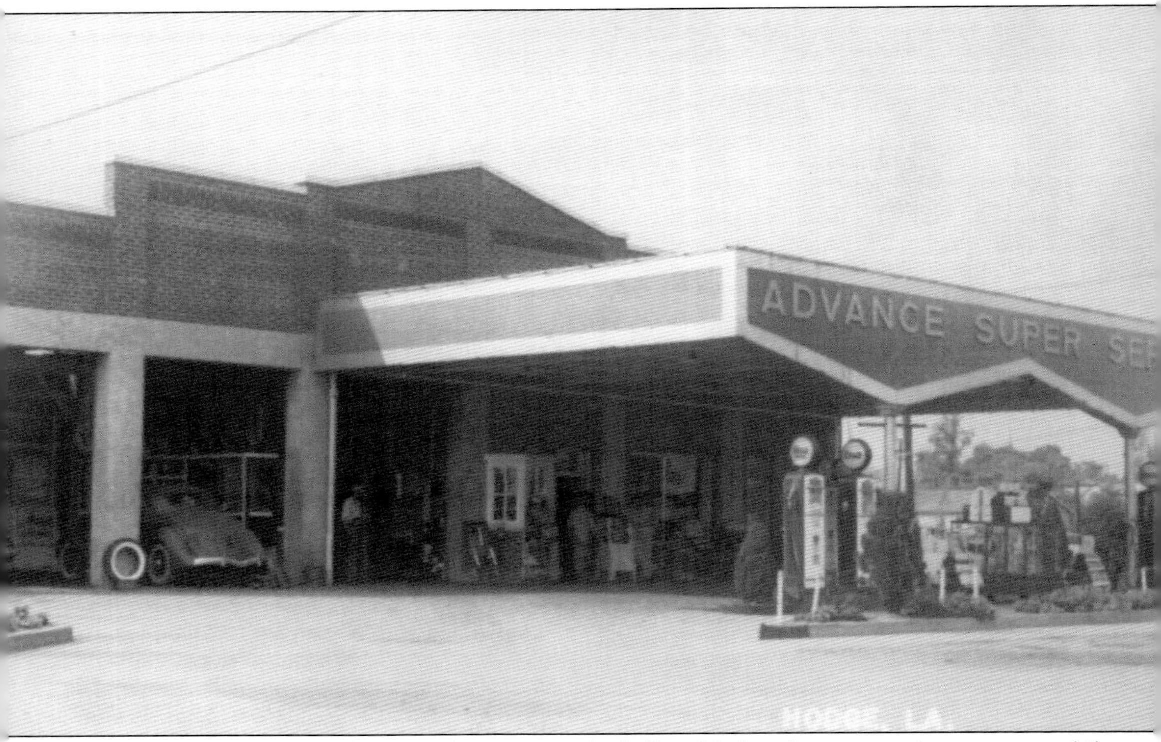


Southern Advance built a petrol station on the hill in Hodge. As more and more automobiles began making appearances, the company decided to help the town with the convenience of a local gas station. This station was located on the site where the Green Clinic currently sits. (Courtesy of Jud Rogers.)

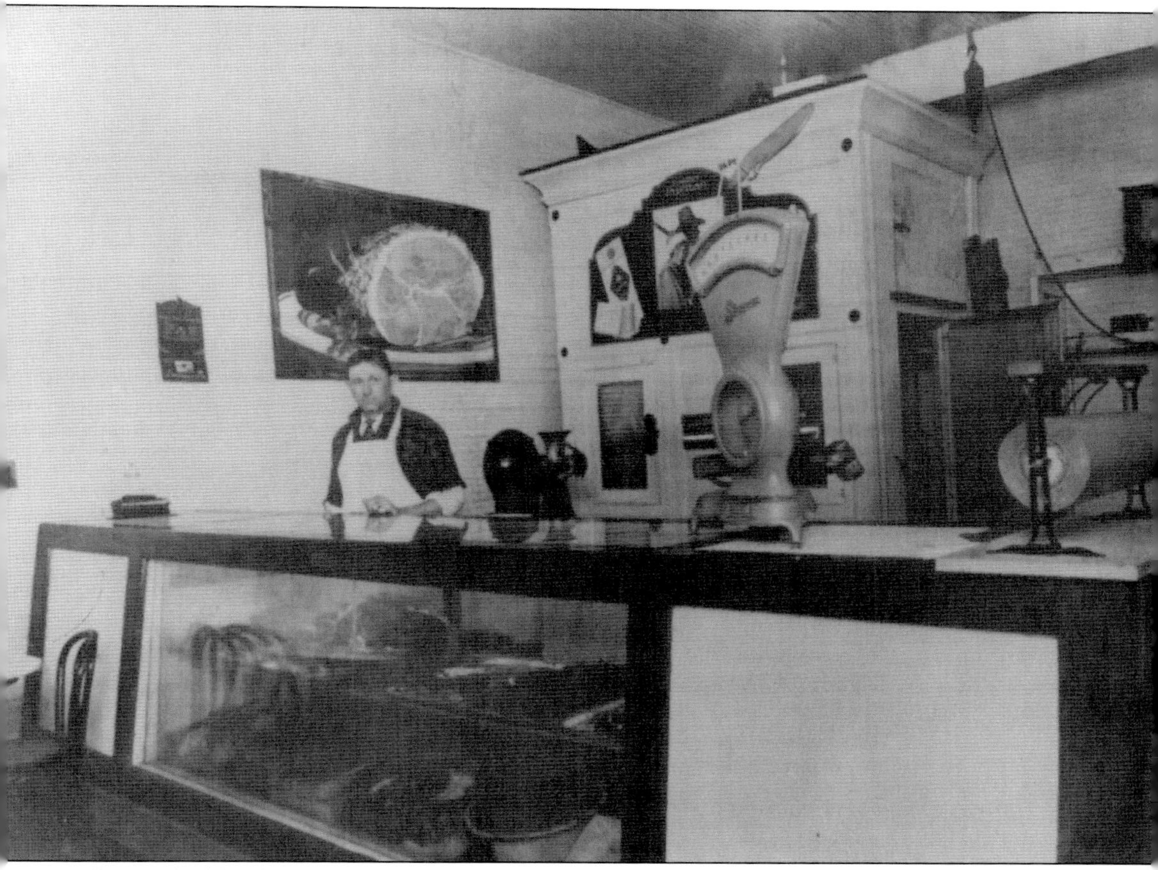

I.J. Allen worked for the Davis Brothers Lumber Company in Ansley for three years and then came to Hodge to work with the Hodge-Hunt Lumber Company. It was here that he saved his earnings and established a meat market. He also handled ice and conducted a cold-drink business. He worked from 1916 until he moved to Jonesboro, where he became half owner of the Jackson Gin and Ice Company. He bought full interest in the company in 1934. (Courtesy of Helon Earl.)

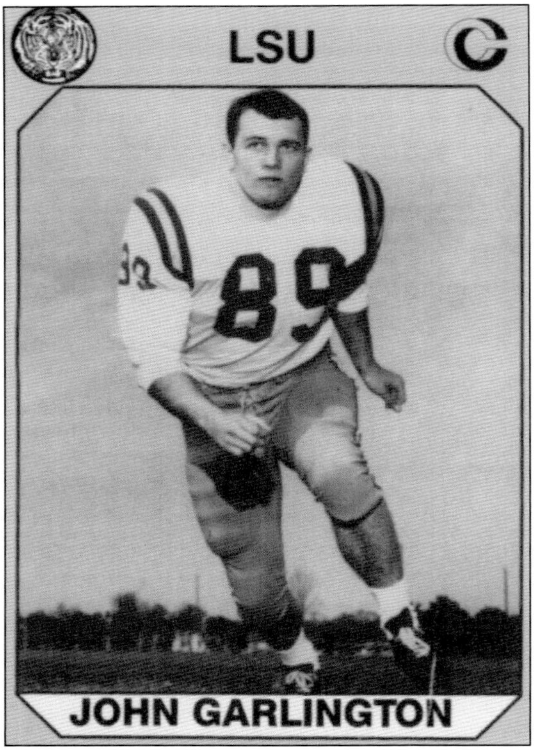


John Garlington was born on June 5, 1946, at the Hodge Clinic. He went to Hodge Elementary and then to Jonesboro-Hodge High School. From there, he received a full scholarship to Louisiana State University and played football as a freshman. He played in many college bowl games and was Defensive Player of the Year at LSU. During his junior year, he signed with the Cleveland Browns and played with the team from 1968 to 1978. Garlington retired and, after several moves, settled in nearby Bienville Parish and worked as the local wildlife and fisheries agent. While working in this capacity, Garlington died in February 2000. He married Karon Walker and had two sons: Moses and Seth. (Both, courtesy of Karon Garlington.)

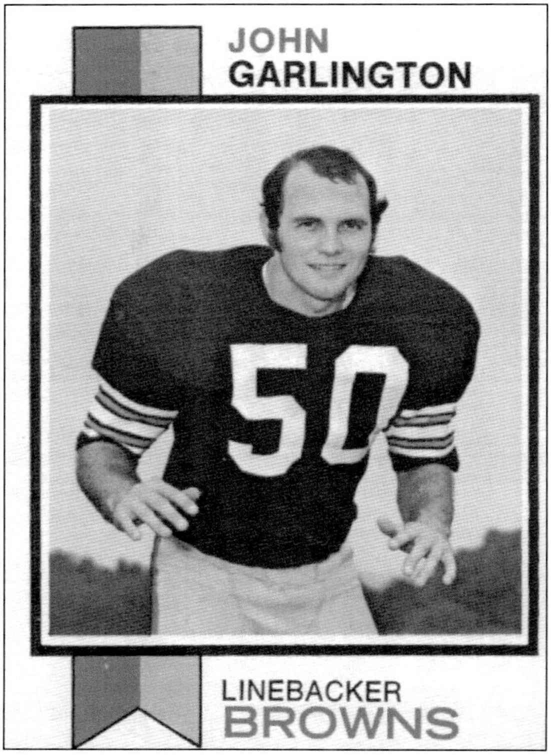

# *Six*

# Northwest Communities

In 1901, the Arkansas Southern Railroad built a rail line about a quarter mile from Allendale, and the post office was moved to a more convenient location near the railroad. Since there was another town named Allendale, the post office and new town were named Quitman in honor of Asbury Quitman Brooks, who was the town's first postmaster. The trains that came through offered the convenience of travel, bringing mail, goods, and visitors. They also brought much to the town of Quitman, helping make it a thriving community with a school, hotel, and livery among many other stores and buildings that made up the downtown. As time progressed, the Depression saw many families leave the area. World War II left the town with few men and boys. In the 1980s, the train packed up its rails, and now all that Quitman has is the Quitman High School, the post office, and a convenience store, along with two churches.

During the time the railroad was being built through Jackson Parish, the Davis brothers, James, Virgil, John, and Robert, came from southern Arkansas looking for rich timberland; they settled on an area called Troy. The brothers, along with many families from their operations in Arkansas, worked for two years to clear an area for a mill and a town. They named this town Ansley in honor of their brother Virgil's wife, Marie Antoinette Ansley. The Davis Brothers mill supplied all the timber to build the town, and for many years, it was a thriving community. The town had a school, a picturesque hotel, a store, and a doctor's office. Even baseball tournaments were one of the many things people in the area could enjoy. When the mill closed 55 years later, the town of Ansley closed with it.

Beech Springs has become synonymous with James Houston "Jimmie" Davis. It was here and in the surrounding communities where Davis grew up in a poor farming family. He went to school in Quitman and graduated from Beech Springs. Friends of Davis built the Jimmie Davis Tabernacle near his childhood home. It is used regularly, but the town itself has disappeared, and all that is left along with the tabernacle is his childhood home and the cemetery he is buried in.

This area is still full of people proud of their legacy, and some work hard to keep it alive.

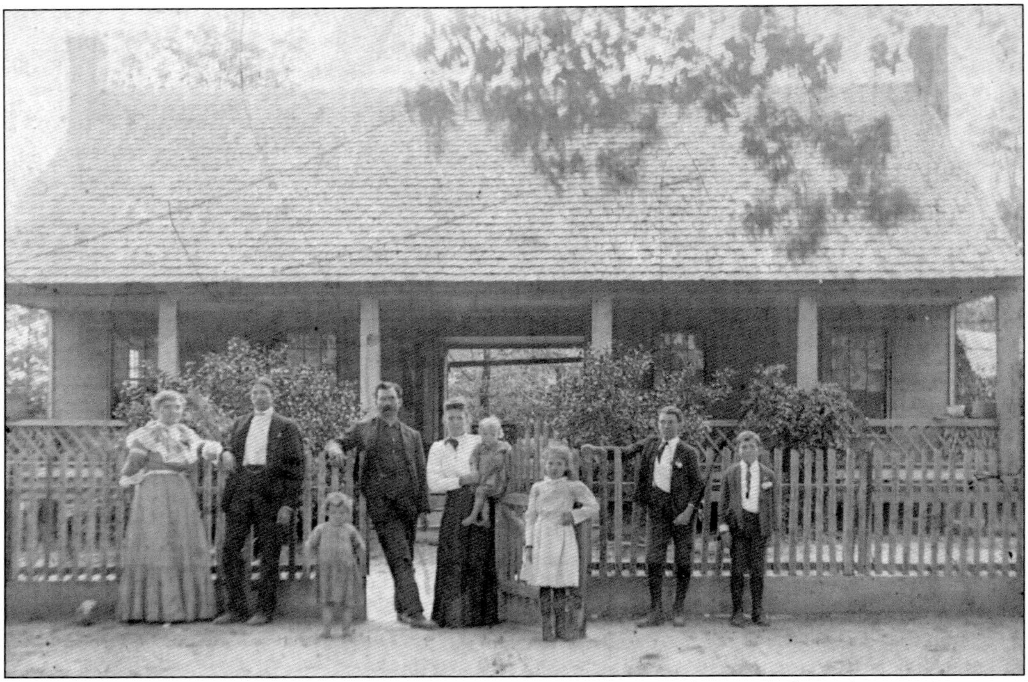

This photograph shows the Clifton-Horton family posing in front of their dogtrot home in Allendale, located about one mile northwest of Quitman. Dogtrot houses consisted of two log cabins connected by a breezeway, or dogtrot. Typically, one cabin was used for cooking and dining, with the other used for a bedroom. There was a chimney on each end of the home serving each side. The dogtrot breezeway provided a cool area for sitting in the hot summers of Louisiana. (Courtesy of Clyde Pointer.)

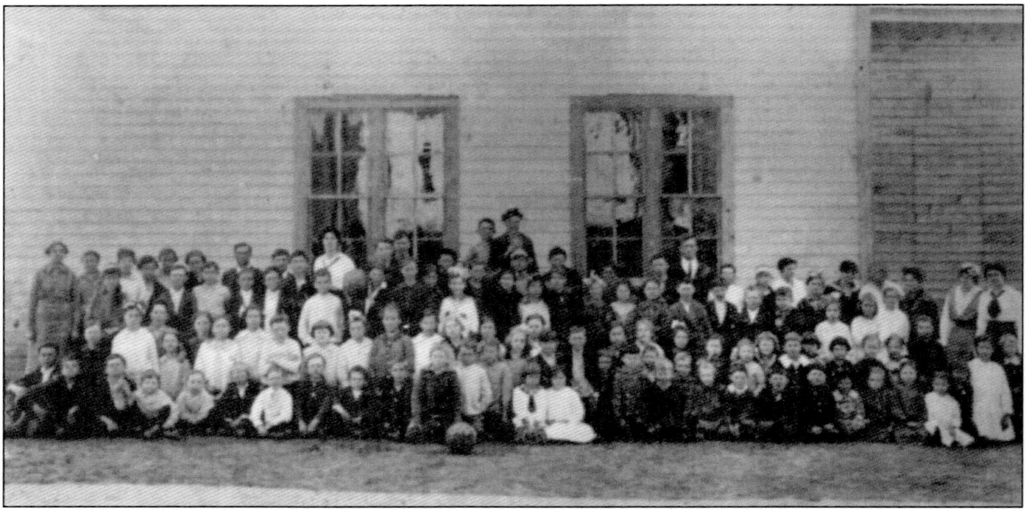

The school at Brooks Chapel, located about two miles northwest of Quitman, was destroyed by fire in 1903. It was decided that a school should be built in the new town of Quitman. A two-room frame building was constructed on the hill were Quitman Baptist Church is now located. This picture shows the students in the 1904–1905 school year. Eight grades were taught by Annie Noble and Jennie Pirkle, and a Mr. Mitchell was principal. (Courtesy of Sylvia Pagan.)

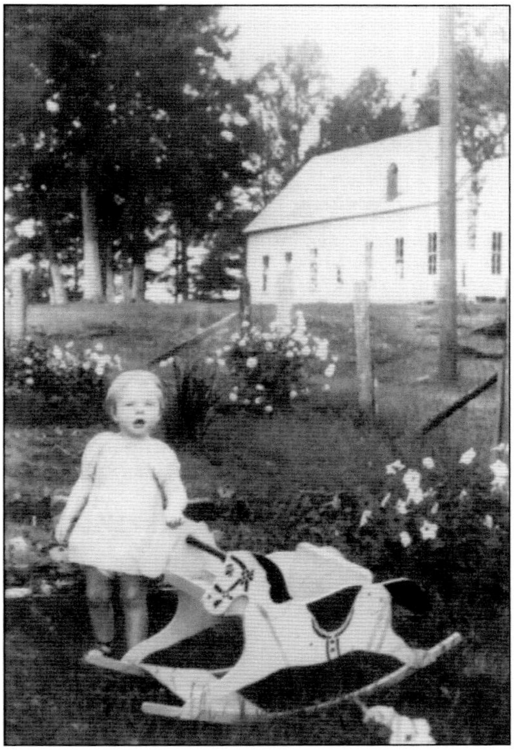

The Quitman First Baptist Church was organized on September 1, 1901. The first building was erected in 1904. The image at right shows Rose Stewart around 1935 in her front yard with the church building in the background. In 1951, a new parsonage was built, and in 1968, ground-breaking ceremonies were held for the construction of a new auditorium. The building was finished and dedicated in July 1968. An education building was added in 1975. At this time, the old church building was torn down. (Right, courtesy of Sylvia Pagan; below, courtesy of Katherine Rowell.)

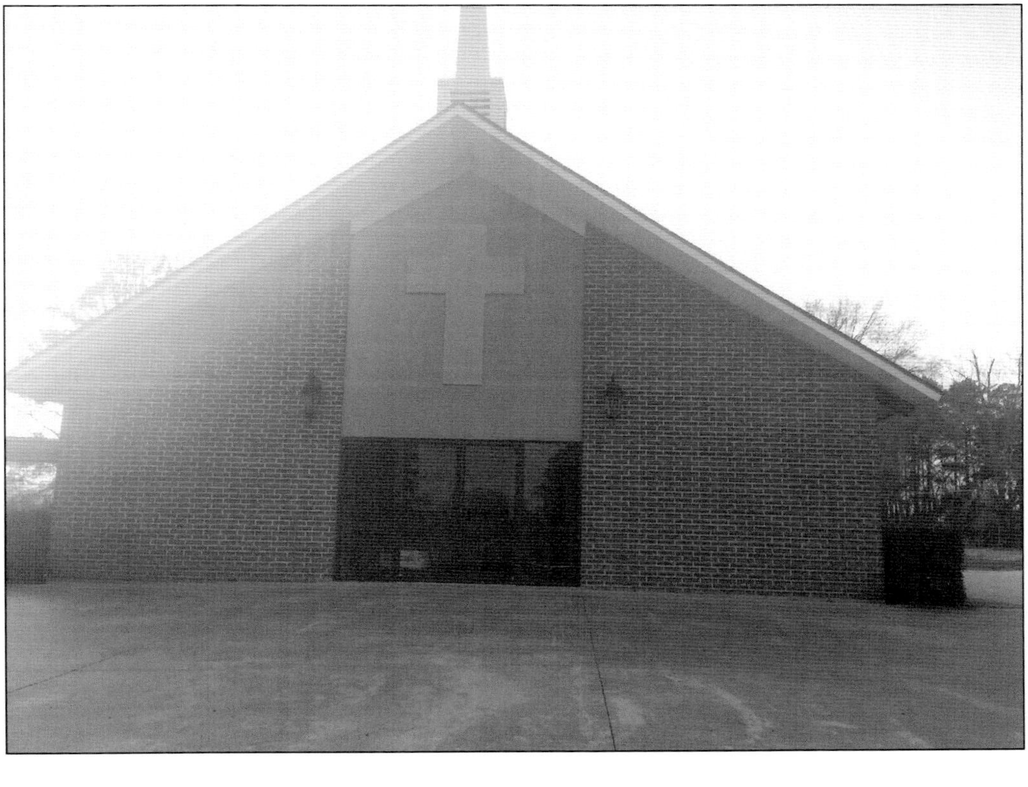

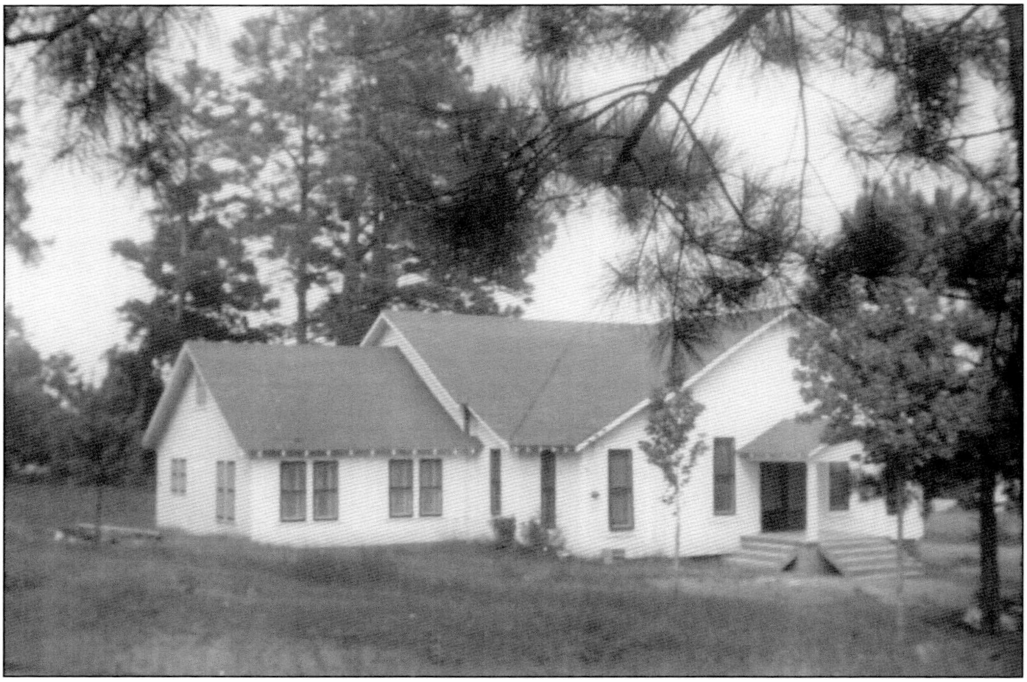

In 1906, a Methodist Protestant church was erected near where the present church sits, across from the First Baptist Church. In 1919, it reformed as Methodist Episcopal, and a new building was constructed at the present site and the old structure was torn down. In 1975, construction began on the current building and was finished in May 1976, and Quitman United Methodist Church was formed. The 1919 building was torn down, and in May 1976, a dedication service was held. The church has grown from its part-time monthly meetings to full-time services. (Above, courtesy of Sylvia Pagan; below, courtesy of Katherine Rowell.)

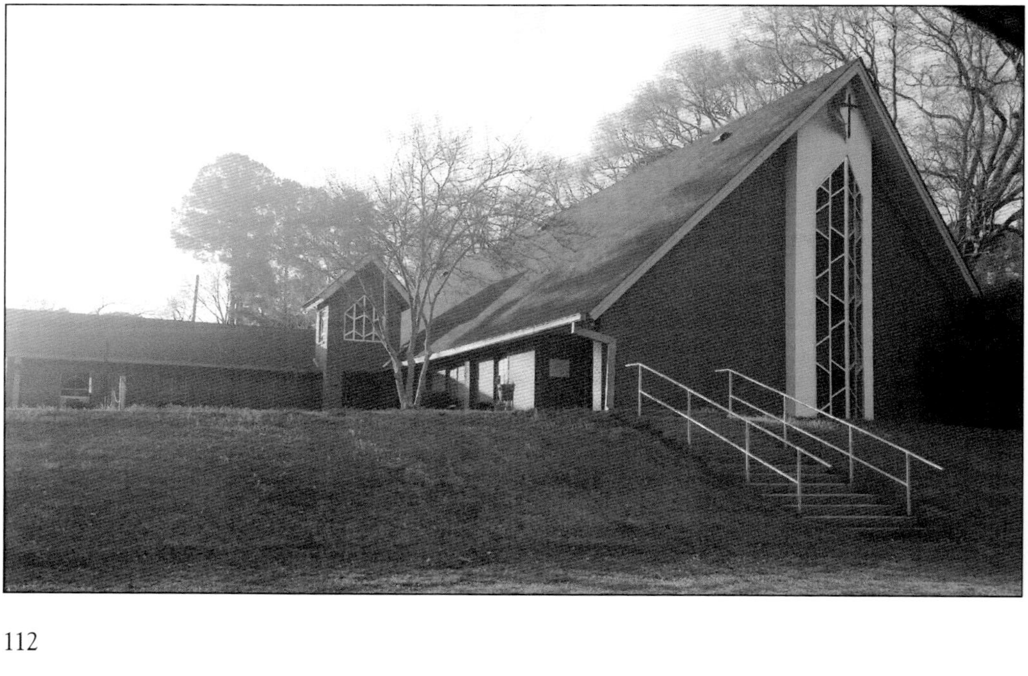

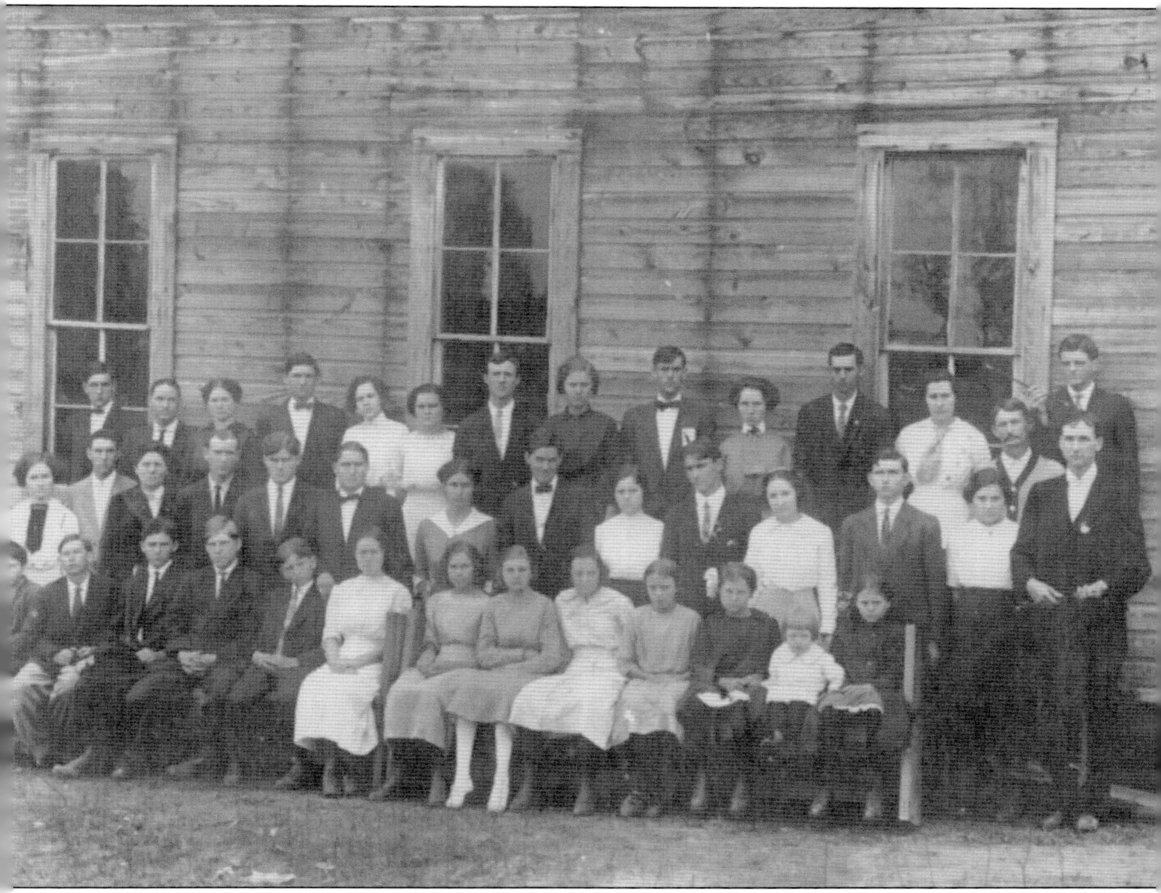

In 1913, the young scholars of Quitman often rode horses and walked many miles while enduring the elements, only to reach the poor facilities of the schoolhouse. This school was also called the "singing school on the hill," because singing and music were taught during the summer months. It was in this setting that James Houston "Jimmie" Davis went to school. There were many singing conventions led by Walter Ponder. This photograph likely shows one of the singing conventions held at the school. (Courtesy of Patricia Maxwell.)

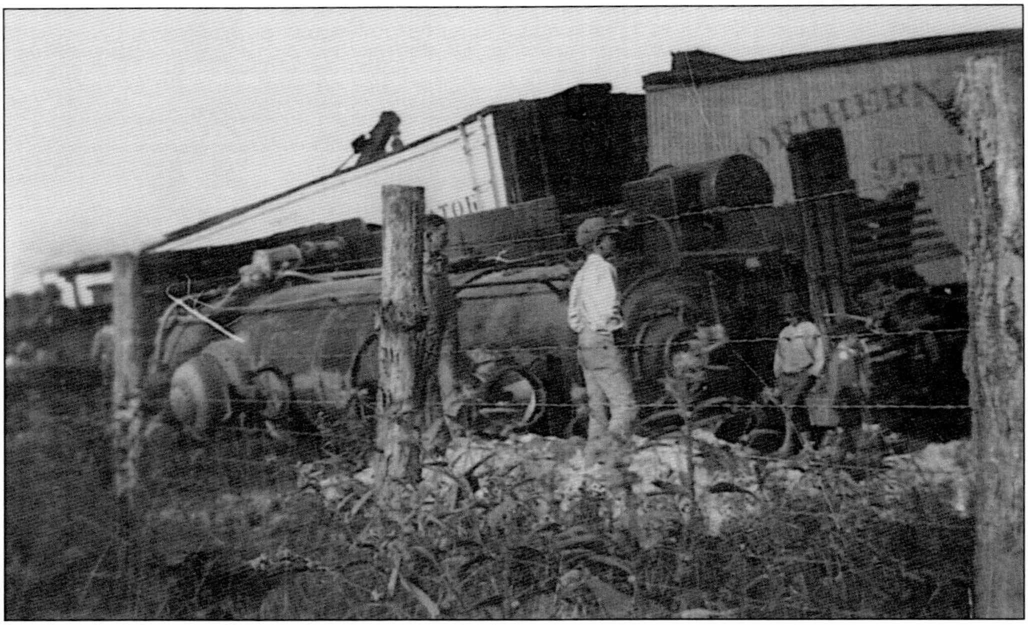

This train wreck was located near the Quitman community during the 1920s. It was told that this wreck happened close to where the current post office sits. Though it is not confirmed, it is said that the train derailed because of a simple bolt coming free and causing the rails to separate, thus sending the train off its track. This train was a lifeline to Quitman, bringing people, news, and goods to the town. There are many stories passed down about the trains that came through and the men who ran them. (Both, courtesy of Sylvia Pagan.)

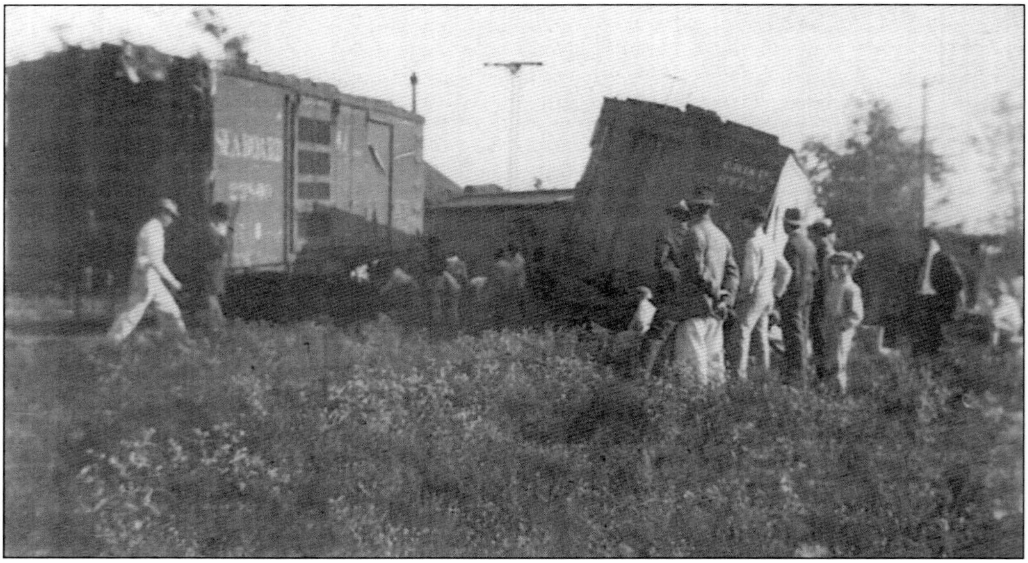

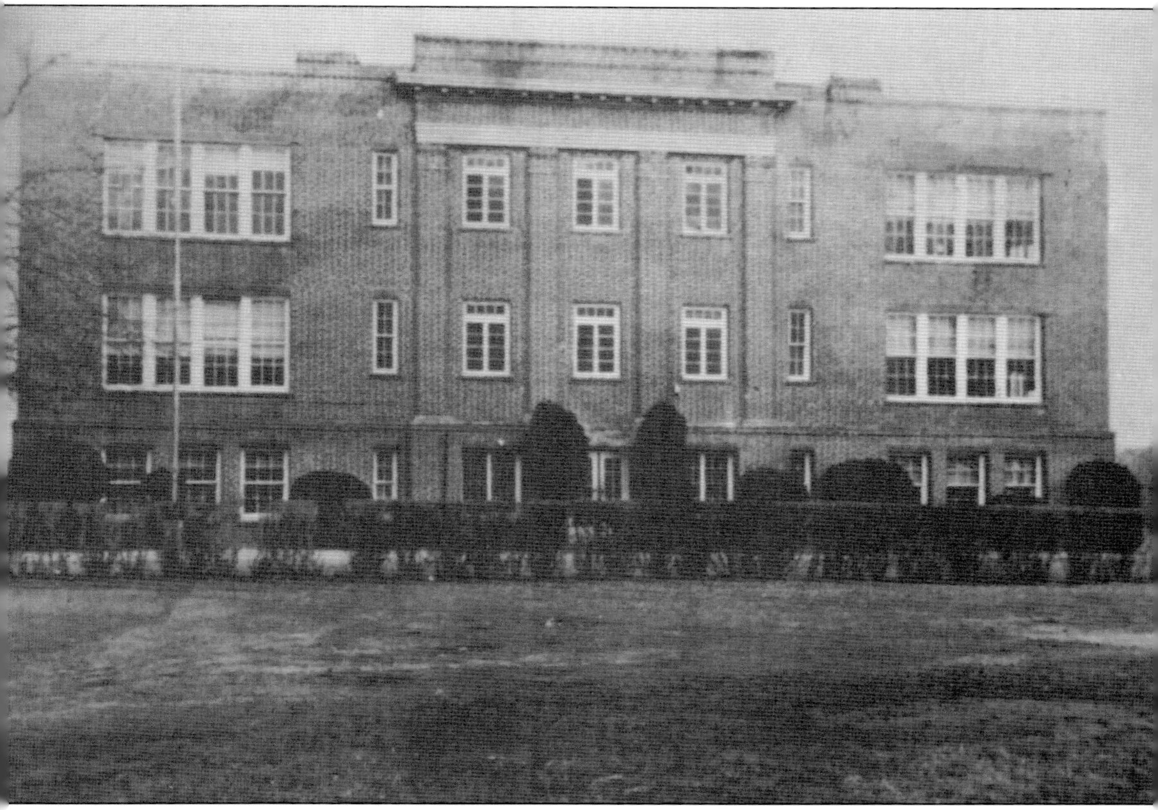

The residents of Quitman soon realized their current school facilities were inadequate and voted for a tax to finance the construction of a new school building. Land was acquired southeast of the railroad, and construction of a three-story building began in 1919. In that year, the school on the hill was closed, and the students moved just south of the railroad. However, the money ran out, and the second and third floors were not completed until 1921. (Courtesy of Sylvia Pagan.)

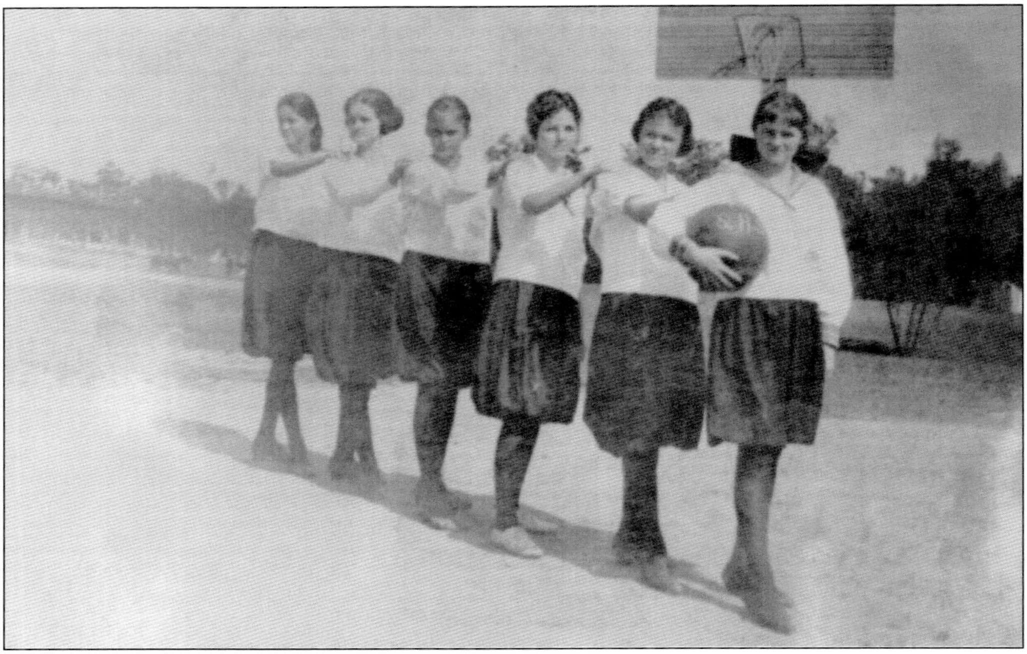

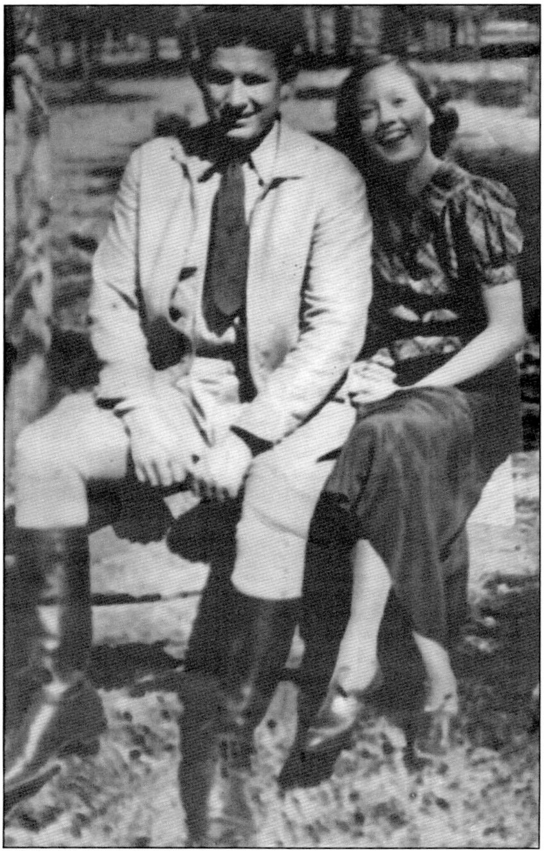

From 1924 to 1926, Quitman had several athletic accomplishments, and both the boys and girls had outstanding basketball teams. The girls' team, coached by a Mr. Shields, was successful for several years. Myra Jones coached the boys to several victories. From left to right are Maggie McIntosh, Cloy Walsworth, Mrytis Brooks, Ella Howard, Maude Pearl, and a Mrs. Howard. (Courtesy of Sylvia Pagan.)

Pictured here are John C. Jones and Virginia Stroud just after they were married in 1934. John was a Civilian Conservation Corp sergeant at Camp Davis in Ansley. He enlisted in the Navy as a machinists mate second class and worked shore patrol as a police petty officer, badge no. 1, on the USS *Shenandoah*. He was town marshal of Quitman in 1950 for about eight years, and then served as mayor until 1962. (Courtesy of Sylvia Pagan.)

Levon Hinton graduated from Quitman High School in 1942 and left to fight in World War II. He went overseas in June 1943 and served on the USS *Mississippi*; he also went to Honolulu and fought on several Pacific islands before coming home. Hinton was one of the many boys who graduated from Quitman and left to fight in the war. (Courtesy of Ellen Hinton James.)

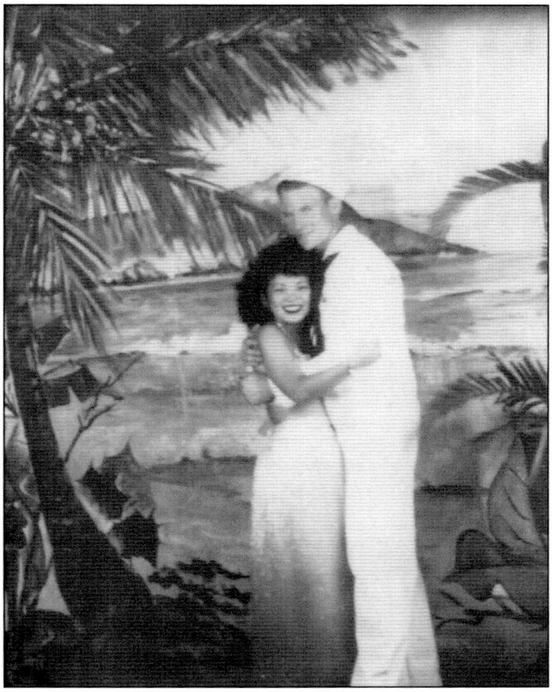

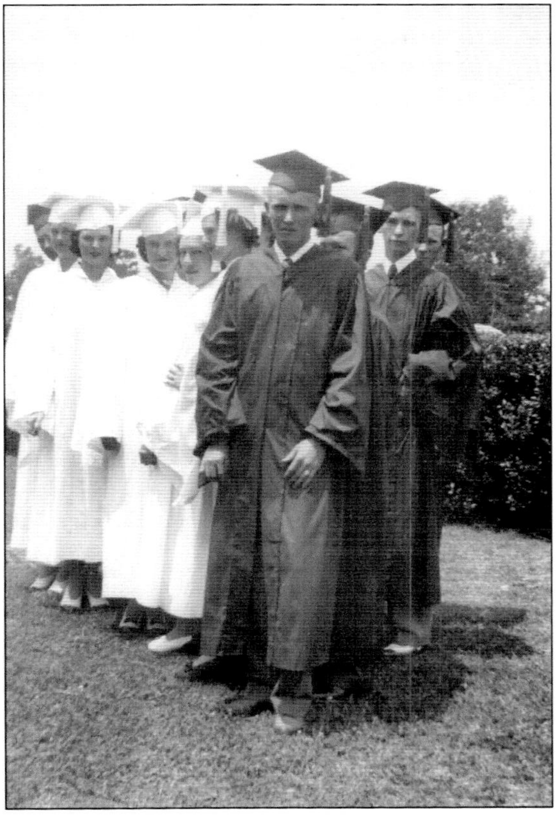

During World War II, the population and school enrollment of Quitman dropped as male teachers and students became scarce. In the years to follow, the smaller schools in the surrounding areas closed due to low enrollment, and Quitman's student population grew. This is a photograph of the 1942 graduation class; five graduates are not pictured, and most, if not all, of the seven boys from this class fought in World War II. In fact, just about all the boys in the classes from 1941 to 1945 joined the war effort. By 1945, only three boys had graduated and they too joined. In 1953, a tornado destroyed the top of the high school building, and a new classroom, along with additional land, was acquired. This proved very useful as more schools closed and sent their students to Quitman. (Courtesy of Ellen Hinton James.)

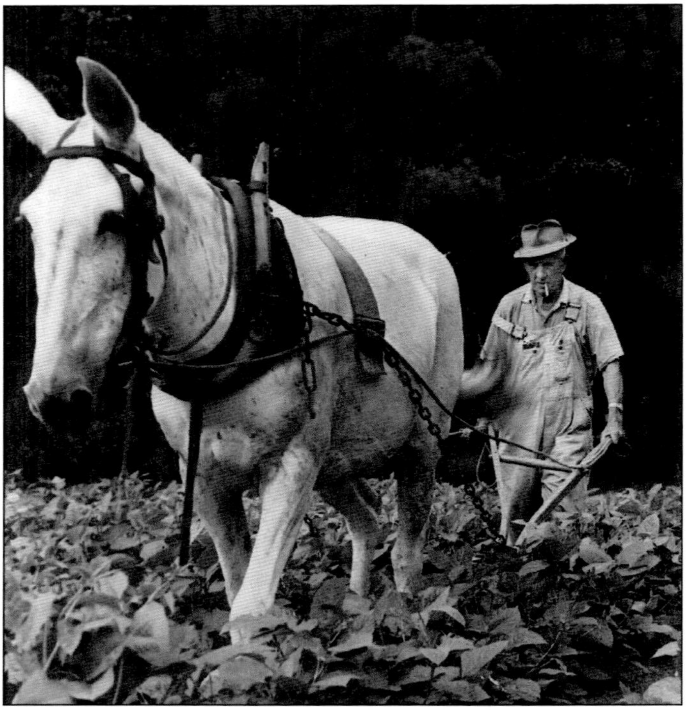

Farming was a way of life for the people of rural Jackson Parish. Here, Jessie Lowe plows the garden with his mule Blue sometime in the 1940s. Lowe lived off Sweetwater Road in Quitman, where he farmed all his life. (Courtesy of Sylvia Pagan.)

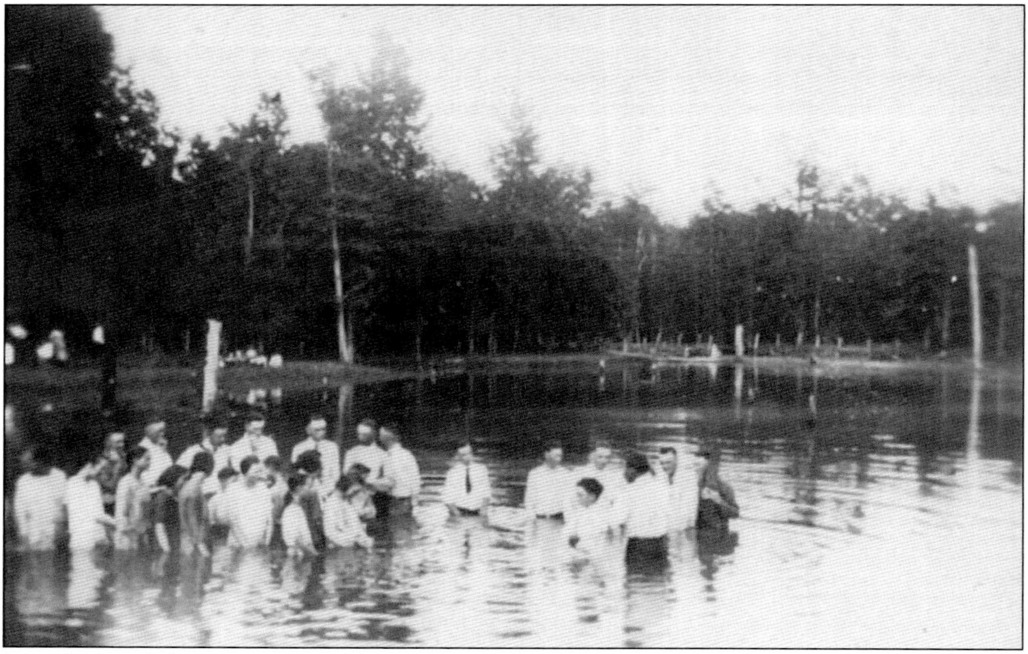

In early church history, it was common practice when someone presented their faith to the church that they would be baptized. The church would hold a baptismal ceremony at a nearby creek, pond, or other water source. Spectators would watch from the shore as their family member or friend was baptized. In some rural areas, these practices carried on into the 1950s. Churches later built a baptism area inside the church. (Courtesy of Paula Smith.)

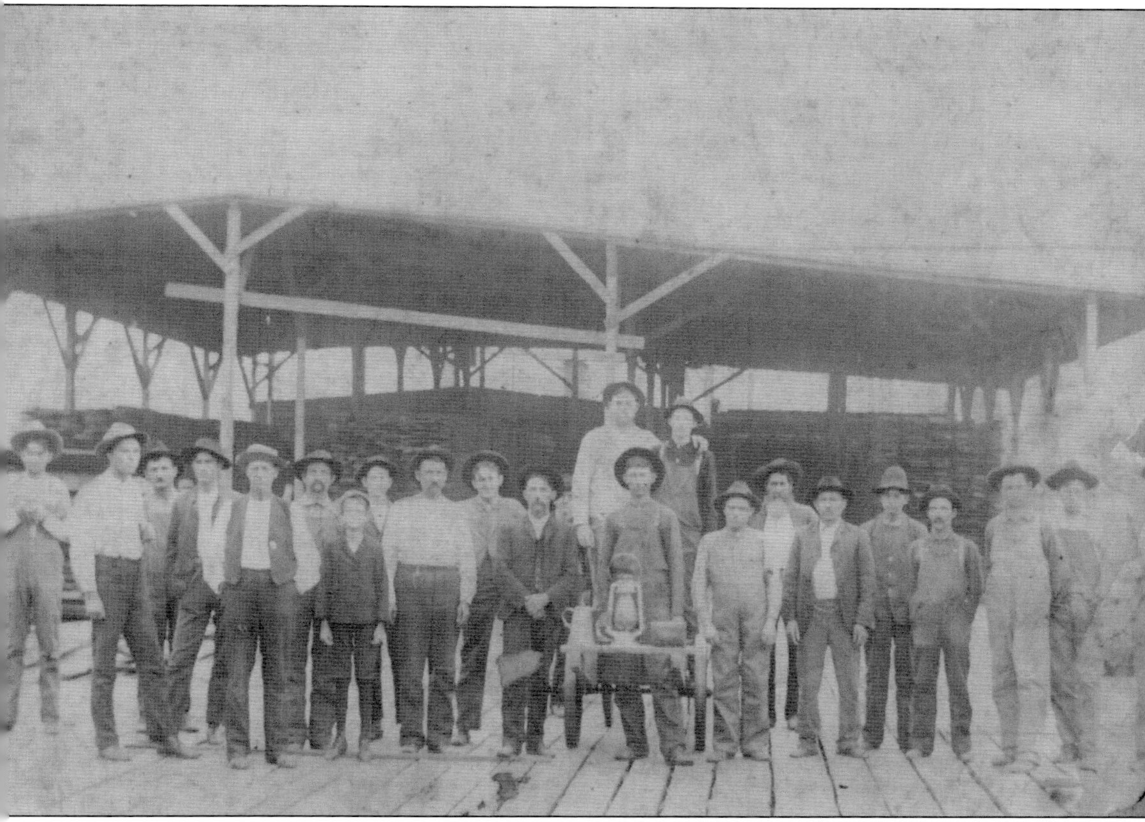

In 1901, the Davis brothers settled about 20 miles north of Hodge and named the area Ansley. About 20 or more families moved from their operations in south Arkansas to Ansley to help build the sawmill and town. It took two years for the workers to pull down the forests to build the town. In 1905, workers at the lumber cooling shed paused for this picture. (Courtesy of Sylvia Pagan.)

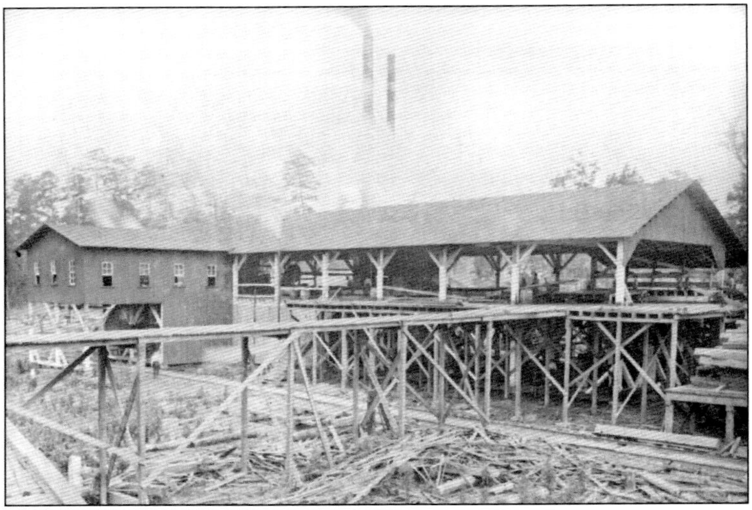

The Davis brothers built and completed this sawmill in 1902, and in December 1902, Davis Brothers Lumber Company was incorporated. Six years later, the company built a planer mill and continued to see success and the growth of the mill and town. The brothers took care of their employees for over 50 years. (Courtesy of the Hunt family.)

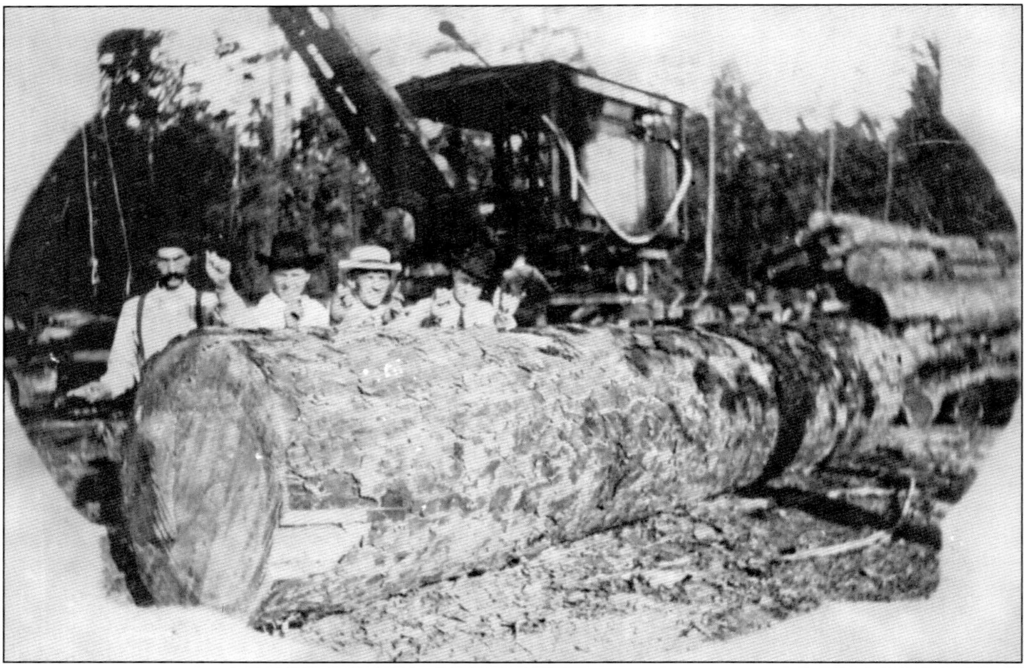

These men posed beside a large, just-cut pine tree with their hands forming letters spelling "Ansley." This pine log—and in the background, a skidder—rest on the East & West Louisiana Railway that Davis Brothers built. By 1907, the brothers had extended the logging railroad five miles northwest through their timber. (Courtesy of the Hunt family.)

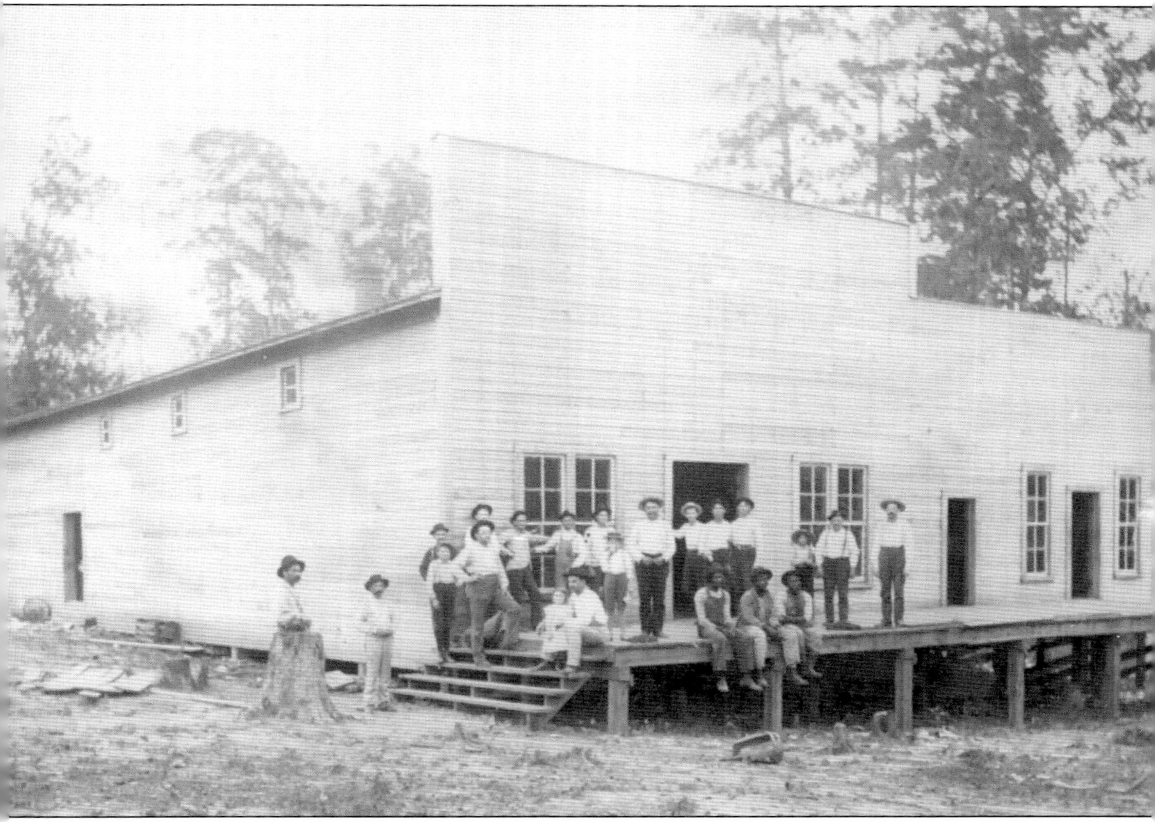

Davis Brothers built a commissary for its workers. This building, "the store," as it was called, housed a meat market and offices for the company. The store carried everything from slabs of bacon to Sloan's Liniment. It closed in 1926, and in that same year, a brick building, modern for its time, was erected a short distance up the hill. During the Depression, when orders were minimal, the mill only ran one or two days a week, and the Davis brothers allowed their employees to charge for food and supplies. Many families left town owing large amounts of money, but Davis Brothers never brought lawsuits to recover the money. (Courtesy of the Hunt family.)

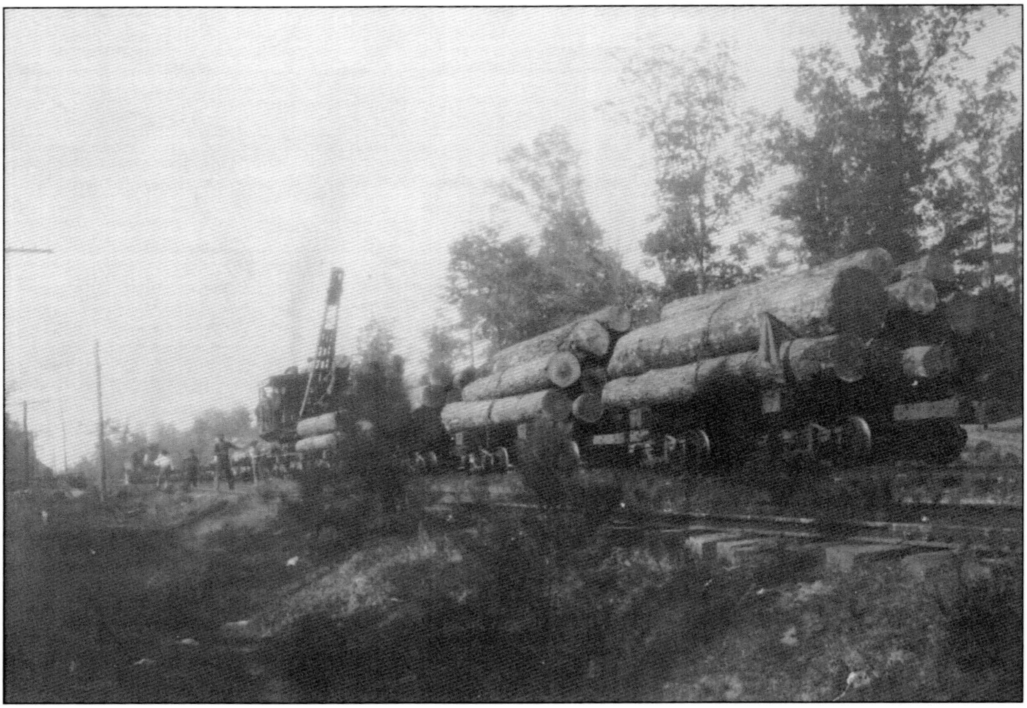

These photographs show a train on the East & West Louisiana Railway, along with a skidder and logs harvested from the Ansley area, in 1903. A skidder is any type of heavy vehicle used in a logging operation for pulling cut trees out of a forest in a process called skidding, in which the logs are transported from the cutting site to a landing. Here, they are loaded onto railroad cars and sent to the mill in Ansley. Working conditions around these machines were very dangerous. (Both, courtesy of the Hunt family.)

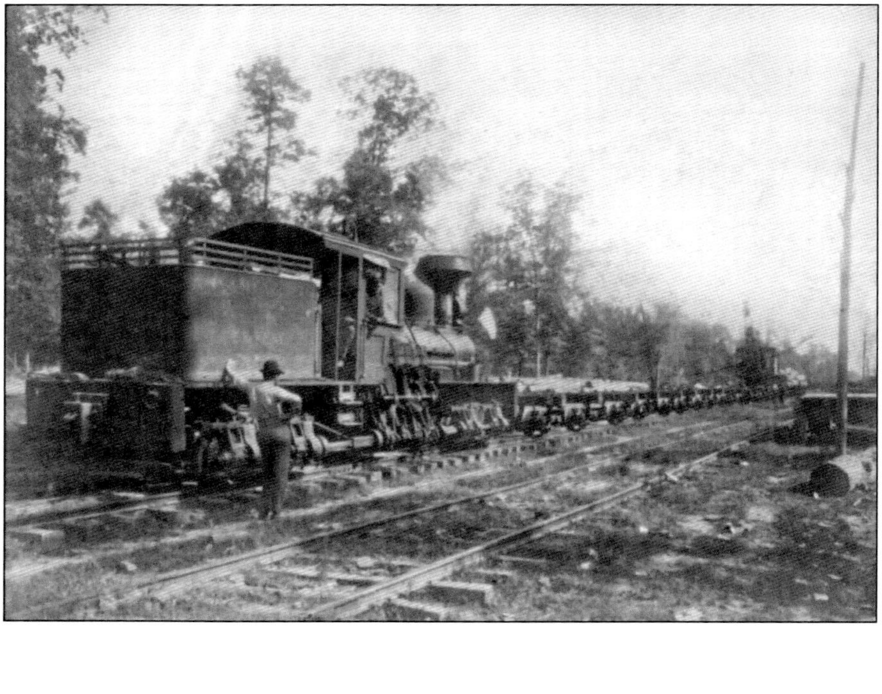

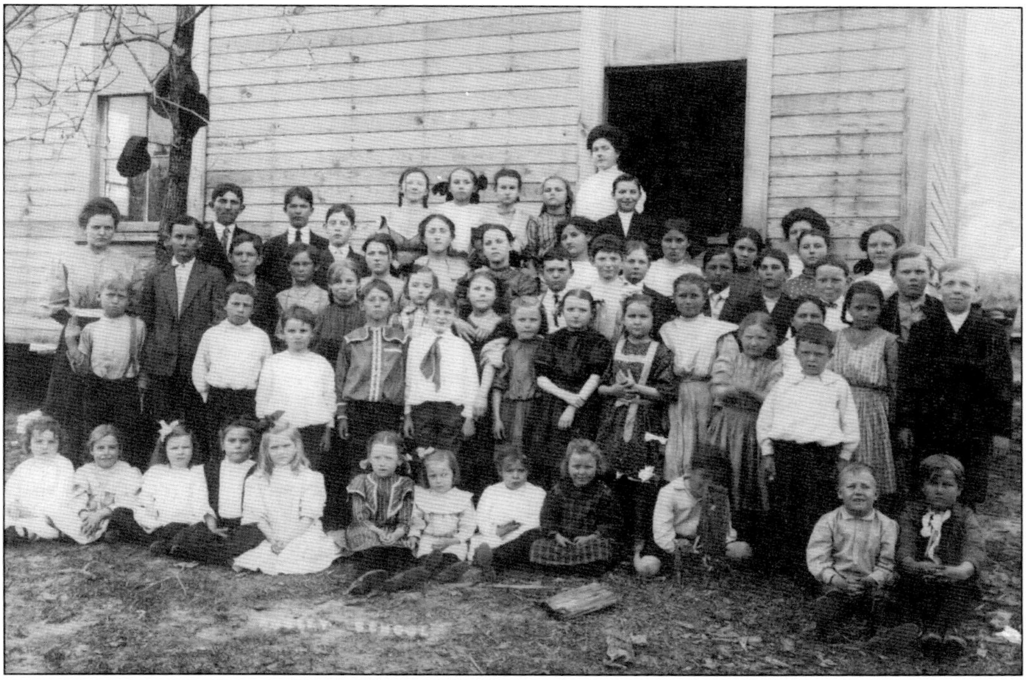

In 1903, Davis Brothers built a two-room building to be used as the Ansley School, just down the hill from the Ansley Union Church. This building was used as a school until 1908, when more room was needed, and it was sold to a young married couple. In 1908, Davis Brothers again built another larger, two-story school building that was later called the Woodmen building. The Woodmen of the World used the second story as a meeting place after the school was moved to another new building. This building, located in north Ansley, burned down in 1933. Ansley was, at one time, one of the largest schools in the parish. In 1936, enrollment was 202, and by 1944, the student population was 105. In 1945, the high school was closed and students were sent to Quitman. By 1951, the entire school was closed, and the end of Ansley had begun. (Both, courtesy of the Hunt family.)

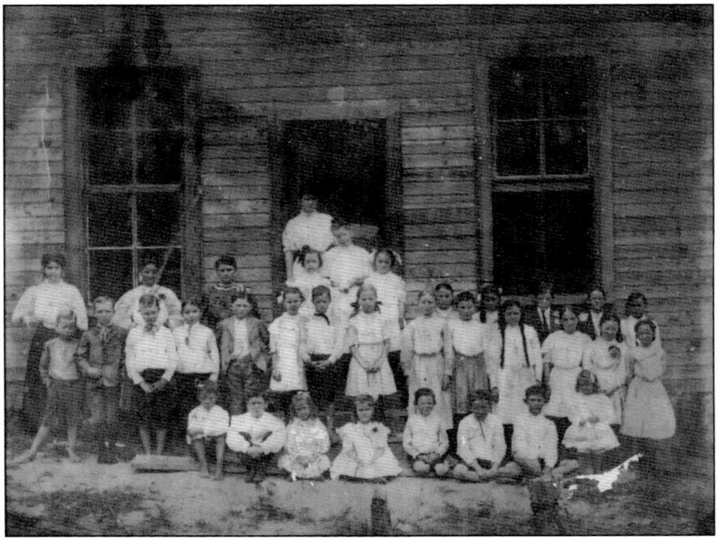

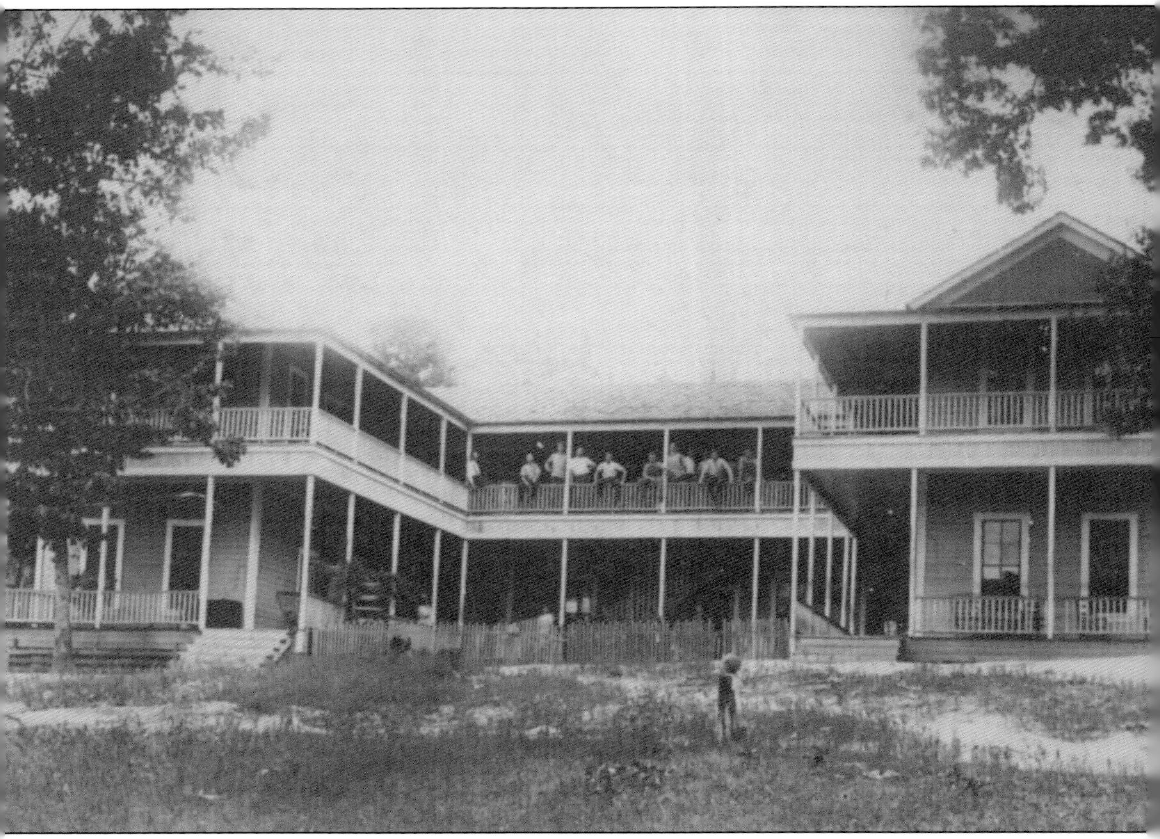

Nellie and Luther Young were the Ansley Hotel keepers in the 1930s, in the hotel built by Davis Brothers in 1903. They passed down many stories of the hotel guests and parties. One such story happened in May 1934, when two strange men dressed in black showed up at midnight. Their fedoras were pulled low over their heads, and they carried what looked like violin cases. They paid for their rooms in advance, and said they would be gone before daylight. The next day, the news spread that Bonnie and Clyde Barrow had been killed. It was never known if these men were involved. The hotel was sold to John Ponder in the early 1950s, and the lumber was recycled to build a house and other things for his family. (Courtesy of the Hunt family.)

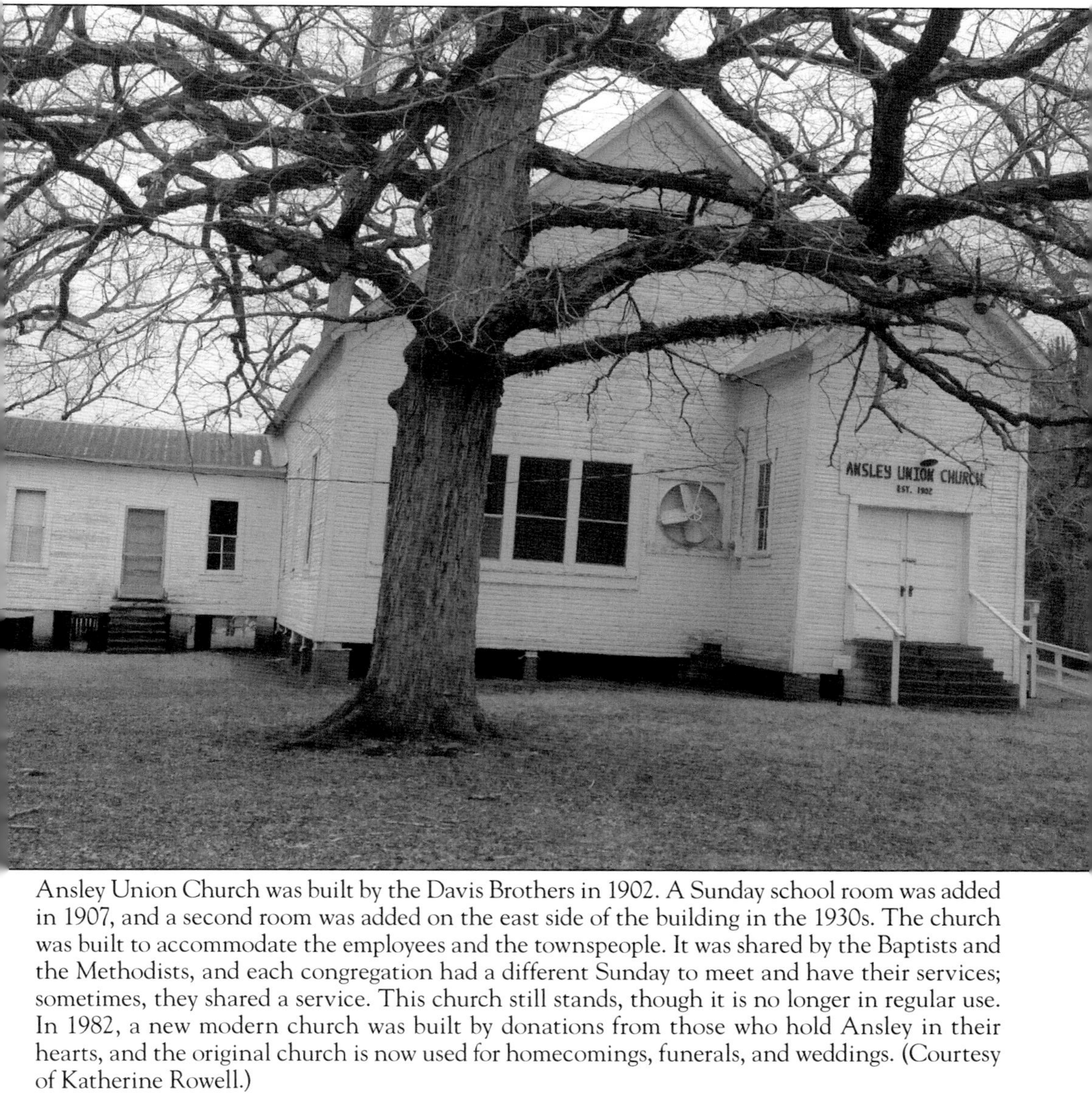


Ansley Union Church was built by the Davis Brothers in 1902. A Sunday school room was added in 1907, and a second room was added on the east side of the building in the 1930s. The church was built to accommodate the employees and the townspeople. It was shared by the Baptists and the Methodists, and each congregation had a different Sunday to meet and have their services; sometimes, they shared a service. This church still stands, though it is no longer in regular use. In 1982, a new modern church was built by donations from those who hold Ansley in their hearts, and the original church is now used for homecomings, funerals, and weddings. (Courtesy of Katherine Rowell.)

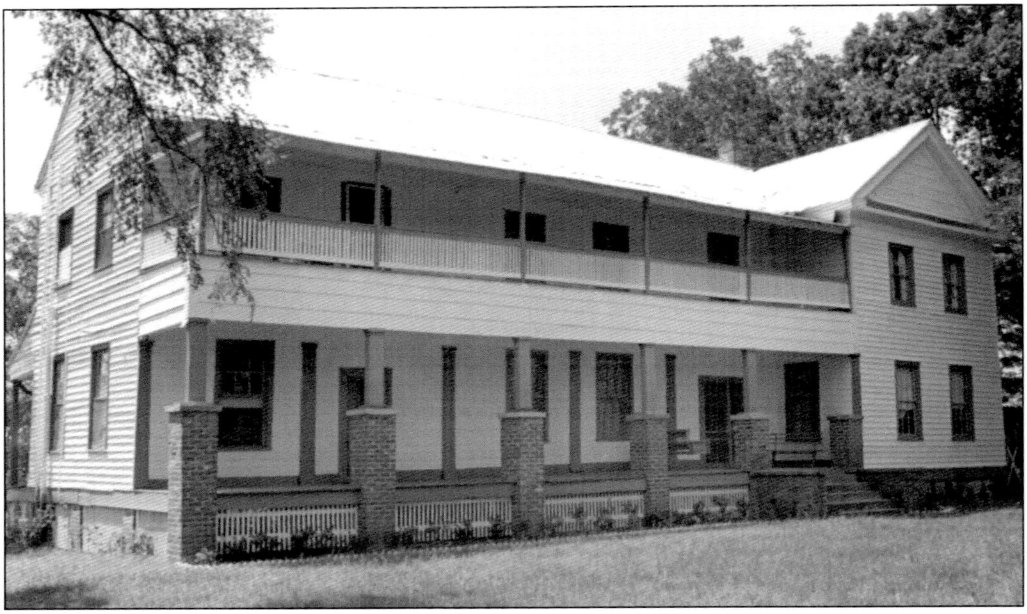

Isam and Aspilla Sims came from Georgia sometime in 1850 and ran a large plantation between Clay and Vernon. Stories tell of the lavish parties and dances before the Civil War that were hosted in their large home. This home is now in the hands of the Ellis family and is one of the oldest homes in the parish. (Courtesy of the T.L. Colvin estate.)

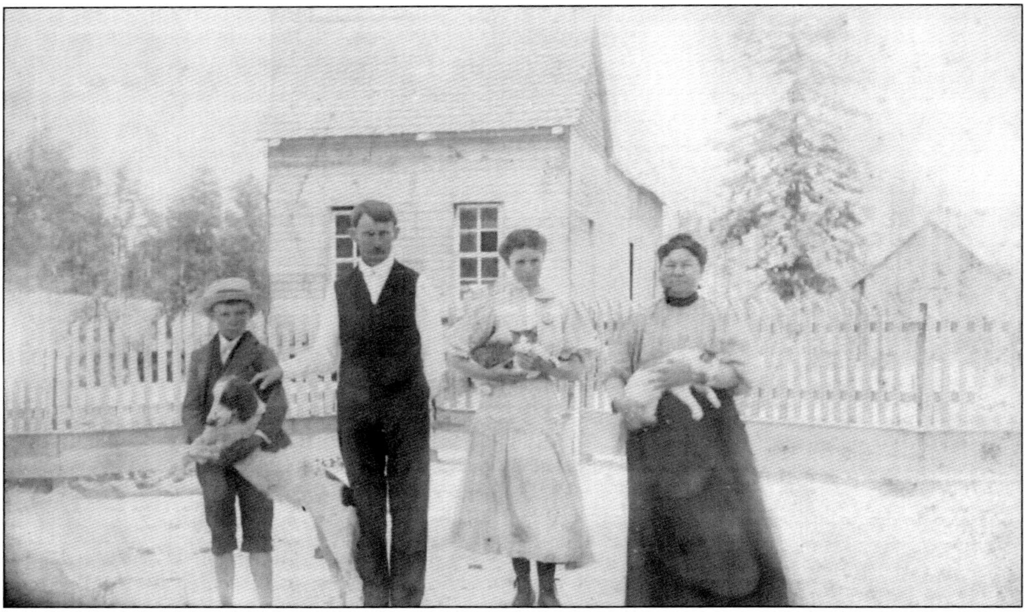

In this 1905 photograph, Walter Hines Ponder, his two children, and wife Louella Duke, along with their pets, pose near their home in Beech Springs. Walter loved animals and acted as a veterinarian for his stock and his neighbors. He worked as a farmer, was well read, and sometimes used the knowledge he gained from books to help family and friends with medical matters and emergencies. Ponder loved singing and often led services at church singing conventions and was involved with the singing school on the hill. (Courtesy of Patricia Maxwell.)

James Houston Davis was born September 11, 1899, to a poor farming family in Beech Springs, now a ghost town southeast of Quitman. "Jimmie" went to school in Quitman and graduated from Beech Springs in 1919. Serving as the governor of Louisiana for two nonconsecutive terms, he became known as the "singing governor" and for riding his horse Sunshine up the steps of the capitol and into his office when he was accused of using excessive money for a limo to drive him to work. He was elected into the Country Music Hall of Fame in 1971. He was also famous for writing "You Are My Sunshine," which he had recognized as the state song in 1977. (Courtesy of the T.L. Colvin estate.)

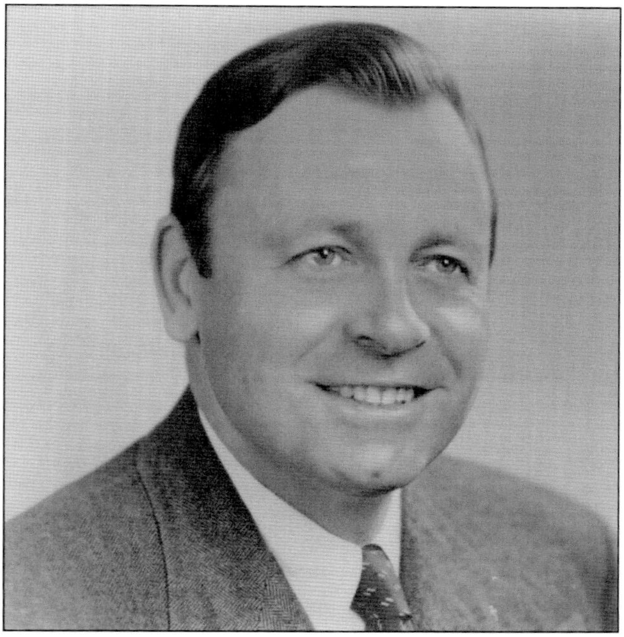

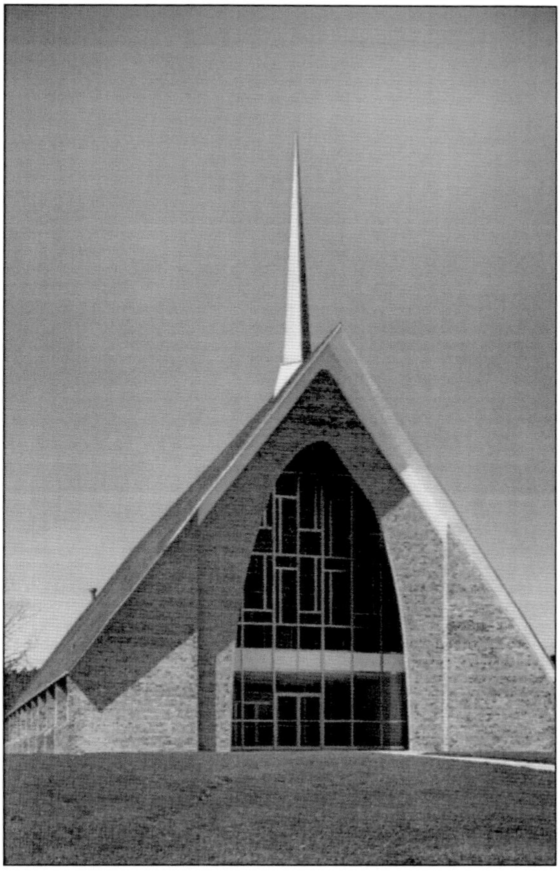

The Jimmie Davis Tabernacle was built in 1964 by friends of Jimmie Davis. It was built in Beech Springs, near the site of his birth and the old site of the Beech Springs High School. This structure was designed to hold 750 people, including a 50-person choir. Every year, the tabernacle held a homecoming, and Jimmie Davis would come to sing and sit under a tree to tell stories. These homecomings came to an end after he died. (Courtesy of the Jackson Parish Bank.)

Consistent with our mission to preserve history on a local level, this book was printed in South Carolina on American-made paper and manufactured entirely in the United States. Products carrying the accredited Forest Stewardship Council (FSC) label are printed on 100 percent FSC-certified paper.

MADE IN THE USA